teach yourself...
Photoshop 4
for Macintosh and Windows

Linda Richards

MIS: PRESS

A Subsidiary of
Henry Holt and Co., Inc.

MIS:Press
A Subsidiary of Henry Holt and Company, Inc.
115 West 18th Street
New York, New York 10011
http://www.mispress.com

First Edition—1997

ISBN 1-55828-532-6

MIS:Press and M&T Books are available at special discounts for bulk purchases for sales promotions, premiums, and fundraising. Special editions or book excerpts can also be created to specification.

For details contact: Special Sales Director
MIS:Press and M&T Books
Subsidiaries of Henry Holt and Company, Inc.
115 West 18th Street
New York, New York 10011

10 9 8 7 6 5 4 3 2 1

Associate Publisher: *Paul Farrell*

Managing Editor: *Shari Chappell*	**Production Editor:** *Anthony Washington*
Editor: *Rebekah Young*	**Technical Editor:** *Jonathan Lipkin*
Copy Edit Manager: *Karen Tongish*	**Copy Editor:** *Karen Tongish*

ACKNOWLEDGMENTS

It's never one person who makes a book happen, but a series of people contributing their part to the whole.

Brian Gill, my agent at Studio B, is a sweetie with vision and did a lot to make my involvement with this very rewarding project possible. I continue to feel good about having my career in his very capable hands.

Rebekah Young, my editor at MIS:Press, is a goddess with a lot of irons in the fire. She nonetheless manages to make everything happen beautifully.

Jonathan Lipkin, my technical editor on this project who had the redoubtable job of checking my every word and always pointed out my stylistic and technical slips with grace. Grace is an under rated quality in tech editors, and he has it.

There are a whole cadre of (to me) nameless people at Adobe who have taken a fabulous program and made it better. If they hadn't done that, I wouldn't have had anything to write about. If they hadn't done it so well, it would have been a less joyous project.

Thanks also to my life partner, David Middleton. Some of his artwork and many of his photographs were used as the basis of a lot of the exercises in this book. Even more important to me are his consistent patience, humor and wisdom: I've relied on this throughout this project as well as through all aspects of life that we share.

Thanks to my son Michael Richards for continuing to be associated with me. Lots of guys would be less patient with having a geek for a mom. ("Sure we can do that, Mike. But first have a peek at my cool new zip drive..." Famous last words.)

Special thanks to my brother, Peter Huber, who dragged me — kicking and screaming — to computers all those years ago. I don't think he knew what he was starting.

Linda Richards
scribe@mindlink.bc.ca

Contents

CHAPTER 14: Image Resolution and Importing Files . . .291

Introduction

The first time I saw Photoshop it knocked my socks off. I was at Comdex many years ago looking for stuff that is hot and new, as high tech writers will. I am a writer, but I am also a graphic designer and photographer by training and heritage, so the Photoshop demonstration floored me. It was magic, right? This, I knew, was the technology that would change the world. And, in many ways, it has.

My mind was blown by that Comdex demonstration. Practically disbelieving what I'd seen, I grabbed the friend I was attending the show with, who was on the other side of the building. I pulled her away from whatever silly thing she was looking at (it couldn't have been more important than this, could it?) and dragged her back to the booth. "Do it again!" I instructed the demonstrator. When he was done, we still weren't satisfied and made him do something else.

All these years later, my mind is still blown by some of the things you can do in Photoshop. Some of it is magic, but it also takes care of some mundane tasks and just makes our lives a whole lot simpler.

NEW IN 4.0

Version 4.0 of Adobe Photoshop adds some features that we couldn't have conceived of a few years ago, simply because the application didn't exist. Internet publishing, for instance, was unheard of just a few years ago. Photoshop 4.0 is one of the first commercial packages to incorporate features especially for Web publishers. I imagine they had to do this: Photoshop has been the standard for graphic designers almost since its release. Since professional designers are now spending a lot of time designing for electronic publication, it just makes sense to build features for the medium into the package.

Tool Tips give you a brief description of the thing you're about to use. They're sort of like constant on-line help without the inherent hassles.

The new Actions commands let you record a script of commands and then play them back at will, even to a whole batch of files. This is incredibly powerful stuff for those of us whose duties include repetitive tasks.

Adjustment Layers give extra power to the layers introduced just a couple of releases ago. Adjustment Layers make it super easy to try on different effects to see how they fit and toss them if they don't.

The jury is still out on Digital Watermarking because you have to go outside the program—and your system—to really make it happen. However, it's nice to see that 4.0 is beginning to address some of the security issues that are becoming apparent in on-line publishing.

The new Guides and Grids help you place your artwork precisely into your image and with other placement issues, another bonus for those designers who do all of their pre-Web work in Photoshop, as many do.

New selection and editing features have made Photoshop's already powerful interface somewhat more elegant to use, as well as easier for the newbie to get the hang of.

New zooming and viewing features also add to Photoshop's overall elegance and ease of use, and the Navigator gives you a whole new—and very helpful—tool to zoom and navigate around your image.

New Gradient and Filter Capabilities and new Blending Modes mean that there are more ways to easily enhance and alter your image.

Free Transform as well as several new transformation features let you flip, rotate, and otherwise skew images more easily than before.

New palettes and palette enhancements incorporate many new features and provide new ways to deal with the old ones.

AN OVERVIEW

Photoshop 4 not only incorporates some truly excellent new features, it has also looked at a lot of the old ones and rethought the way they are used and implemented. The result is a really new package that will be easier for new users to work with and more elegant and powerful for old hands once they get used to the changes. Unlike a lot of software upgrades that seem like little more than a feeble grab for upgrade bucks, Photoshop 4.0 is—on several levels—a genuine reworking of an already excellent product.

Teach Yourself ... Photoshop 4 for Macintosh and Windows was written to help you learn the program as quickly and efficiently as possible. Its lessons, language, and goal are simple: to get you doing cool stuff with Photoshop in the least amount of time possible. Right now is even better than later.

Teach Yourself ... Photoshop 4 for Macintosh and Windows includes these features:

PROGRESSIVE LESSONS

You don't need to know anything about Photoshop to use this book. You'll start with the basic tools and concepts and then move on to more complex topics. For reinforcement, some of the key principles will be repeated from time to time as new information is added.

The book is intended to be taken as one big meal—starting at the beginning and working through to the end in sequential fashion. However, human beings and deadlines being what they are, it is expected that some readers may want to skip ahead to the very thing they have questions about this instant. That, too, is all right. Do keep in mind, however, that the book builds on lessons learned from a simple beginning. If you skip ahead and find yourself lost at sea, back up a bit until you feel comfortable.

HANDS-ON EXERCISES

Most of us learn best by doing, so this book offers opportunities to practice in nearly every chapter. In the beginning, you'll find the exercises to be very literal, telling you every keystroke to use. In later lessons, it is assumed that you've mastered the fundamentals, and the exercises focus more on learning new material. Screen shots are included throughout the book to give you at-a-glance information.

THE CD-ROM

The CD-ROM included with this book offers several extras to the reader. On one level, the disc is a living color section. Color examples of the work shown in the book are included on the disc to give you a rendering you can work with.

As a special bonus, we've included a selection of color royalty-free images from the Hyogen-sha, Inc. Royalty Free Stock Photo Collection. Volume 0 includes 100 images of the same quality and can be ordered through their Web page or directly from them. The images included on the CD, however, are royalty-free, so you can use them and manipulate them in any way you like.

We've also included some useful and interesting filters and demo software. See the About the CD-ROM page of the book.

CHAPTER SUMMARIES

Each chapter concludes with a brief summary of the material that you've learned. Use this to review the most important concepts and techniques.

OPTIMIZING YOUR COMPUTER FOR PHOTOSHOP 4.0

Photoshop 4.0 is a big and powerful program, so it's not that surprising that it runs best on a big and powerful computer—the bigger and more powerful, the better. If you're still thinking about what type of system to buy, get the most powerful computing beast you can afford. A (very) general rule of thumb is that the more powerful the processor and the more RAM you have, the better Photoshop will perform for you. However, if you're not computer shopping this week (and most of us aren't) Adobe has set down some basic parameters for Photoshop.

System Requirements on the PC

You'll need a minimum of an Intel-based 486 processor running Windows 3.1 with MS-DOS 5.0 or later, Windows 95, or Windows NT version 3.5.1 or later.

Plan on having at least 16 MB of RAM available for Photoshop, but as I said, more is better.

Free up at least 25 MB of space on your hard drive, but plan on making more available if you'll be working with large images.

You'll need an 8-bit (256-color) display adapter card, and a mouse or some other pointing device that you know is compatible with the program (the manufacturer will be able to tell you if it is).

If you plan to use the CD-ROM set that ships with the software, you'll need a CD-ROM drive. These days, the floppy disk–based version of Photoshop is the exception, not the rule.

That's the minimum configuration. Adobe's "best performance" recommended system is:

- A Pentium or Pentium Pro processor
- Windows 95 or Windows
- At least 32 MB of RAM
- A 24-bit (millions of colors) video display card
- A PostScript printer
- Acceleration products bearing the Adobe-charged logo

System Requirements on the Macintosh

To run Photoshop on the Macintosh, you need a minimum of an Apple Macintosh computer with a 68030 processor or a Power Macintosh.

Plan on having at least 16 MB of RAM available for the application, but as I said, more is better.

Photoshop runs only on Apple's System 7.1 or later (7.1.2 on the Power Mac). Photoshop 4.0 doesn't run under System 6 or earlier.

Free up at least 25 MB of space on your hard drive, but plan on making more available if you'll be working with large images.

If you plan to use the CD-ROM set that ships with the software, you'll need a CD-ROM drive. These days, the floppy disk–based version of Photoshop is the exception, not the rule.

That's the minimum configuration. Adobe's "best performance" recommended system for the Macintosh is:

- A Power Macintosh
- Apple System software 7.5 or later
- At least 32 MB of RAM
- A 24-bit (millions of colors) video display card
- A PostScript printer
- Acceleration products bearing the Adobe-charged logo

Additional Hardware

There are some things you don't absolutely need to run Photoshop but are nonetheless nice to have around. You might think about adding some of these to your system if you don't already have them:

- A flatbed (reflective), slide (transparency), or three-dimensional object scanner
- A back-up storage system, such as a SyQuest, DAT, or magneto-optical system
- 24-bit (true color) video
- A digitizing tablet with a stylus for drawing
- Uninterruptible power supplies for your computer, hard disk, and monitor
- A PostScript printer
- A video input/output card for multimedia use
- Third-party acceleration products that speed up Photoshop processing

And we're off!

CHAPTER 1

Getting Familiar with Adobe Photoshop

In this chapter…

- Installing and launching Adobe Photoshop
- The Toolbox
- The palettes
- Measuring, magnifying, and reducing
- Creating and saving your first document

Adobe Photoshop is a huge, sophisticated, and incredibly complex program. If it weren't, it's unlikely it would be so popular with digital and graphic arts professionals around the world. All that sophistication and complexity can be pretty overwhelming for the Photoshop neophyte. I mean, the graphics department at *Time Magazine* are making Photoshop do backflips and the folks at *The Enquirer* have never had it so good. That can be pretty intimidating for a new user.

But take a step back. One of the reasons Photoshop has gotten such a huge following in a relatively short time is because, at its core, it's essentially very easy to use. Let's face it, the folks using Photoshop at the professional level are mostly artists, and as artists, they like to do art.

A decade ago when someone at a magazine wanted to create a cover image that superimposed a photograph of a horse jumping over a rainbow, they called in a photographer. The photographer would get two excellent images and sandwich them in the darkroom. This would take a lot of time, a lot of effort, and—from the magazine's perspective—a lot of money. And all before you ever got to the final film stage. Photoshop puts the power back into the hands of the person with the concept. While some photographers aren't happy about that, a lot of them have gone out and purchased computers and Photoshop. Welcome to the 90s!

Becoming a Photoshop guru will take lots of hours of just sitting there and playing with your computer—and this book—and tweaking and bending your creations until you get them just right.

On the other hand, you probably already have the skills you need to perform some very basic—yet all-important—functions. The very complexity of the program allows it to function on many levels and the step from beginner to guru might be just a few intense sessions away.

In this chapter, we'll look at some of those basic functions: the first steps you need to take toward guruhood. We'll start with installing and starting up the program and then move on to creating a file, saving your work, and then quitting. In the process, you'll learn many of the basic tools and techniques, as well as a few handy shortcuts.

The objective of this section is to give you a feel for the program without overloading you with all the possibilities and options of each of the tools, palettes, and menus. There will be time enough for that in later chapters as you build your skills.

Photoshop is an advanced drawing and painting program as well as a program for correcting and manipulating photographic images. The documents you create can be very simple or extremely involved, depending upon your creative goals. You will, however, need many skills for every project regardless of size or complexity. Some of these are:

- Opening an existing file or creating a new file
- Using drawing, painting, and selection tools
- Modifying your work
- Saving your work

INSTALLATION AND INITIAL STARTUP

Installing Adobe Photoshop on a Macintosh

If you have the disk version of Photoshop, make back-up copies of all your master program disks. If you have the CD version, remember not to use the disc to reheat pizza; you might want to reinstall a fresh version at some point in the future.

To install Photoshop:

1. Insert Installer Disk 1 in your internal floppy disk drive, or insert the CD-ROM. When the installer icon appears, double-click to open it. After the Installer dialog box and the Photoshop Big Electric Cat appear, click **Continue**.

2. A second dialog box will appear, offering two choices of installation from a pull-down list at upper left. If you choose **Easy Install**, the Installer will place everything on your hard disk. If you select the **Customize** choice, only certain selected items will be installed. If you are a first-time user, you must install everything.

3. The Installer will do the rest, prompting you to insert disks periodically if you're loading from floppy disks.

4. When the Installer is finished, you will be notified whether the installation was successful or not. Click **Quit**, and the computer will restart itself.

Installing Adobe Photoshop on a PC

If you have the floppy disk version of Photoshop, make back-up copies of all your master program disks. If you have the CD version, remember not to use the disc to reheat pizza; you might want to reinstall a fresh version at some point in the future.

The Photoshop installer will determine what version of Windows you are running and will install the correct version of Photoshop for your configuration:

1. Start Windows if you haven't already.

2. Insert Installer Disk 1 in your internal floppy disk drive or insert the CD-ROM. When the installer icon appears, double-click to open it. After the Installer dialog box and the Photoshop Big Electric Cat appear, click **Continue**.

3. In Windows NT or Windows 95, choose **Install Photoshop**, and move directly ahead to step 5. In Explorer or Windows 3.1, 3.11, or NT 3.5.1, find the Adobe Photoshop directory on the Photoshop CD-ROM and open **Disk 1**.

4. Double-click the **Setup.exe** file. The installer dialog box appears.

5. Click **Next**.

6. Follow the instructions on your screen, including adding company information and serial number. The serial number appears on the registration card that shipped with Photoshop 4.0.

7. Click **Next**, and then click again to confirm your information.

8. Choose the appropriate install parameters from the options presented:

   - **Typical** is the most common setup and will give you access to all Photoshop options.

   - **Compact** will configure a setup that gives you the minimum required options and places the least demand on your system.

   - **Custom** gives you control of which files you wish to install. Select the files you want, and then click **Next**.

9. Create a program folder, or use an existing one. Click **Next.**

10. Clicking **Next** confirms the selections you've made and starts the installation. You'll be prompted when the installation is finished.

11. If prompted to do so, close all other applications so the installer can restart Windows for a fresh, clean start.

If you're looking forward to seeing the movies in the Photoshop CD-ROM set, be sure to install QuickTime for Windows. The QuickTime installer is located on the Photoshop 4.0 CD-ROM.

N O T E

Starting Photoshop for the First Time on the Macintosh

1. Find the Adobe Photoshop 4.0 folder, which was installed on your hard disk. Open the folder and double-click on the **Photoshop** icon to launch the program (Figures 1.1 and 1.2).

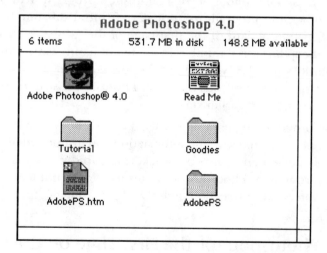

Figure 1.1 *Adobe Photoshop 4.0 folder: View by Icon.*

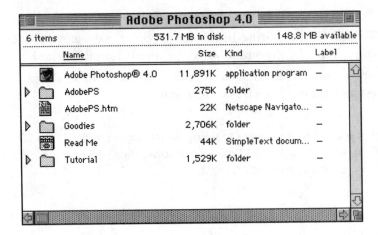

Figure 1.2 *Adobe Photoshop 4.0 folder: View by Name.*

2. Since this is the first time you are using the program, you will see a dialog box that asks you for information so that your copy of the program can be personalized. Enter your name and the name of your organization by clicking in each box. Use the **Tab** key to move from box to box.

3. Enter the serial number of your Photoshop program. Without the serial number, the program will not start. To find this number, look on your registration card or the first page of the Adobe Photoshop *User's Guide*. Keep this serial number in a safe but handy place. You'll need it to identify yourself if you call Adobe for technical support. If you are upgrading from a previous version of Photoshop, use the serial number provided with that earlier version.

As the program begins, you will see a color Photoshop startup splash screen personalized with the information you just provided. At the bottom of the screen, words are flickering rapidly. This is part of the startup routine as Photoshop searches its folders and loads in the necessary filters, color selection tables, and preference information.

Starting Photoshop for the First Time on the PC

There are two ways to start Photoshop on the PC. In Windows 3.1, 3.11, or Windows NT, use the Program Manager to open the program folder you specified at installation. Double-click the **Photoshop** icon to launch the program.

In Windows 95 or Windows NT, choose **Start:Programs:Adobe:Adobe Photoshop 4.0**, provided you installed the program in the Adobe folder. If not, choose the folder you did install it in.

THE PHOTOSHOP DESKTOP

Your first view of Photoshop gives you a good overview of the tools that will change your artistic world. If you've never opened the program before, you will see a menu bar at the top of the screen, along with several windows (Figure 1.3). We will open other windows, but let's start with these basics. Because of differences in screen resolution, platforms, and other variables, your screen may not look exactly like the one illustrated.

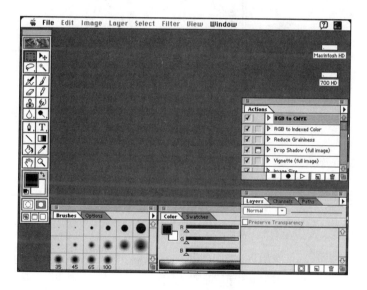

Figure 1.3 The Photoshop desktop.

The Photoshop menu bar has pull-down menus under the categories File, Edit, Image, Layer, Filter, View, and Window. Later, we will look at the menus and submenus under each of these headings. Put the mouse pointer on one of these headings and click to reveal the menu choices. You'll notice that most of the commands are grayed out, with only the File menu and the Window menu showing items that can be selected. That is because there are currently no files open.

TOOL TIPS

If you let your pointer rest briefly on one of the Tool icons in the Toolbox, a small yellow box that tells you the name of the tool appears (Figure 1.4). This is called a *Tool Tip*. If you let your pointer rest briefly on various elements within the Palettes, Photoshop will give you a Tool Tip to tell you either the name of the thing you're pointing at or, in very simple terms, its use. This can be very helpful with the less frequently used elements of Photoshop, which can be difficult to remember.

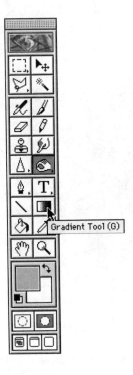

Figure 1.4 A Tool Tip.

NOTE Depending on the processor speed of your machine, the Tool Tip might take several seconds to appear. This is because the program takes a few seconds to determine that it's a Tool Tip you're after and not just a slow selection of the Tool itself. If you get a Tool Tip when you weren't asking for one, don't worry. Tool Tips don't get in the way of Photoshop's functionality.

Turning Tool Tips Off

Things like Tool Tips make some people crazy. If you'd rather have Tool Tips just go away and leave you alone, simply turn them off by choosing **File:Preferences:General** and deselect **Show Tool Tips**. To turn them on again, simply check that box in the Preferences file.

PALETTE ORIENTATION IN PHOTOSHOP

Many individual Photoshop tools, commands, and options are arranged into a series of palettes. These are nothing more than separate, floating windows with icons, dropdown lists, check boxes, and other controls.

Photoshop's main palettes—other than the Toolbox, which is also a kind of palette—are grouped together in several windows, each of which contains two or more separate palettes arranged in overlapping fashion. A tab displays the name of each palette in the window, making them easy to identify. Just click on a tab to bring a given palette to the front of the window and make that palette active. When you choose a palette from the menu bar at the top of the screen (e.g., **Window:Show Brushes**), the window containing that palette is displayed, with the selected palette in the front of the window and ready for you to use.

Other available palettes in that window are behind the one being displayed with only their tabs showing. In this way, several palettes can be available at the click of the mouse. The Photoshop desktop with several palette windows visible is shown in Figure 1.3.

You may grab and drag a tab with the mouse to move a palette into a window of its own or to drop it into another group. Some Photoshop palettes, like the Toolbox, which appears on the left side of the screen, contain nothing but icons representing tools for image creation and image modification. Like any window, the Toolbox and other palette windows can be moved by clicking and dragging the gray bar at the top. Each tool in the Toolbox has special options that are controlled by another palette. These options appear in windows of their own.

PALETTE GROUPS

One default group includes Brushes and Options tabs. The Brushes palette controls the size and shape of painting and editing tools, color mode, paint opacity control, and other features for customizing your tools. The Options palette lets you set special features for the currently selected tool (Paintbrush, Magic Wand, etc.).

Also at the bottom of the screen is another palette window with Color and Swatches tabs. Each of these palettes can be used to select colors. You also may move this window to any location on the screen you wish.

The third window on the screen displays Layers, Channels, and Paths palettes. These are used to work with individual layers (for now, think of them as clear overlays), channels (such as the separate red, green, or blue components of your image), and paths (outline-oriented shapes). The default desktop and its palettes is shown in Figure 1.3.

A fourth window, the Actions palette, is new to Photoshop and supports task automation and batch processing. Actions lets you record a sequence of editing steps as an Action list that can then be applied to another selection in the same image, to another image file, or even to hundreds of files in a batch operation. The Actions palette is shown in Figure 1.5, below.

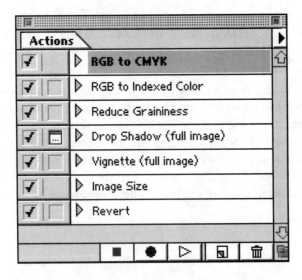

Figure 1.5 Actions palette.

SHORTCUT

To hide the palette windows and the Toolbox, press the **Tab** key. To bring them back, press the **Tab** key again. If all your palettes and the Toolbox suddenly disappear from the screen for no reason, don't panic. You've probably hit the **Tab** key by mistake.

This next section will provide an overview of the major functions of each of Photoshop's palettes. We'll get into detailed functions later as we begin to use each tool.

ABOUT THE TOOLBOX

The Toolbox is divided into five parts.

- Clicking on the arresting eye gets you basic information about Photoshop.
- There are 20 selection, painting, drawing, filling, and editing tools.

SHORTCUT

To toggle between the Rectangular and Elliptical Marquee tool, select one or the other from the Options palette, or hold down the **Option** key when you select the Marquee, and the Marquee icon will change to the appropriate tool to reflect your choice.

- Below the editing tools is a color control box, which lets you change background and foreground colors.
- Next is a mask mode box, which provides the choice of normal or quick mask mode.
- Finally, there's a screen display mode box, which gives you different views of your work.

Selecting a tool or a mode is as easy as clicking on it once. Many, but not all, of the tools have additional options associated with them. To see these options, double-click on the tool and then access the choices from the palette that becomes active. (If the relevant palette is not currently open on the screen, Photoshop will open it when you double-click on the tool.) Until you have a file open, the mask mode and screen mode areas will remain inactive. The Toolbox is shown in Figure 1.6, and the key functions are listed in Table 1.1.

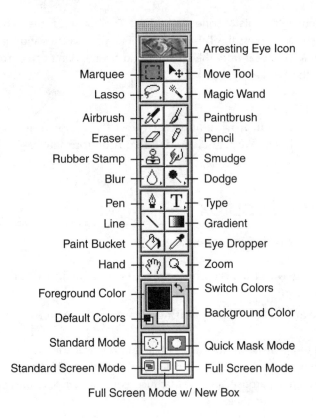

Figure 1.6 *The Toolbox.*

Table 1.1 The Toolbox Top 20

Tool	Type of Tool	Function
Marquee	Selection	Selects square, rectangular, round, or elliptical areas
Move Tool	Selection	All moving functions
Lasso	Selection	Selects freeform areas
Magic Wand	Selection	Selects areas based on a determined range of color values
Airbrush	Paint	Paints a soft-edged line
Paintbrush	Paint	Paints a soft-edged line

Table 1.1 The Toolbox Top 20 (continued)

TOOL	TYPE OF TOOL	FUNCTION
Eraser	Editing	Erases all or part of an image
Pencil	Paint	Paints with hard-edged line on image
Rubber Stamp	Paint	Clones (duplicates) an image
Smudge	Editing	Smudges an image like a finger dragging
Blur	Editing	Sharpens or blurs part of an image
Dodge	Editing	Lightens or darkens part of an image
Pen	Line	Creates Bezier curves
Type	Type	Creates text
Line	Line	Creates straight lines of varying width with optional arrowheads
Gradient	Fill	Fills areas with blend between foreground color and background color
Paint Bucket	Fill	Fills areas with foreground color
Eyedropper	Color selector	Selects color from the image through a chalk pastel or wet paint
Hand	Positioning	Moves image in any direction within the window; useful when working on magnified views of an image that will not completely fit in the window
Zoom	Magnification	Allows enlargement or reduction of image up to 16 times normal and down to 1/16 size of normal

The Rectangular/Elliptical Marquee, Sharpen/Blur, and Dodge/Burn tools are each combined into a single box. When you double-click on one of the tools, the Option palette becomes active, offering you the choice of any of the tools.

THE COLOR CONTROL BOX

The color control area displays the current foreground and background colors for the document. Clicking on the two-headed arrow reverses the foreground and background colors. Try it, and observe the effect.

NOTE   The default colors (black foreground, white background) are indicated by the small color swatch below and to the left of the large color swatches. This information is stored in the Photoshop Preferences file. Clicking on this small patch resets the large swatches back to their default values.

To demonstrate the two areas at the very bottom of the Toolbox, you'll need to have a file open. To create a new file, either select **New** from the File menu or press **Command-N** (Mac) or **Ctrl-N** (PC) on the keyboard. The New File dialog box will appear with option boxes requesting file-size information (Figure 1.7). By clicking on the pop-up menu, change the units from inches to pixels for both height and width. Enter **640** for the width and **480** for the height. (These dimensions will create a full-screen file on a 13-inch monitor.) Click **OK**. A new untitled file will open.

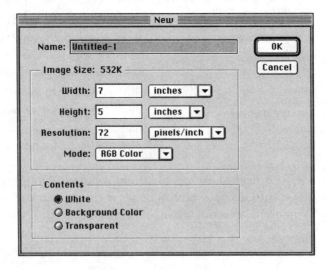

Figure 1.7 *New File dialog box.*

THE MASK MODE BOX

Photoshop offers you the ability to make quick masks to rapidly select certain limited, defined areas in which to paint or edit an image. The Mask Mode box tells you whether or not you are in the standard or quick mask mode by the position of the rectangular bar under one of the two icons. When a file is open, you can click on either icon to change modes. If there is no file open, this option will be unavailable.

THE SCREEN DISPLAY MODE BOX

The bottom box contains three icons that designate screen display mode. The left-hand box shows the window with menu, title, and scroll bars. In this mode, you can see all open documents, which may be stacked one behind another. (In Photoshop you can have more than one file open at a time.) The center icon provides the menu bar only and obscures all other open documents. The last icon removes all menu bars for a full-screen view of the top document only. As in the Mask Mode box, the bar underneath the icon designates your choice.

MENUS

Photoshop has seven menus; four have their own detailed branching submenus. Most of the commands are too complex to explore in detail here, but it's worth a moment to get an overview of the kinds of operations they cover (Table 1.2). Where defined, command keys are listed on the menu.

Table 1.2 Menus and Their Functions

MENU	FUNCTIONS
File	Opening and closing files, acquiring and exporting images to various formats. Printing. Setting application preferences.
Edit	Undo and Redo functions; Copy, Cut, and Paste, along with special Paste functions; commands for cropping images, filling, and creating borders on selected areas; Publisher options; definition of patterns and composite controls; Snapshot option.

Table 1.2 Menus and Their Functions (continued)

MENU	FUNCTIONS
Image	Image-enhancement commands for color correction, image rotation, flipping, distortion, etc. Also includes powerful commands for channel calculations, as well as changing image size and image resolution, creating traps, and viewing a histogram. Trapping is done here, too.
Layer	Sophisticated layer control. As well as layer masks, grouping controls, full transform and free transform commands, as well as merging, flattening and matting.
Select	Manipulation and enhancement of selection borders through the use of special tools. Selection commands work closely with channels.
Filter	A mind-boggling array of image-processing choices including filters that blur, sharpen, distort, twirl, add noise, stylize, and customize selected portions of images in unbelievable ways.
View	All the window commands. Make things appear bigger and smaller as well as special monitor controls.
Window	Creation of new windows, with commands for zooming in and out. This menu also has commands for showing and hiding all palettes (Brushes, Color, Info, Channels, Path) as well as showing and hiding Rulers. Multiple open files appear by name in this window and can be brought to the front via the pull-down menu.

BRUSHES/OPTIONS WINDOW

The Brushes/Options window (Figure 1.8) opens by default when Photoshop starts up for the first time. If the window is not open (e.g., if the window was closed in an earlier session), you can open it by selecting **Window:Show Brushes** or **Window:Show Options** from the Window menu or by pressing **F5**.

The Brushes palette, labeled with its own tab, controls the size of the tool being used. The second tab is used to set options. Some of the options in the Brushes/Options palettes apply not only to the Paintbrush tool but to the Pencil, Airbrush, Rubber Stamp, Line, Type, Paint Bucket, Gradient, Smudge, Blur, Sharpen, Dodge, and Burn tools. You must select one of these tools (such as the Paintbrush) from the Toolbox to see all the options. When a tool is selected, the label on the second tab changes to reflect the currently active tool. It will read *Smudge Tool Options, Paint Bucket Options,* and so forth.

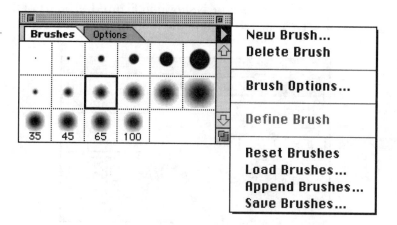

Figure 1.8 Brushes/Options window, showing Brushes palette.

The Options palette in this window also controls features of the Selection tools, such as the Marquee, Magic Wand, or Lasso. When one of these tools is active, any changes you make in the Brushes palette have no effect.

The Brushes Palette

The Brushes palette has two parts:

- The Brush Size and Shape boxes show the relative size and shape of the tip (including whether it's hard-edged or soft-edged) of the Paintbrush or other painting tool. You can create and store many different brush shapes including the custom shapes you create. These shapes may change depending upon the tool chosen. A scroll bar lets you view additional brushes that may have been defined or loaded into the palette, and you may resize the palette using the Zoom and Resize boxes like other Macintosh display windows.

- The Brushes menu is a fly-out menu with options for loading or creating new brushes, including **New Brush**, **Define Brush** (create a brush from the current selection in your image), **Reset Brushes**, **Load Brushes**, **Append Brushes**, and **Save Brushes**.

The Options Palette

The choices available in the Options palette change as you move from one tool to another. The Options palette is shown in Figure 1.9. Some of the types of options that may be available include the following:

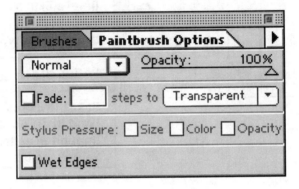

Figure 1.9 The Options palette.

- For painting tools like the Pencil and Paintbrush (and the Eraser), a slider control labeled *Opacity* lets you determine the transparency or opacity of the paint. Lower percentages mean more transparent paint. Higher percentages mean that the paint is more opaque. For the Airbrush, Smudge, and Blur/Sharpen tools, this slider determines the amount of pressure with which the effect is applied. For the Dodge/Burn tool, the slider determines the lightening or darkening effect in terms of exposure.

- Most of these tools also select a painting mode, which gives you a choice of ways to apply paint. Depending upon the mode, the underlying image will be affected in different ways. More about all these painting tool features in Chapter 3.

- Some tools offer different options available on this palette. For example, the Magic Wand Options let you set a brightness range, within which all similar pixels will be selected. Rubber Stamp Options determine how portions of images are duplicated from one picture to another.

COLOR/SWATCHES WINDOW

This group of palettes has the controls you need to set colors that will be used by your tools. To locate the Color/Swatches window, select **Window:Show Color** (or **Show Swatches**).

SHORTCUT

You may also press **F6** to display this window with the Color palette in front.

The Color Palette

The Color palette has five parts:

- The color sliders at left indicate the composition of the foreground and background colors. The default color mode is RGB (red, green, blue), so the colors are displayed as proportions of these three colors. Other color modes have different sliders.

- The two large and overlapping boxes on the right display the current foreground and background colors, just as they do in the color control area of the Toolbox. The foreground color is the color that is applied to the document whenever you use a drawing or painting tool or fill with a solid color. The background color is the color that is revealed when you use an eraser on the screen or when you cut out and move a selection. Click on one or the other to activate it, and then specify its color using the sliders or the Eyedropper tool as described later.

- At the bottom is a spectrum containing default color selections that can be used for painting or filling. To select a color, click on the foreground or background squares, click on the **Eyedropper** tool, position it over a color, and click again to select the color.

- An exclamation point inside a triangle (see Figure 1.10) appears whenever you have specified a color that does not have an equivalent in the CMYK color model (representing cyan, magenta, yellow, and black, the colors used in four-color process printing), which means that you'll find that color difficult to reproduce with any system that uses CMYK, such as an offset printing press. The closest valid color to the one you've specified appears in a swatch next to the triangle. Click in that area with the eyedropper to replace your specified color with the valid hue.

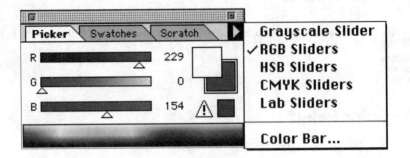

Figure 1.10 The Picker palette.

- The right-pointing triangle at the right of the palette is a fly-out menu that can be used to select a color model (i.e., grayscale, RGB, HSB, CMYK, or LAB) and to specify which of these color models is used for the spectrum at the bottom of the palette. We'll get to the differences between these color models in later chapters.

THE SWATCHES PALETTE

This palette is a grid of colored squares that can be selected with the Eyedropper tool by clicking (foreground) or **Option**-clicking(Mac) or **Alt**-clicking(PC) (to set the background color). Swatches are a useful way of keeping sets of colors that you want to reuse together. The fly-out menu on this palette lets you load, save, and append sets of swatches to create custom groups of colors.

THE LAYERS/CHANNELS/PATHS WINDOW

Three useful palettes that control channels, paths, and layers are contained within this window.

The Channels Palette

Choose **Window:Show Channels** to display this palette, shown in Figure 1.11. When the Channels palette opens in the RGB mode, you'll see three channels listed—a red channel, a green channel, and a blue channel—plus a composite of the previous three, the RGB image. Each of these has a keystroke combination assigned to it. Individual channels can be viewed separately and can be painted, edited, and manipulated with all of the Photoshop tools.

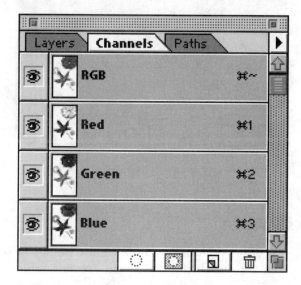

Figure 1.11 Channels palette.

The eye icons mean that a channel is being viewed.

The fly-out menu (revealed when you click on the palette's arrow) provides options for creating additional noncolor channels, deleting channels, and performing other channel manipulations.

Channels will be discussed in more detail in later chapters.

The Paths Palette

The Paths palette is used with the Pen tool. To open the Paths palette, select **Window:Show Paths**. The Pen tool can be used to define selection areas.

These selections can then be saved as mathematically defined (PostScript) paths or as selection borders.

The Paths palette is shown in Figure 1.12.

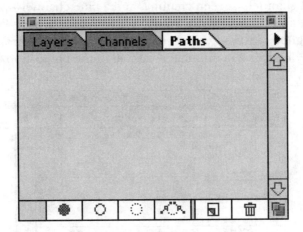

Figure 1.12 *The Paths palette.*

The Layers Palette

The Layers palette offers options for choosing the particular overlay you are working with from among all the layers you create, including the relative opacity of a layer. There's a small trash can at the bottom of the palette that can be used to discard or delete a layer. This palette's fly-out menu provides options for creating, merging, and duplicating layers. The Layers palette is shown in Figure 1.13.

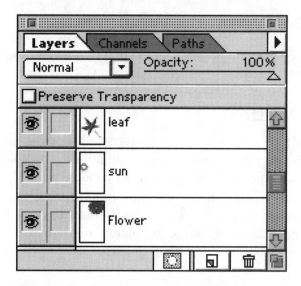

Figure 1.13 *The Layers palette.*

The Actions Palette

Actions allows you to record a sequence of editing steps in the form of an Actions List. You can apply the list to the another selection in the same image, another image file, or a large number of files in a batch operation. Using the Actions palette (Figure 1.14), Actions are easily saved and later "played" back to duplicate complicated, tiresome, or redundant editing steps.

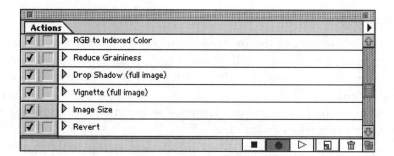

Figure 1.14 *The Actions palette.*

THE INFO/NAVIGATION WINDOW

These palettes share a window to help you find your way through your artwork at a glance.

The Info Palette

To make the Info palette appear, choose **Window:Show Info** or press **F8** (Figure 1.15). This palette gives you different information about the position of the mouse and the color directly under the mouse pointer.

The first two sections define the color in terms of RGB components or CMYK components. Press the small arrow in each of these boxes to select other ways to display color values. Alternately, the right arrow fly-out menu lets you set palette options for both of them.

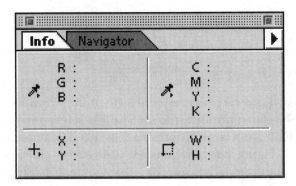

Figure 1.15 Info palette.

The lower-left section of the Info palette shows the position of the mouse in an open window by giving you its X and Y coordinates with the X coordinates representing its horizontal orientation and the Y coordinates representing its vertical orientation. The lower-right section gives you information on a live area within the marquee. You can request this information be given to you in the measurement type of your choice.

If you don't see any changing numbers in the Info palette, your mouse is pointing outside the window.

To find the numerical value of any screen location:

1. Place the mouse in the upper-left-hand corner of the window without clicking it. Both the X and Y coordinates should read 0.

2. Move the mouse horizontally across the window, keeping it as close to the top as possible without clicking or dragging. The X values will increase, but the Y values will remain at or close to 0. Continue all the way to the upper-right-hand corner.

3. Now move the mouse vertically to the lower-right-hand corner. The X values will stay the same, but the Y values will increase.

4. When the mouse is in the absolute lower-right-hand corner of the screen, the Info palette indicates the maximum screen size. This size is measured in pixels, inches, centimeters, points, or picas. To see the options for screen measurement, press on the small arrow near the X, Y coordinates box. A pop-up menu will appear indicating these choices.

The Navigation Palette

The Navigator lets you zoom to any part of your image, as well as resize your artwork with a single pull of the resizing slider. Alternatively, you can specify zoom levels numerically by increments of 0.44% to 1600%.

RULERS AND GRIDS

To show rulers on the top and left sides of a document window, choose **Show Rulers** from the Window menu or press **Command-R** (Mac) or **Ctrl-R** (PC). When the rulers appear (Figure 1.16), the units will be the same as those you last selected in the Info palette. You can reset the units in the Info palette or through the Units submenu of the Preferences command from the File menu.

As you move the mouse in the window, you'll see faint grayed-out lines in the rulers, mirroring your movements. These positioning lines will become useful when you want to draw a box or a line of specific dimensions or create a centered shape in the window. You can also use these guidelines to position the Type tool, as we will when you create your first document.

There may be times when you want to change the 0,0 point on the rulers. To do this, click in the left-hand corner box where the rulers come together and hold the mouse button down. As you drag out into the window, you will see that the mouse pointer has turned into a set of crosshairs that extend up into the ruler area. When you release the mouse button, the on-screen crosshairs will disappear and the 0,0 point will have moved in the rulers (Figure 1.17).

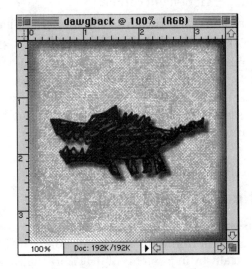

Figure 1.16 *Window with Rulers option active.*

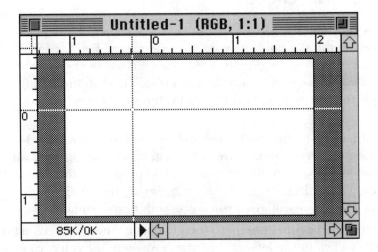

Figure 1.17 *Rulers with repositioned 0,0 point.*

To reset the 0,0 point back to its default position in the upper-left-hand corner, click in the crosshairs box just below the Close box.

MAGNIFYING AND REDUCING YOUR VIEW

To see the effect of the Magnifier/Reducer tool, you need to have an image on your screen. Remember that these tools enlarge the image only for display purposes, they do not increase or decrease the size of your actual file (Figure 1.18).

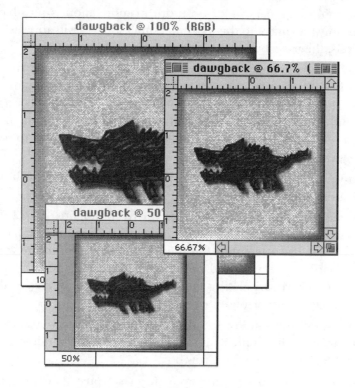

Figure 1.18 *One file in three working sizes.*

To change the size of an image:

1. Choose the **Eyedropper** tool and select the color of your choice in the Picker palette. Click on the **Paintbrush** tool and draw a squiggle in the middle of the open window.

2. Without changing tools, press **Command+** (Mac) or **Ctrl+** (PC) to enlarge the window. You can use the plus sign on the basic keyboard or on the number pad on the extended keyboard. When a new window is created, it is first displayed at a smaller window size and can be enlarged in this way.

3. Select the **Magnifying** tool and click on the squiggle to enlarge the image. Each click will enlarge the image by a factor of two, and the menu bar will indicate this enlargement. The first click will enlarge the window from 100% (actual size) to 200% (double actual size). You can enlarge the image 16 times to 1600%. The plus sign in the middle of the tool disappears when no more magnification is possible. As you magnify the image to this extreme, small squares will appear. These are pixels, the basic building blocks of a digitized image.

4. To reduce the image by factors of two, press the **Option** key (Mac) or **Alt** key (PC) while you click in the window with the Magnifying tool. You'll know you're in a reduction mode because the plus sign in the middle of a glass changes to a minus. Click to reduce the image until you've brought it down to actual size. Continue clicking to reduce the image to fractions of actual size.

5. To reset the image to actual size, double-click in the box for the Magnifying tool.

6. To zoom into the window using keyboard commands, press **Command+** (Mac) or **Ctrl+** (PC). To zoom out, press **Command-** (Mac) or **Ctrl-** (PC). You can use either the plus and minus signs at the top of your keyboard or the plus and minus signs on the keypad if you have an extended keyboard. Using these keys increases or decreases the size of the image by single-digit increments.

7. To expand the window to full-screen height you can also click in the **Zoom** box in the upper-right-hand corner of the window or drag the window larger using the Grow box.

8. We don't want to save this squiggle masterpiece, so close the file by selecting **Close** from the File menu or pressing **Command-W** (Mac) or **Ctrl-W** (PC). When the Alert box prompts you to save the file (Figure 1.19), click **Don't Save.**

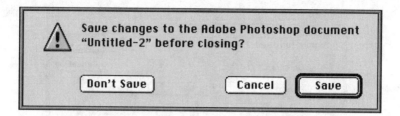

Figure 1.19 Alert box.

WARNING

Whenever you see the exclamation mark in a triangle in Photoshop (Figure 1.19), the program is warning you that you're about to do something more or less irreversible. When you see it pop up in a palette or a dialog box, stop and think about it. Is this something you *really* want to do?

EXERCISE 1.1: CREATING YOUR FIRST DOCUMENT

We're going to create a handbill for a party supply company. The image will consist of three overlapping balloons with the name of the firm at the bottom.

Creating a New File

1. Create a new file by selecting **New** from the File menu or by pressing **Command-N** (Mac) or **Ctrl-N** (PC).

2. When the New dialog box appears, change the units from pixels to inches using the pop-up menu (Figure 1.20). Enter **3** inches for width and **3.75** inches for height. Don't worry about screen resolution for now; leave it at 72 pixels per inch. (You can press the **Tab** key to move among the option boxes or double-click in each box to activate it.) Click **OK** when you're finished.

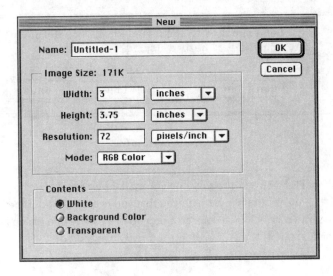

Figure 1.20 *Changing units in the New box.*

Making a Selection

1. Make sure the Info, Brushes, and Colors palettes are open and that the rulers are visible. Select these items from the Window menu if needed.

2. Select the **Elliptical Marquee** tool from the Toolbox.

3. Move the mouse into the window. Starting near the upper-left-hand corner, click and drag downward to create an oval shape. The mouse pointer will turn into crosshairs as you do. Release the mouse when the oval is approximately 1 inch high (you can tell by reading the height and width display that appears at the bottom of the Info palette; see Figure 1.21). Don't worry about getting precise shapes and numbers for now; we're just learning basic concepts here.

The oval wiggling shape you see is called a *selection* or a *selected area* (Figure 1.22). The *marching ants* around the edge are the active selection border. The selection defines an area in which you can draw, paint, and edit the image. Outside of this area, tools are ineffective. This selection will remain active until you do something else with a selection tool, deselect the selection by clicking outside the selection area, or press **Command-D** (Mac) or **Ctrl-D**

(PC). If you accidentally make the selection go away, the pull-down Edit menu will offer **Undo Deselect** as the first option.

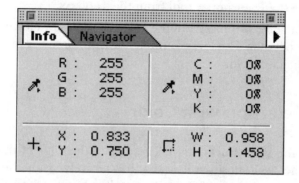

Figure 1.21 Info palette showing selection height and width.

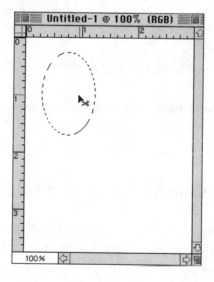

Figure 1.22 An elliptical selection.

To undo any action, press **Command-Z** (Mac) or **Ctrl-Z** (PC) or select **Undo** from the Edit menu. Photoshop supports only one level of undo. This means that if you execute more than one action, you can undo only the last one.

Picking a Color

1. Choose the **Eyedropper** tool from the Toolbox.
2. Select a color you like from the color swatches by clicking once on the square of color. The foreground color icon on the Toolbox will fill with your selected color.

Filling a Selection with Color

1. Select the **Paint Bucket** tool. The drip at the edge of the bucket is the tool's hot spot. Position it so that it is entirely inside the oval selection border, and click once. The selection border fills with color; this is your first balloon! To temporarily hide a selection border (also called *marching ants*, the *crawlies*, etc.), press **Command-H** (Mac) or **Ctrl-H** (PC). When you do this, the selection has not been deactivated, only hidden. To make the edges of the selection appear, press **Command-H** (Mac) or **Ctrl-H** (PC) again.

2. Press **Command-D** (Mac) or **Ctrl-D** (PC) to deselect the elliptical selection permanently.

3. Select the **Elliptical Marquee** tool again. Place it below and to the right of the first oval and drag to draw a second oval. You can make this oval larger if you like and make the second oval overlap the first.

More Ways to Choose Colors and Fill Selections

1. Choose a second color you like from the Color Swatch palette. The tool changes to an eyedropper automatically. Click on the color choice.

2. Hold down the **Option** key (Mac) or the **Alt** key (PC) and press **Delete**. The second oval turns your chosen color, demonstrating a second way to fill a selected area. Deselect the area by clicking with the **Elliptical** tool outside of the yellow oval. This is another way to deselect an active selection.

3. Using the Elliptical tool, draw yet a third oval, this time above and slightly to the right of the second oval. Again, make sure they overlap. Select yet another color from the Color Swatch palette. Select **Fill** from

the Edit menu. The Fill dialog box appears specifying a fill with the foreground color at 100% opacity in normal mode (Figure 1.23). Click **OK** or press **Return** to make this choice. The third oval fills with blue. This is a third way to fill a selection border. Deselect the oval by pressing **Command-D** (Mac) or **Ctrl-D** (PC).

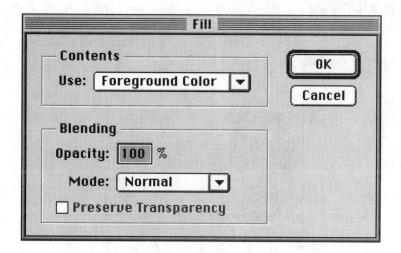

Figure 1.23 *The Fill dialog box.*

Now, we'll give the balloons strings.

Painting with the Paintbrush Tool

1. Select the **Paintbrush** tool from the Toolbox. If the Brushes palette is not open, open it. Select the second smallest brush size in the top row.

2. Move the Paintbrush tool into the Picker palette and, as it turns into an eyedropper, pick a medium gray. Every Toolbox tool turns into an eyedropper when moved across the swatches of the Picker palette.

3. To give each of your balloons a string, position the Paintbrush tool at the bottom of an oval. Press the mouse button as you drag a line downward. Release the button at the end of the stroke and reposition the mouse on the next oval. (Don't worry about being neat—it's supposed to be a wavy line.) Do this for each of the three ovals.

Using the Magic Wand Tool and Applying a Filter

Next, we'll apply a filter to the balloons to give them a more realistic look. Filters create special effects and can be applied to the entire file or to a specific area. In this case, the filter will be applied only to the first balloon.

1. Pick the **Magic Wand** selection tool. Move the wand into the document window, and click it once in the first balloon. The wand selects all pixels of similar color and value, extending the selection all the way to the edge of the balloon (Figure 1.24).

Figure 1.24 Balloons in progress.

2. From the Filter menu and the Other submenu, select **High Pass**. The High Pass dialog box will open (Figure 1.25). Leave the radius at 10.0 pixels. The High Pass filter looks for the highlights and brightest areas in an image and emphasizes them. Used in this way, the High Pass filter gives a feeling of dimension.

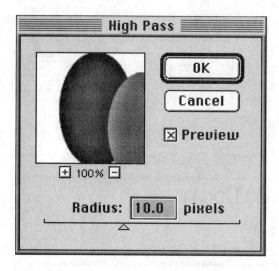

Figure 1.25 High Pass filter dialog box.

3. Repeat steps 1 and 2 with the other two balloons. Deselect the blue balloon when you're finished.

Finally, we'll add some type to the poster:

1. Use the eyedropper to change the foreground color to black.
2. Select the **Type** tool (the large *T* in the Toolbox). The mouse arrow will turn into a shape that designates a text insertion point.
3. Using the positioning marks in the rulers as a guideline, move the mouse so that it is centered in the lower half of the screen (*X* = 1.5, *Y* = 2.25). The *X* and *Y* values in the Info palette will help you. When you've positioned the mouse correctly, press the mouse button and click. The Type Tool dialog box will appear (Figure 1.26).

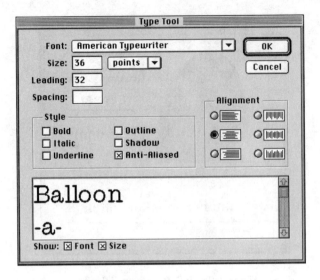

Figure 1.26 *Type Tool dialog box.*

4. Select a font (typeface) by clicking on the pop-up menu. A list of type-faces will be displayed. We've chosen **American Typewriter**, but you can choose any typeface you have installed in your system.

5. Enter **36** for the type size.

6. Enter **32** for the leading. Leading (pronounced *ledding*) is the space between lines. Specifying 32 means the lines will be a little tighter together than if you selected a more normal leading of 36 for 36 point type.

7. Set spacing (letter spacing) to **0** or leave the box blank.

8. For type style, check only **Anti-Aliased**. Anti-aliasing gives PostScript type smooth edges.

9. Choose **Center** for the alignment of the text.

10. Finally, place the pointer in the open area at the bottom of the window. Type **Balloon -a- Rama** on three separate lines, hitting **Return** or **Enter** after each section you want to appear on a different line.

11. Click **OK** to close the Type Tool dialog box. The type will appear floating over the background, stacked and centered, with an active selection border visible. If your screen does not look this way, select **Undo** from the Edit menu, or press **Delete** to remove the floating type and start over from step 3.

Copying and Pasting a Floating Selection

Now we will place a copy of the type on top of itself to create a drop shadow effect. You won't see any changes on the screen yet:

1. Copy the floating type selection by pressing **Command-C** (Mac) or **Ctrl-C** (PC) or choosing **Copy** from the Edit menu. You won't see any changes on the screen yet.

2. Paste this copy on top of the type by pressing **Command-V** (Mac) or **Ctrl-V** (PC) or choosing **Paste** from the Edit menu. It will seem as though nothing has happened, but what you've done is placed a copy of black type on top of black type. (Stay tuned.)

3. Select a light color that you like from the color palette. Press **Option-Delete** (Mac) or **Ctrl-Delete** (PC) to fill the black selection with the new color.

4. Use the directional arrow keys on your keyboard to move the selected lightly colored type down and to the right. Click twice on the up arrow and twice on the left arrow. A black drop shadow should appear to peek out from behind the green selected area (Figure 1.27).

SHORTCUT

If your keyboard doesn't have directional arrows, you can move the selection (step 4) by positioning the Type tool inside the selection border of any of the letters until the pointer changes into an arrow. Then, click and drag the green selection very slightly up and to the left, and let go. If you go too far, press **Command-Z** (Mac) or **Ctrl-Z** (PC) to undo and try again. Even if you have directional arrows on your keyboard to nudge the selection, this is a good skill to practice.

Figure 1.27 *Moving copied selection to reveal drop shadow.*

5. Press **Command-D** (Mac) or **Ctrl-D** (PC) to deselect everything. You're finished.

6. To see the finished effect, hide the rulers (**Command-R** on the Mac or **Ctrl-R** on the PC) and select the full-screen display in the screen mode box, which will set off your artwork against a black background.

7. To prepare to save your document, return to either of the two screen display modes that include a menu bar.

Saving Your Document

To save your document, choose **Save** from the Edit menu or press **Command-S** (Mac) or **Ctrl-S** (PC). A Save dialog box will appear prompting you to enter the name of the file and the format in which you wish to save it (Figure 1.28). Photoshop supports a wide range of formats. Some of these formats can be seen by clicking on the Save box pop-up menu. The specifics of these formats will be discussed in a later chapter. For now, you can save the file in the basic Photoshop format, which comes up as the default:

1. Press **Tab** to select the Title box if it is not already selected.
2. Enter the name of the file and click **OK** or press **Return**.

WARNING

Even though we left saving your work for the end of the lesson, it's a good idea to save your file early and often when you are working on a complex project to avoid unexpected data loss. (A sadder but wiser user tip: Invest in a battery-operated power supply for both your computer and monitor. These power supplies can buy you enough time to save your work and turn off your computer safely in case of a power outage.)

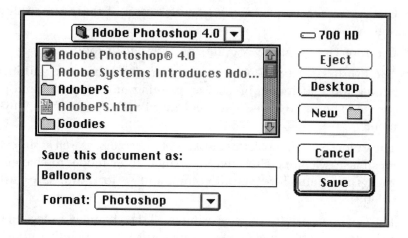

Figure 1.28 Save dialog box.

What You've Learned

Installation and Startup

- Installing Photoshop 4.0 on a Macintosh computer
- Installing Photoshop 4.0 on a PC
- Launching Photoshop and personalizing your copy

Tools, Palettes, and Rulers

- Use the Toolbox to choose tools for selecting, painting, and editing images
- Use the Color Control mode to select background and foreground colors, to reverse the two, and to reset the colors to their defaults—black foreground, white background
- Use the Mask Mode to choose between quick mask on and quick mask off
- Use the Screen Display mode to choose one of three screen display options
- Use Tool Tips to quickly scan the use of a specific tool
- The Brushes palette displays controls for all the painting and image-editing tools, including brush size, painting mode, opacity, and pressure or exposure. Choose **Load and Save Brush** options from a fly-out menu
- The Color/Swatches palettes display default colors, as well as sliders for creating new colors. Use them to change color mode, to change the background and foreground colors, and to load and save custom palettes
- The Channels palette allows viewing of all the channels associated with a document. The number of channels will vary depending upon the mode being used. The Channels palette lets you selectively view and write on one or a combination of color and/or black-and-white channels simultaneously
- Watch the Info palette for information about mouse position, pixel color values, height and width of selected objects, angle of rotation of selected areas, and distance measurement
- Use the Paths palette to make and save selections with the Pen tool
- Use rulers and grids to assist with mouse placement and drawing shapes or lines of exact dimensions. Ruler units can be changed on the Info palette

Document Display Reduction and Magnification

- Change the display image size with the Magnifying/Reducing tool from the Toolbox. Click in the window to enlarge by factors of two or **Option**-click (Mac) or **Alt**-click (PC) to reduce the image by factors of two

- The keyboard alternative is to change the display image size by factors of one by pressing **Command+** (Mac) or **Ctrl+** (PC) to increase and **Command-** (Mac) or **Ctrl-** (PC) to decrease.

Creative Skills

- Choose areas to manipulate using selection tools
- Fill selected areas with foreground color using a variety of techniques
- Paint using anti-aliased brushes
- Create type using the Type tool
- Apply filters to selected areas
- Copy, paste, and move selections to create multilayered effects
- Manage your documents
- Create a new file by selecting **New** from the File menu
- Save a file with the **Save** or **Save as** *filename* command from the File menu

CHAPTER 2

Adobe Photoshop Principles

In this chapter...

- Object-oriented and paint-type programs
- Additive and subtractive color models
- Bits, bytes, and megabytes
- Color, grayscale, and bitmapped modes
- Identifying file size, channels, and mode
- Preferences file

How Computers Create Images

Understanding basic Photoshop concepts and why Photoshop does what it does so well will help you use the program.

There are two primary forms of graphics-creation programs:

- bitmap programs such as Adobe Photoshop, Fractal Design's Painter, and PixelPaint Professional
- object-oriented illustration programs such as Adobe Illustrator, Aldus FreeHand, and Deneba Canvas

About Paint-Type Programs and Pixels

Paint-type programs create pictures with minuscule dots called *pixels*, which are the smallest units of measure on a computer screen. Scanned photographs and artwork are paint-type images represented by pixels. To transfer a photograph or drawing onto the computer screen for image processing, it must first be *digitized*, that is, turned into numerical data by a scanner. Only then can data be displayed on a computer screen as a large collection of pixels. When viewed at 800%, it is easy to see the pixels that comprise an image (Figure 2.1).

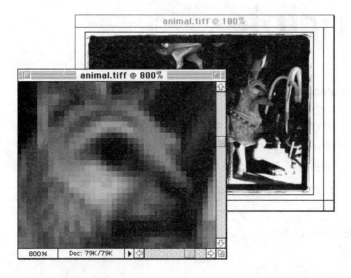

Figure 2.1 *When viewed at 800%, it's very easy to see the pixels that make up the image.*

Exercise 2.1: Learning about Pixels

1. Create a new file by selecting **New** from the File menu.

2. In the New dialog box, make the size 640 pixels wide by 480 pixels high. Leave the screen resolution at the default setting of 72 pixels per inch and set the mode as RGB.

3. Enlarge the screen to 100% by pressing **Command-+** (Mac) or **Control-+** (PC). Change the foreground color to a bright yellow by selecting a yellow swatch on the Swatches palette. Select the entire screen by pressing **Command-A** (Mac) or **Ctrl-A** (PC); then press **Option-delete** to fill the screen with yellow. Make sure the background color remains white.

4. Select the **Paintbrush** tool and click on the largest brush in the top row of the Brushes palette (the large hard-edged brush). Change the foreground color to black, as you did earlier with yellow.

5. Draw a squiggle in the middle of the image. It will appear to have smooth edges.

6. Using the Navigator palette, slide the control to the extreme right, which will bring your image to 1600%. Still using the Navigator, drag the live area box over the small representation of the image until you have reached the place where your squiggle is. On the main screen, small squares will have become visible around the edges of the painted line. These are pixels.

7. Select **View:Show Rulers** to get a sense of the size of the image.

8. From the View menu, select **New View**. This will create another view of your work, but not a new document. The new window will have the same title (*Untitled-#*), but the magnification amount will be different, and what you do in one window happens simultaneously in the other. Move the second window to the side to see the first window if you need to.

 When more than one window is open, clicking anywhere in any window behind the active window makes it active and brings it to the front. If the other windows are smaller, they will be obscured. To see the smaller windows, either reshape the large window to reduce it or select the other windows by name from the bottom of the Window menu.

NOTE

In the enlarged window, notice that what gives the line its smooth edge is the averaging of pixel values between the yellow and the contrasting black brush stroke. This is the essence of Photoshop: painting on pixels. Even though you can move a floating selection around, as you did when you offset the floating type in the Balloon-A-Rama exercise, you cannot simply grab a chunk of pasted-down pixels and move them elsewhere as if they were a self-contained object. To see what happens when you try to move pixels in Photoshop, try this:

1. Select the **Lasso** from the Toolbox.
2. Move the Lasso into the document window. Press the mouse button and draw a rough circle in the area where your yellow background and black squiggle meet. Release the mouse button, and you have a selected area.
3. Select the **Move** tool from the Toolbox. Position the Move tool inside the selection border.
4. Press the mouse button and drag the selection slightly upward. Notice the jagged border that appears as you drag; this border is composed of the edges of the pixels (Figure 2.2).

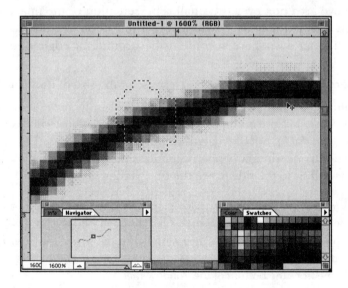

Figure 2.2 *Selecting a cluster of pixels. Note the Navigator's positioning on the image.*

5. Let go of the mouse button. Behind the selection your background color (white) is revealed (Figure 2.3).

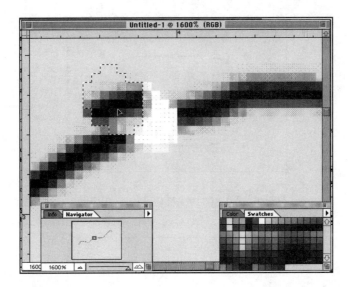

Figure 2.3 *Moving a cluster of pixels with the Move tool reveals the background color.*

6. Press **Command-Z** (Mac) or **Ctrl-Z** (PC) to undo your last move and put the selection back where it belongs.

7. When you're finished, double-click the **Eraser** tool to erase the entire image. Press **OK**. If your background color is still set to white, the window will turn white.

In a paint-type program such as Photoshop, you can literally change an image one pixel at a time. This is great for retouching, creating natural textures, and representing the objects of the "real world" in a photo-realistic manner.

About Object-Oriented Programs

Object-oriented programs such as Adobe Illustrator create images in a completely different manner from pixel-type programs. In object-oriented/illustration programs, shapes and lines are created with mathematical instructions, rather than dots of color (Figures 2.4 and 2.5), so that they become solitary objects. In a sense, object-oriented graphics are like paper cutouts that can be endlessly shuffled, overlaid, resized, and rearranged.

Adobe's PostScript has become the universal language for the creation of these equation-drawn lines and shapes.

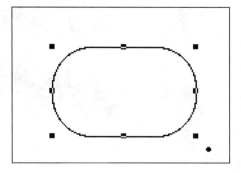

Figure 2.4 *A line created in Adobe Illustrator.*

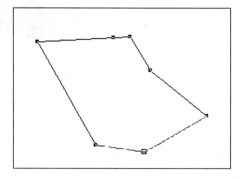

Figure 2.5 *A freeform shape created in Adobe Illustrator.*

For example, when you draw a shape in an object-oriented program, you tell the computer the size, outline, and dimensions of the shape; whether or not the shape should have a border; and how thick the border should be, what color to use as a fill, and so on. Through PostScript, these instructions are coded into each object you create, so that you can move objects around on the screen or copy and paste them into other documents without affecting them or their backgrounds. These circumstances are quite different from what happened earlier when we drew on yellow pixels with a black brush and then moved a cluster of pixels by lassoing them.

Pixel Programs versus Object-Oriented Programs

The advantage of object-oriented graphics is that shapes and lines can be rearranged and resized larger or smaller as many times as necessary, without any loss of detail when they are printed. They are excellent for the creation of line illustrations and hard-edged text. Their drawback (from one point of view) is that because they are defined mathematically, they have a computer-drawn look and feel. You can't properly retouch a photograph or create the same kind of subtle painterly effects that you can in Photoshop.

In summary, both types of programs are excellent tools, each with specialized uses. Why should this matter to a Photoshop user? Two big reasons:

- Until Photoshop, you couldn't layer images and then shuffle them around as you can with object-oriented programs. Once a pixel is changed, it's changed, unless you press **Undo**. For the most successful results, it's important to plan the order in which you'll work and to save interim versions of your project as you go.

- Each time you rotate or resize a selected Photoshop image (or portion of an image) you affect the picture quality on a pixel-by-pixel basis. For example, you add pixels when you enlarge an area and you take them away when you reduce.

Repetitive enlarging and reducing have no effect on image quality in an object-oriented program because there are no pixels to manipulate, just formulas, but it makes a big difference in Photoshop, and the cumulative results may not be what you desire.

COLOR

Color is described differently on the computer than in print. On a computer, color is additive. In print, color is subtractive.

Additive Color: The Sum of All Colors Is White

In grammar school you learned that red, yellow, and blue were primary colors, and that when you combined them you got a muddy brown. But those were actually primary pigments, the components of paints or inks, which are completely different from the primary colors that make up most of the visible spectrum. When you describe light, the primaries are red, green, and blue, as Isaac Newton discovered with a prism more than 300 years ago.

Each color that a human sees occupies a different position on the spectrum and has its own distinctive wavelength and frequency. When your eye sees all the colors of light together in equal intensity, the perception is that you're seeing white light. By the same token, when no light strikes the retina, we have the illusion that we're seeing black.

Because the colors red, green, and blue (RGB) can be combined to make the colors we can see as well as white light, they are called *additive* colors. When you watch TV or experience combined lighting effects at a concert, you're experiencing the effects of additive color.

Subtractive Color: The Sum of All Colors Approaches Black

Back in grammar school, starting with a clean, white paper, the more full-strength red, yellow, and blue finger paint you added, the darker and muddier the color became. Because combining these primary colors absorbs reflected light and creates the impression of black, they are called *subtractive* colors. Each additional color overlaid on paper subtracts from the amount of light that bounces back for your eye to see.

Subtractive colors form the basis of all printing on paper. The pigments cyan, magenta, yellow, and black (CMYK) are combined in various percentages to create the colors of the spectrum. (K is the abbreviation for black in four-color printing, to avoid confusion with the B used to represent blue in the RGB model.)

It's important to recognize the difference between these two color models, because here lies the challenge of converting what you see on your computer monitor (an additive model) to what you want to see on the printed page (a subtractive model). Photoshop gives you the tools and techniques to translate between these two basic color models, as we'll learn later, in Chapter 14, which explores creating color separations for printing.

Hue, Saturation, and Brightness: A Way of Describing Color

As you read this section, keep your Color palette open. Click on the arrow at the side of the palette. As the pop-up menu appears, select the **HSB** color model. You will notice now that the sliders describe the foreground color as HSB instead of RGB or another model (Figure 2.6). You can move the sliders and observe the effects on the foreground color.

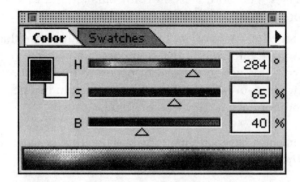

Figure 2.6 *The Color palette ready to calculate hue, saturation, and brightness.*

Color has three different attributes that give its unique position in three-dimensional color "space." Each color can be described in terms of:

- *Hue*—a description of the absolute place of the color on the spectrum according to its wavelength. In the visible spectrum from infrared to ultraviolet, orange-red has a long wavelength compared to the shorter wavelength of indigo. The slider bar for hue looks like a rainbow.

- *Saturation*—the intensity of a color, or its purity. In video, saturation is also known as *chroma level*. The saturation of a color is related inversely to the amount of its opposite's color that it contains. For example, a fully saturated red contains no green or blue. Add equal parts of green and blue to pure red, and you lower the saturation.

- *Brightness*—a description of how bright or dark the color appears in terms of how much light is reflected back to the eye. Another word for brightness is *value*. When you add black to a hue, you lower its value. Adding white raises or increases its value.

Although **HSB** is a viewing option on the Colors palette menu, it is not a true mode like RGB, CMYK, or Grayscale. It is merely a way of viewing and evaluating the color in an image.

BITS, BYTES, AND MEGABYTES

Perhaps you've heard color described as 8-bit or 24-bit and seen references to bitmapped images. The word *bit* is short for binary digit. Bits are the smallest units of measurement of computer data.

Eight bits together make a *byte*, but a byte contains more than eight times the information of a bit. Each of the eight bits in a byte can be turned on or off, so a byte contains two to the eighth power of information (2^8)—or 256 possibilities. Twenty-four-bit color images contain eight bits per pixel for each of the three components: red, green, and blue.

Two-hundred-fifty-six is a magic number—you will see it repeatedly throughout Photoshop to describe color and grayscale values.

N O T E

A thousand bytes is called a *kilobyte*, abbreviated by the letter *K* (no relation to the *K* in CMYK). A thousand kilobytes is called a *megabyte* (MB). A file that is 1234K could also be represented as a 1.2-megabyte file, abbreviated 1.2 MB. Word processing files are usually in the double-digit kilobyte size, sometimes more if they're very long. Paint-type files, however, can routinely be in the megabyte range, which is why a lot of random access memory (RAM) and a large hard disk are essential for Photoshop success: Photoshop demands room to run (RAM, again) and the hard drive space to store all your creations.

EXERCISE 2.2: GRAYSCALE, COLOR MODES, AND MORE

Photoshop supports a number of different color modes, some of which will receive special attention in later chapters. There are four primary modes, however, that you must understand in order to take advantage of Photoshop's many tools.

Grayscale Mode

In Photoshop's grayscale mode, 256 shades of gray, from pure white (255) to solid black (0) make up the picture (Figure 2.7). Not all those shades have to be used, however. The median color in the grayscale spectrum has a value of 128. When you are in grayscale mode, you can use all the painting and editing tools, including Photoshop's many plug-in filters.

Figure 2.7 *The same image in grayscale and bitmap modes.*

RGB Mode (Color)

Because RGB is an additive color model, all colors of the spectrum can be created using red, green, and blue in varying degrees of brightness (value). Each of these component colors occupies its own channel.

1. Your open file should be all white, and the foreground color should be white. On the Color palette fly-out submenu, change the mode from HSB to **RGB**. All three RGB sliders will be to the far right.

2. Select **Preferences** under the File menu. Select **Displays & Cursors** and make sure that the **Color channels in color** box is checked.

3. Open the Channels palette. This isn't necessary for our next step, but it will help show you the relationship between viewing channels and the Channels palette.

4. Press **Ctrl-1** (PC) or **Command-1** (Mac). The red channel will appear.

5. Press **Ctrl-2** (PC) or **Command-2** (Mac). The green channel will appear (Figure 2.8).

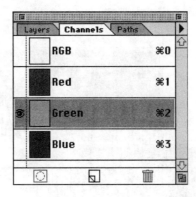

Figure 2.8 Channels palette displaying green channel only.

6. Press **Command-3**. The blue channel will appear (Figure 2.9).

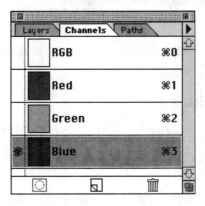

Figure 2.9 Channels palette displaying blue channel only.

7. Press **Command-Shift-~**. The composite of all three channels will reappear (Figure 2.10). There is no RGB "channel" per se, which is why the channel number is zero. What you see when you press **Command-0** is the sum of the combined red, green, and blue values of the three component channels.

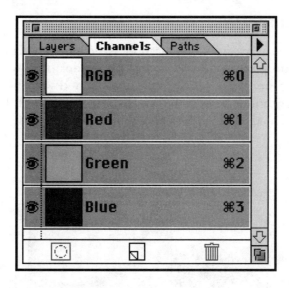

Figure 2.10 Channels palette displaying R, G, and B channels simultaneously.

Because 24-bit color uses eight bits of information (256 possibilities) for each pixel component of red, green, and blue, 24-bit color gives you 256 x 256 x 256 possibilities, or 16,772,216 colors, which should be enough for any designer.

Any of these 16.7 million colors can be represented with varying brightnesses of red, green, and blue in their respective channels. In each channel, 0 is the darkest value (black) and 255 is the lightest (white).

CMYK Mode

Just as the RGB mode has three channels composing an image, the CMYK mode has four channels: cyan, magenta, yellow, and black. As discussed earlier, the CMYK colors represent the inks used in the four-color printing process; therefore, they are called *process colors*. Translating an image from the computer screen (RGB mode) to the printed page requires color separation, and RGB files must be converted into CMYK files before separations can be created. RGB-to-CMYK file conversion will be discussed in later chapters.

Bitmapped Mode

In contrast to the grayscale and color modes, the bitmapped mode offers only black and white pixels—no colors and no shades of gray (Figure 2.11). Although many wonderful effects can be obtained working in this mode, bitmapped files cannot be scaled, distorted, or treated with Photoshop's filters. To convert a color file to bitmapped mode, it must first be converted to grayscale.

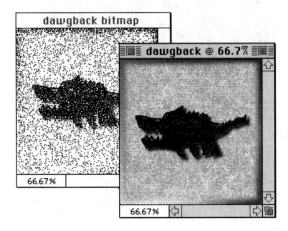

Figure 2.11 A bitmapped image with a diffusion dither, behind the same image with a grayscale treatment.

Grayscale, RGB, CMYK, bitmapped, and other Photoshop modes will be covered again in later chapters.

GETTING INFORMATION ABOUT AN OPEN FILE

The lower-left-hand corner of an open window lets you know the percentage of your file as you view it as well as the size of your open file in kilobytes (Figure 2.12). Also shown in the box is the size the file will be when saved in compressed format. A fly-out menu that lets you choose from actual document size or scratch size (the amount of memory or disk space Photoshop needs to maintain both the file and copies needed to undo actions) is available.

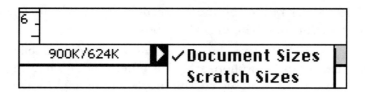

Figure 2.12 *File size box.*

Hold down the **Option** key while you click on the File Size box, and you will see a pop-up display (Figure 2.13). It will tell you the following:

- height and width of the file
- number of channels the file contains
- mode (color or grayscale)
- resolution of the image in pixels per inch

If you wish to see the height and width displayed in inches or centimeters as well as in pixels, change the units in the Info palette (under the pop-up menu attached to the x, y box) or in the **Preferences:Units** submenu under the File menu.

```
    Width: 190 pixels (2.639 inches)
   Height: 243 pixels (3.375 inches)
 Channels:   3 (RGB Color)
Resolution:  72 pixels/inch
```

Figure 2.13 *Pop-up display with more file information.*

Preferences

The Preferences menu allows you to customize Photoshop to suit your working style and your printing and color separation requirements (Figure 2.14).

There are eight general-purpose dialog boxes within the Preferences menu:

- **General**—allows you to choose the type of color picker and designate the way new pixels will be created when a file is resized or resampled through the interpolation options. Many of these items will be covered in detail later in the appropriate sections. For now, the default selections will function best for your purposes.

- **Saving Files**—offers you the option of downward compatibility with earlier versions of Photoshop, as well as other specialized saving options. Here, you're also best served with the default settings for now.

- **Displays & Cursors**—faster or smoother CMYK composites, dithering and diffusions options, and options for viewing some of the cursors in different ways. You will want to change some of these as your expertise develops.

- **Transparency & Gamut**—allows you to set transparency and color for the Gamut Warning indicator as well as options for how the grid is viewed.

- **Units & Rulers**—select how you want your document to be measured: inches, pixels, centimeters, picas, or points. You can also set the Column Size Width and Gutter to correspond with dimensions in your desktop publishing program, if you are preparing a file to fit into a predetermined space.

- **Guides & Grid**—select the color and measurement system for your grid and guides. You might try playing with some of these if any of the current colors bother you. I've known artists, for example, who were horribly bothered by the default light blue. Also, resetting the width of the grid might bring it more in line with a publishing program you are familiar with, making it easier to identify with the program.

- **Plug-ins & Scratch Disk**—use this option to select the folder in which your plug-ins will be kept. Plug-ins include the filters that appear under your Filter menu as well as Acquire and Export options (such as scanning and file-compression modules) that appear under your File menu. For the Scratch Disk options, Photoshop uses hard disk space as "virtual" memory to perform file operations when there is not enough RAM available. Select your choice of primary and secondary scratch disks in this dialog box. Your primary scratch disk should be your fastest hard disk if you have more than one. You must have empty hard disk space to take advantage of this option. Your choice will not take effect until the next time you open Photoshop.

- **Image Cache**—refers to the level of RAM desired for working images. Photoshop 4 defaults to four levels, which should be adequate for most purposes.

NOTE

The Photoshop preference defaults have been set to be adequate for most basic purposes. A rule of thumb: If you're not sure if it should be changed it probably doesn't need to be. When you've gained the expertise to want the program to provide more functionality, you'll know what to change.

There is a separate Preferences fly-out menu directly below the Preferences menu that includes four options specifically for printing and the preparation of color separations:

- **Monitor Setup...**
- **Printing Inks Setup...**
- **Separation Setup...**
- **Separation Tables...**

These preferences will be covered in a later chapter.

WHAT YOU'VE LEARNED

Photoshop Fundamentals

- There are two main types of graphics programs: object-oriented and pixel-type.
- Adobe Photoshop is a pixel-type program that creates images out of pixels.
- Object-oriented programs create images with mathematical equations using languages like PostScript.
- On the computer, color follows an additive model; the colors red, green, and blue combine to create white, just as different colors of the light spectrum combine to create white light.
- In four-color process printing, the pigments cyan, yellow, magenta, and black combine to create colors on paper.
- Color can also be described in terms of hue, saturation, and brightness.
- Information is stored in memory increments of bits, bytes, kilobytes, and megabytes.

- Photoshop works with two primary color modes: RGB and CMYK (16.7 million colors) and the grayscale mode (256 levels of gray). There are other modes for specialized purposes.

File Information

- The lower-left-hand corner of an open window tells you the file size in kilobytes (K) and the size of present operations.
- Press the **Option** key while you click on this box to learn file dimensions, channels, color mode, and resolution.

Preferences

- Use **Preferences…** (**File:Preferences** menu) to set preferences for the color picker, grid display, and other utility features.

CHAPTER 3

Image Creation Tools

In this chapter…

- Using painting and drawing tools
- Creating new brushes
- Using different painting modes
- Cloning images
- Painting with patterns
- Creating lines and arrows
- Erasing and restoring images

PAINTING CONCEPTS

Anti-Aliasing

When you took a close-up view of the black squiggle you drew in Chapter 2, you saw that the pixels surrounding the solid black line gradually changed in color until they matched the yellow of the background. In the normal view, however, all you saw was a smooth black line. The smoothing of a line, shape, selection, or a piece of type with respect to its background is called *anti-aliasing*. It helps the edges of images blend smoothly into the background upon which they're pasted, painted, cloned, and so forth. Many of Photoshop's tools feature anti-aliasing either as an option (Paint Bucket and Type tools) or as a built-in feature (Paintbrush, Airbrush, Rubber Stamp, Smudge, Sharpen/Blur and Dodge/Burn tools).

Foreground and Background

When we say *foreground* and *background* in Photoshop, we may be referring to one of two different concepts:

- The foreground and background colors are those defined on the Color palette and in the Color Control box as the current color you paint with (the foreground) and the color that would remain if you used the Eraser tool to erase part of the present image (the background). The foreground and background colors are used as the beginning and ending points of a gradient blend. They may also be used as the starting and ending colors of an individual brush stroke if you have a digitizing tablet and a pressure-sensitive pen.

- However, when we speak of a brush stroke being anti-aliased into its background, we mean the surface to which the brush stroke is applied—a solid color, a pattern, a photograph, and so forth. But this is not the ultimate background, which is the underlying, hidden color that appears only when a piece of the picture is erased, cut, or moved. The word *background* is used frequently in both ways in Photoshop, but it should become clear in context which sense of the word is meant.

EXERCISE 3.1: CHANGING FOREGROUND AND BACKGROUND COLORS

Using the Large Color Selection Boxes and Small Color Swatches

1. Change the foreground color by clicking on the uppermost of the two large color swatches, either on the Color palette or in the Toolbox. A double border will highlight the active color swatch (Figure 3.1). Move your mouse pointer over to the small color swatches (it will turn into an eyedropper). Click to make your choice. (Other methods of color selection and color mixing will be discussed in later chapters.)

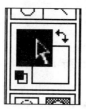

Figure 3.1 Highlighting an active color swatch.

2. Change the background color by clicking on the lower of the two large color swatches. Select your background color as you did the foreground color.

Using the Eyedropper Tool to Sample Image Color

1. Create a new document (640 x 480 pixels) using the default colors of white background, black foreground. Make sure your Color palette is in RGB mode. If it is not, change it by clicking on the arrow to the right of the palette to reveal the fly-out menu and select **RGB Sliders**.

2. Using the Eyedropper tool, click to select a medium blue among the colors. You can click on the **Swatch** palette, if you wish, to choose from the fixed range of swatches presented there.

3. Open the Brushes palette if it is not open by selecting **Window:Show Brushes**. Select the box with the number **35** in the circle. This is a large brush shape with a diameter of 35 pixels and a very soft edge. Select the **Paintbrush** tool.

4. Draw in the new document with the Paintbrush. The color will be intense blue in the middle, feathering out to soft blue at the edges.

5. Select the **Eyedropper** tool from the Toolbox. As you click and drag it around the swatches, the foreground color and the sliders will change. When you release the mouse button, a new color will be selected.

6. To change the background color, hold down the **Option** key as you click and drag the Eyedropper around the image.

Changing the Foreground Color While Using a Painting Tool

1. While using the Paintbrush, release the mouse button and press the **Option** key and your Paintbrush will turn into an Eyedropper.

2. Click and hold the mouse button as you drag the eyedropper around the image. You will be sampling the color, and the foreground color box and sliders will change accordingly.

3. If you let go of the **Option** key and click the mouse button again, you will be painting again, so be careful.

4. Reset your foreground and background colors to black and white by clicking in the miniature default color icon in the Toolbox.

5. Double-click in the **Eraser** tool box to bring up the Eraser Options palette. Click the **Erase Image** button. When the Erase Entire Image? alert box appears, click **OK**.

Notes on the Eyedropper

You can set the Eyedropper to sample individual pixels or to average a 3 x 3 or 5 x 5 pixel area around the pixel the Eyedropper passes over. Use the Eyedropper Options palette to set this feature.

EXERCISE 3.2: USING BRUSHES

Millions of Brushes in One!

Photoshop brushes are very adaptable tools. You can use them to paint freeform or straight lines or smooth, fuzzy, or rough-edged lines. Their shapes can be round, oval, calligraphic, or a shape that you create. The paint can be applied continuously, intermittently, or as a dotted line, and the paint can range from opaque to completely transparent. You can even paint in different brush modes that allow you to lighten or darken only selected pixels in an image. Consider the rule of multiplying possibilities to come up with the number of choices: there are millions of brush effects you can use to express your creativity.

In this section, we'll learn about the Brushes palette as it applies to the Paintbrush, although most of what you learn in this section will apply to the other painting tools as well (Airbrush, Rubber Stamp, Pencil). Special qualities and/or different options relating to the Paintbrush and other painting tools will be discussed later.

Selecting the Brush Shape

1. Start with a clean, white screen, with black as your foreground color. Make sure your **Paintbrush** tool is selected in the Toolbox.

2. With the Brushes palette open, click in one of the brush shape boxes to choose the shape of the tip of the Paintbrush (Figure 3.2). Draw a line in the open document.

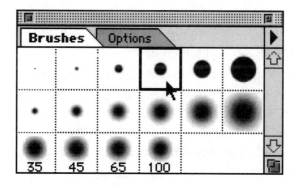

Figure 3.2 Selecting a brush shape.

3. Experiment with different brush diameters and degrees of softness.

To use any tool more precisely, press **Caps Lock** and the tool icon will change into a cross-hair shape (Figure 3.3). You can use this option with all the painting, editing, and selection tools as well as with the Paint Bucket and Eyedropper tools.

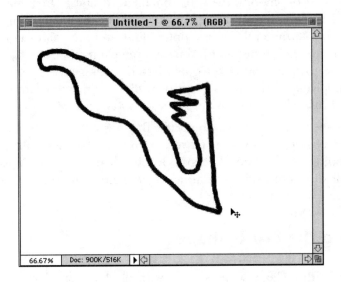

*Figure 3.3 Normal Paintbrush tool and cross-hair icon with **Caps Lock** in use.*

Drawing a Vertical or Horizontal Straight Line with Any Brush

1. Position the brush where you want the line to begin.
2. Press the **Shift** key and hold it down.
3. Click and drag the mouse to draw the line. The action of the brush will be constrained to the vertical or horizontal axis, depending upon the direction in which you drag.
4. Release the **Shift** key and then release the mouse button.
5. Practice drawing lines of different thicknesses (Figure 3.4) by selecting different brush sizes.

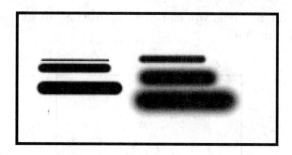

Figure 3.4 Paintbrush lines of varying thicknesses.

6. To draw another separate line, click the mouse to start the line before pressing the **Shift** key.

Drawing Connecting Straight Lines (at any Angle) with Any Brush

1. Click once to determine the beginning of the line. Release the mouse button.
2. Press and hold down the **Shift** key.
3. Move the mouse to where you want the line to end. Click the mouse button. The line will be drawn as the dots are connected (Figure 3.5).

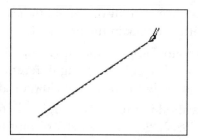

Figure 3.5 Drawing a straight line with the Paintbrush.

4. Still holding down the **Shift** key, move the mouse to a new end point and click. You can do this as many times as you want. The line you draw is not limited (constrained) to any angle. You can make the angle as acute or obtuse as you want.

5. With a little practice, you can draw a fairly decent star using this technique (Figure 3.6).

Figure 3.6 Drawing a star using the dot-to-dot technique.

Creating New Brushes

Photoshop comes with 16 ready-made brushes in the Default Brushes palette, but you may want to create others of different sizes, shapes, angles, and degrees of hardness:

1. Select **New Brush** from the fly-out menu indicated by the arrow at the right of the palette, or click in the next available space with any tool.

2. The New Brush dialog box will appear (Figure 3.7). In this window you can generate a new brush by entering different numbers. Watch your new brush take shape in the box in the lower-right-hand corner.

3. Diameter is measured in pixels. The larger the number, the larger the diameter of the brush. Set the diameter of your new brush to **50** pixels.

4. *Hardness* is the softness or hardness of the brush as measured by the percentage of the brush that is hard. A completely hard-edged with no hard center brush would be 100% hard, from core to edge. A completely soft brush with no hard center would be 0% hard. Set the hardness for this brush to **80%** by entering numbers in the Option box or using the sliders.

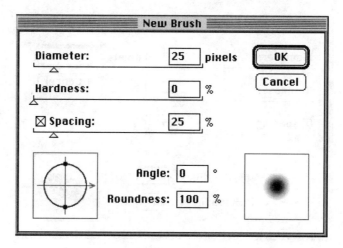

Figure 3.7 *New Brush dialog box.*

5. *Spacing* determines the amount of space between brush-tip impressions in a full stroke. Twenty-five percent is the right amount to get a good overlap to create a continuous line. If you wanted to make a dotted line, you would increase the spacing to more than 100%. The higher the percentage, the wider the spacing: up to 999%. If you turn the **Spacing** option off, the distance between brush strokes will be determined by how fast you drag the mouse (faster speed means more distance between strokes, sort of a stone-skipping effect.) For this brush, leave the spacing setting on, at **25%**.

6. *Roundness* allows you to change the shape of a brush. A brush stroke doesn't have to be completely round. For a stylized look, you may prefer to have a chiseled brush tip, like the nib of a calligraphy pen. To change roundness, you can either enter a number less than 100 in the Roundness box, or, using the model in the left-hand corner, move the dots on either side of the cross-hairs to compress the circle into an ellipse. Set the roundness for the new brush to **50%**. The New Brush dialog box should look like Figure 3.8.

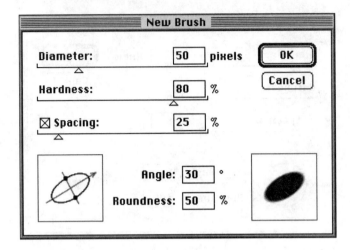

Figure 3.8 New Brush dialog box with new brush data entered.

7. When you've completed these settings, click **OK**. Your new brush is the last item on the menu, a circle with the number 50 in it.

Reviewing the Settings for Any Brush at Any Time

To review the brush settings, do one of the following:

- Select **Brush Options** from the Brushes palette right-hand side fly-out menu.
- Double-click on the picture of the brush you'd like to inspect.

Saving Brushes

1. Select **Save Brushes** from the Brushes palette fly-out menu.
2. An empty dialog box will appear. Using the hierarchical menu, locate the **Adobe Photoshop 4.0** folder. Open the folder by double-clicking on it. Inside you will find a folder titled **Brushes & Patterns**. Open the folder and type **My New Brushes** in the empty box (Figure 3.9). This will create a New Brush file.

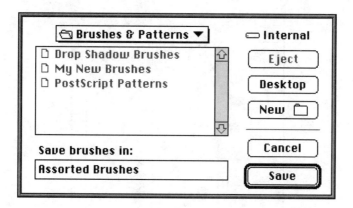

Figure 3.9 *Save dialog box.*

3. Click **Save** to return to Photoshop.

Loading Brushes

Now that you've had a chance to practice with the basic brushes, it's time to see some of the more exotic choices that Adobe offers:

1. Select **Load Brushes** from the fly-out menu.
2. Locate the **Adobe Photoshop 4.0** folder through the hierarchical file system. As before, within the Photoshop folder you will find another folder named **Brushes & Patterns**. Inside this folder you will find several files of brush palettes.
3. Select **Assorted Brushes** and click **Open**.
4. A dazzling new array of brushes will appear (Figure 3.10). You can draw with these unusual shapes using any painting tool.

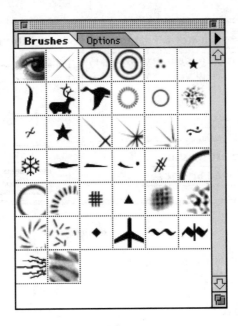

Figure 3.10 Assorted brushes in the Brushes palette.

5. Take a few moments and practice using these brushes (Figure 3.11).

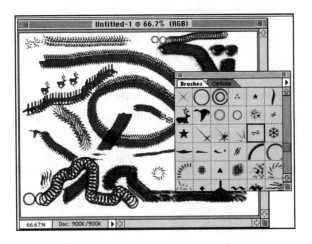

Figure 3.11 Painting with assorted brushes.

WARNING

If you make changes to a default preset brush, that brush will be permanently changed in the Brushes palette. If you accidentally ruin a brush you wanted to keep, you can reload the **Default Brushes** folder from your original Adobe Photoshop program disc or reenter the original values from Table 3.1. If you reload **Default Brushes** from the program disk, any new brushes you've added to your Default Brushes palette will be lost.

Table 3.1 Default Brushes Settings

Row	Diameter in Pixels	Hardness	Spacing	Angle	Roundness
Top	1, 3, 5, 9, 13, 19	All 100%	All 25%	All 0°	All 100%
Middle	5, 9, 13, 17, 21, 29	All 0%	All 25%	All 0°	All 100%
Bottom*	35, 45, 65, 100	All 0%	All 25%	All 0°	All 100%

*Round brush shapes that are too large to fit in a box are represented by a fixed-size circle with the pixel diameter printed underneath.

Creating a Custom Brush

1. Load the Brushes file you created (**My New Brushes**) by selecting **Load Brushes** from the Brushes palette fly-out menu and following the procedure in the preceding Loading Brushes section.

2. When the brushes are loaded, select the second brush from the left in the top row. It will be 3 pixels in diameter, no hardness, 25% spacing, 100% roundness, no angle.

3. Create a clean white space in an open window. Set the foreground color to black.

4. Draw a small *X* with the brush.

5. Select the **Rectangular Marquee** tool in the Toolbox. Click and drag a selection box around your small *X* until it is enclosed by the wiggling selection border (Figure 3.12).

Figure 3.12 *Selecting a drawing to define as a brush shape.*

6. Select **Define Brush** from the Brushes palette fly-out menu. The new brush will appear to the right of the small brush previously created.

7. You can now use your new brush to paint with, in any foreground color you'd like.

8. Don't forget to save this brushes palette as **My New Brushes** before you open any other palette, including the **Default Brushes** file.

NOTE   Brushes are saved in shades of gray so that they can be used to paint with any color. If you create a custom brush stroke while using a color brush, it will appear as a gray brush shape in the palette and will seem semitransparent when you paint with it, even when you paint with solid black paint. The bottom line: if you want a custom brush to be totally opaque when used, create the brush in black.

EXPERIMENTING WITH PAINT OPACITY

The opacity of any Painting tool can be varied from 1% to 100%. Press the number keys to change the opacity in multiples of 10 (i.e., 1 = 10%, 2 = 20%, etc.). One hundred percent opacity (complete coverage) is zero. Here's how to vary opacity:

1. Create a new white screen, at least 4 inches x 4 inches.

2. Draw three parallel horizontal lines: one red, one blue, and one green. Use the **Shift** key while dragging the mouse to keep lines straight.

3. Next, select a vivid yellow.

4. Using the same brush width, draw ten short vertical lines crossing and overlapping the three long horizontal lines. Starting with 10% opacity, create one line for each 10% opacity increase. As the opacity increases, less of the background color shows through.

USING THE PAINTING MODES

Photoshop offers ten different painting modes: Normal, Darken, Lighten, Hue, Saturation, Color, Luminosity, Multiply, Screen, and Dissolve. You'll find these modes on the fly-out menu at the top left of the Brushes palette. All painting modes are available with the Paintbrush, Pencil, Airbrush, and Rubber Stamp tools. The best way to understand the function of each mode is to experiment with them yourself:

1. Start with a clean white screen. Allow an area at least 5 inches x 5 inches to work in. Using the fly-out menu, set your Picker palette to **RGB** view mode.

2. Create a new brush with a diameter of 65 pixels, 100% hardness, 25% spacing, no angle, and 100% roundness. Draw a black horizontal line with this brush at the top of the window.

3. Beneath this line, draw four more horizontal lines with these RGB values: red (198, 0, 38), blue (0, 131, 193), green (30, 135, 64), and gray (144, 144, 144). Use the RGB sliders on the Picker palette to create them.

4. Change the foreground color to gold (236, 152, 0).

5. Select the **Normal** mode from the Brushes palette and draw a line perpendicular to the four lines you have already drawn, holding down the **Shift** key to keep the line straight. In normal mode, the foreground color will completely cover the other four lines.

6. Changing the mode on the fly-out menu between brush strokes, paint the second gold line in Darken mode, the third in Lighten mode, and so on, until you've used all the options. (Before you paint the last line in Dissolve mode, change the brush hardness to 0%. Change it back to

100% after you've painted the line.) Give each vertical line enough space so that you can see its effect.

Painting modes are differentiated by the effect of the overlying brush stroke on the underlying pixels. Each mode affects pixels in a unique way. As you read this, keep in mind that each color is the numerical representation of its RGB values.

To understand how these modes work, you need to think of three different colors involved in the process:

- *Blend color*—The color you're using to paint with, which Adobe calls the blend color. The blend color can be applied with complete opacity (100%) or some degree of transparency, selected from the Options palette's slider.

- *Base color*—The base color is the underlying color that you're painting on top of—the color of your image.

- *Result color*—The result color is the color you get after applying the blend color on top of the base color.

The different modes described here produce different result colors with the same two blend and base colors, using rules that I'll describe briefly. Your best bet, however, is to try these out to see what they do for you:

- *Normal mode*—The blend paint covers underlying base pixels completely when in the 100% opacity mode. This is the most common painting mode.

- *Darken mode*—In the darken mode, only base pixels lighter than the blend color are changed. In our exercise, you'll notice that the black, red, and green pixels are unchanged, but the blue line is darkened, as well as the white spaces between the lines. Use your magnifying glass and look carefully at the anti-aliased edges around each of the horizontal black and colored lines. The lighter areas have taken on a light gold tone.

- *Lighten mode*—In the lighten mode, only pixels darker than the blend color that you are painting with are changed. So here's a brain twister: How can you paint gold over blue in lighten mode and get pink? The answer is simple—the higher number (lighter value) dominates, as you'll see in Table 3.2.

Table 3.2 Example of How Brush Strokes Interact Using Mode Painting

COLOR	BLUE BRUSH STROKE	GOLD BRUSH STROKE	GOLD PLUS BLUE*
Red	0	238	238
Green	131	163	163
Blue	193	23	193

*Combination when painting with gold in lighten mode

Remember how we learned in Chapter 2 that the RGB model uses additive color? Here's proof. Painting gold over blue involves calculations on all three RGB channels. The gold color has lighter pixels on both the red and green channels, so those pixels are changed to those in the gold color. However, in the blue channel the pixels are lighter with a value of 193, so those pixels are left alone. Put it all together, and you get R 234, G 152, B 193 or lavender-pink!

We won't go through this math exercise with every mode—you can do that yourself if you're curious—but it should give you an idea that there's more happening than meets the eye when you paint using different modes. It's all in the numbers, and it's all perfectly logical when you know the rules:

- *Hue mode*—When you paint over pixels in hue mode, their hue changes to that of the blend color (in our case, gold), but they maintain their saturation (intensity) and luminosity (a measure of brightness). Notice that the white between the stripes does not change to gold. In the HSB model, the "white" could be described as any hue, no saturation, and 100% brightness. (Prove this by selecting any area of white with the Eyedropper. Move only the hue slider on the Picker palette, and you'll see it has no effect on the large white color swatch.) That's because the saturation and brightness stay the same in the hue mode, white stays white even when you paint over it.

- *Saturation mode*—Painting in saturation mode changes the saturation of the underlying base pixels but leaves their hue and luminosity alone.

- *Color mode*—Painting in the color mode changes underlying base pixels to the blend color. The hue and saturation of the pixels is changed, but not the luminosity. You can see the effect most vividly where the brush has painted over the gray line, that is, the pixels have changed to gold, but the luminosity is no different than when it was gray. This mode is good for colorizing grayscale artwork (like photographs) without changing the gray levels.

- *Luminosity mode*—Painting in the luminosity mode affects only the lightness of the pixels; the color values are not affected. When the gold color is applied in the luminosity mode, the lightness of the underlying base pixels changes to that of the gold blend color, but their hue does not change. (Therefore, in this mode the black brush stroke and the white spaces between lines change, in luminosity.) The luminosity mode is the exact opposite (inverse) of the color mode. Use this mode when you want to change pixel lightness while leaving the hue alone.

- *Multiply mode*—Drawing over the image in multiply mode darkens the image by multiplying the color values according to a mathematical formula. The best way to see the effect of this is to paint with a clear yellow on a pure white background. Paint over the same area, releasing and repressing the mouse button between strokes. (The yellow will gradually get darker and darker, as though you're painting with felt-tip markers.) You will not get the darkening effect in the normal mode, even if you're painting brush strokes with partial opacity. The most you will get is 100% opacity of your color.

- *Screen mode*—When you paint in the screen mode, you lighten the pixels you're painting over while giving them the tint of the blend color. Consequently, the white is not affected, but black, gray, and other colors are affected. The screen mode is the opposite (inverse) of the multiply mode.

- *Dissolve mode*—In dissolve mode, the blend color replaces the underlying base pixel color at random, based on the density of the applied paint at any specific pixel location. To exaggerate the effect in our example, we changed the brush hardness to 0%. If the brush hardness had been 100%, you would not have seen an effect because the density of the paint would have been the same throughout the extent of the brush stroke. The softer the brush, the more "spattered" the results.

- *Overlay mode*—In overlay mode, the base color is mixed with the blend color, preserving the highlights and shadows of the original image while overlaying the new color on top.

- *Soft light mode*—The soft light mode provides the effect of shining a diffused spotlight on the image. If the blend color is lighter than a base pixel, the pixel is lightened. If the blend color is darker than the base pixel, the pixel is darkened.

- *Hard light mode*—The hard light mode provides the effect of shining a harsh spotlight on the image. The same type of calculations are performed as previously, but pixels are made much lighter or much darker, as required, to produce a stronger effect.

- *Behind mode*—The behind mode is used when you are working with layers (discussed later in this book). It allows you to apply color only to transparent areas.

- *Difference mode*—The difference mode calculates the difference between the blend and base color, and the result color becomes the value that is determined.

While the subtleties of illustrating color will be lost in a black and white book (Figure 3.13), some of the practicalities are not. To hand-color small portions of this black and white photograph, I alternatively used **Overlay Mode** and **Color Mode** to preserve the background detail of the photograph. As illustrated, the Navigator was a big help in zooming in on the portion of the document to be colorized, and the brushes were kept nearby to quickly select the best one for the job at hand. The colorized original has been included on the *teach yourself...Photoshop* CD-ROM.

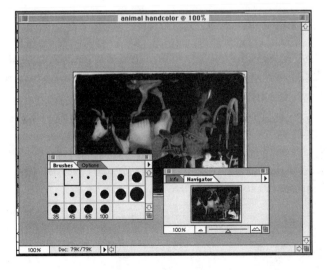

Figure 3.13 Mode color.

SPECIAL SETTINGS FOR INDIVIDUAL BRUSHES

In addition to Brush options (which can be set for any painting and editing tool), each brush has unique settings, which can be accessed by double-clicking on the specific tool icon in the Toolbox.

PAINTBRUSH OPTIONS

To change Paintbrush options, double-click on the **Paintbrush** icon. The Paintbrush Options palette will appear (Figure 3.14).

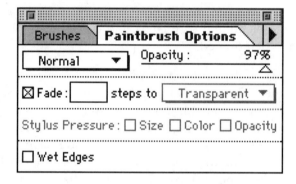

Figure 3.14 Paintbrush Options palette.

Fade

Fade means the distance in pixels over which the brush stroke will last before it fades out. Use **Fade** to create the effect of a real paintbrush running out of paint at the end of its stroke:

1. Enter **25** in the dialog box.
2. As soon as you select a Fade distance, two more options will appear.
3. Select **Transparent** if you want the brush stroke to become transparent and disappear at its end (Figure 3.15).

Figure 3.15 Paintbrush with fade to transparent.

4. Select **Background** if you want the brush stroke to start with the fore-ground color and finish with the background color (Figure 3.16).

Figure 3.16 Paintbrush with fade to background.

Stylus Pressure

Digitizing tablets, such as those manufactured by Wacom, Kurta, and CalComp, feature pressure-sensitive styluses that give the Photoshop artist more ways to be expressive. Photoshop has included in the program stylus options that you can set according to your creative objective:

- Size allows the brush stroke to be thicker or thinner, depending upon how much pressure is used (Figure 3.17).

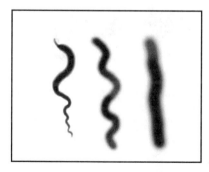

Figure 3.17 Pressure-sensitive brush strokes varying by size, color, and opacity.

- Color changes the color of the brush stroke. Light pressure gives you the background color, medium pressure gives you a color between background and foreground, and the heaviest pressure gives you the foreground color (Figure 3.17).

- Opacity changes the brush stroke to become more opaque with more pressure (Figure 3.17).

AIRBRUSH OPTIONS

- Unlike the Paintbrush, with the Airbrush, paint builds up when you continue to hold it in one place and press the mouse button—it "puddles" just as a real airbrush would (Figure 3.18).

- Set Brush Options for the Airbrush as you did for the Paintbrush (Brush palette).

- Set Airbrush Options (Fade, Stylus Pressure: Color and Pressure) just as you did for the Paintbrush.

- What is called *opacity* (on the Brushes palette) is called *pressure* when the Airbrush tool is active. Increasing pressure increases the darkness of the stroke.

- Use the Airbrush for soft retouching effects, especially when colorizing grayscale drawings and photographs. The airbrush paints a soft spray of color that is unequaled for hazy glows and sheer overlays of hue.

Figure 3.18 Painting with Airbrush.

PENCIL OPTIONS

- The pencil is considered to be a painting tool even though it paints a hard-edged line that is visibly not anti-aliased.

- Use the pencil whenever you want a coarser look (Figure 3.19). All the brush sizes, painting modes, and opacity options apply, just as they did with the Paintbrush and Airbrush.

Figure 3.19 *Example of pencil drawing.*

- Set the Fade and Stylus Pressure options for the pencil by double-clicking on the **Pencil** icon, just as you did for the Paintbrush and Airbrush (Figure 3.20).

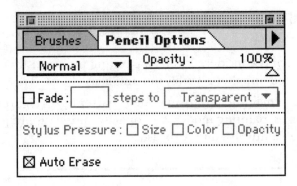

Figure 3.20 *Pencil options.*

Auto Erase

Auto Erase is a feature exclusive to the Pencil tool. To practice:

1. Select a **9-pixel** pencil (fourth from the left on the Brushes palette) and set your foreground color to solid black. Background color should be white.

2. Double-click the **Pencil** icon to open the Pencil Options palette. Click on the **Auto Erase** box. You may leave the other boxes unchecked.

3. Draw a black line against a white background. Release the mouse button. Press the mouse button again as you draw over the black line you just created.

Just like that, the line erases. Actually, this looks more mysterious than it is—what you're doing is painting with the background color when you erase. When the background color is the same color as your window, it seems as though you're erasing. To prove it, do the following:

1. Set your foreground color to a bright red.

2. Click on the background color swatch and set it to purple.

3. Press **Ctrl-A** (PC) or **Command-A** (Mac) to select the entire open window.

4. Then press **Alt-Delete** or **Option-Delete** to fill the window with the red foreground color (it's a shortcut).

5. Press **Ctrl-D** (PC) or **Command-D** (Mac) to deselect everything. Now change your foreground color to blue.

6. Using your pencil, draw a blue line with the mouse button pressed down. Release the mouse and press it again. If the tip of the pencil is in the blue area when you start your next stroke, it will paint with purple. If it's not in the blue, but in the red, it will continue painting with blue. Reposition the pencil in a blue area again and paint. It still paints with purple.

7. Close the window when you're finished. You don't have to save the document.

RUBBER STAMP OPTIONS

The Rubber Stamp tool provides much of the magic associated with Photoshop. With the humble Rubber Stamp, you can sample one part of an image and paint what you're sampling on another part of the screen. This is called *cloning*. You can even clone an image from one window into another.

Because the Rubber Stamp is technically a Painting tool, you can use any of the brushes, including your own custom brushes. All the painting modes apply (Lighten, Darken, etc.), and you can control opacity just as you do with the other tools. The stylus pressure varies size, opacity, or both.

The Rubber Stamp tool has seven additional Cloning and Painting options (Figure 3.21).

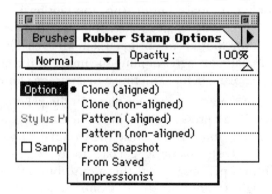

Figure 3.21 *Rubber Stamp options.*

Rubber-Stamping an Aligned Clone

1. Reset the colors to the black foreground/white background defaults. Create a new document, at least 5 inches x 5 inches. Give yourself plenty of area to work in.

2. We need an image to clone, so draw a star using the Paintbrush tool. Use the 5-pixel diameter brush, 100% opacity, and normal painting mode. Remember to hold the **Shift** key down to connect the strokes (see Figure 3.6).

3. When you're finished drawing the star, select the **Rubber Stamp** tool from the Toolbox. Double-click on the **Rubber Stamp** icon to open the Rubber Stamp Options dialog box.

4. From the drop-down Option list, select **Clone (aligned)**. Leave the Stylus Pressure unchecked if you have a digital tablet.

5. Position the Rubber Stamp over the lower-right leg of the star. Hold down the **Option**(Mac), **Alt**(PC) key while you click the mouse button to sample that area. You will notice that the triangle inside the rubber stamp turns white when the **Option**(Mac), **Alt**(PC) key is held down. It is as though the Rubber Stamp is memorizing the part of the screen from which it will start sampling.

6. Now move the Rubber Stamp into the upper-left-hand corner of the document, giving yourself at least 2 inches above and to the left of the star.

7. Pressing only the mouse button (not the **Option** key), start painting with the mouse, using small strokes. You'll see the outlines of the star emerging. If you look at your original star, while clicking and dragging, you'll see a small plus sign sampling the image as the copy of the star is made. Stop copying before you finish making the clone (Figure 3.22).

8. Try moving the mouse to another place on the palette and try to paint another star. Don't press any keys, just try to paint by clicking and dragging the mouse. You can't because the cloning is precisely aligned to where you first started painting. Go back to your duplicate star and continue painting, pressing down the mouse button, and you'll see it picked up right where you left off. Continue painting until the star is complete.

Figure 3.22 *Cloning aligned with Rubber Stamp.*

CASE EXAMPLE: CLONING A TREE

- There are never enough trees in the forest. We started with a lonely forest scene. (See the two tree images in the Chapter 3 folder on the CD-ROM.)

- We selected the **Rubber Stamp** tool and chose the **Clone (aligned)** option from the Rubber Stamp Options box.

- Using a medium-sized round brush of about 9 pixels, we first painted the outline of the second tree while sampling the first tree.

- It was not necessary to be extremely careful about painting the edges of the leaves because we knew we were painting the second tree against a busy forest background. This is important to keep in mind when cloning.

- Next, we rubber-stamped the shadow area and finished by filling in the leafy center of the tree.

Figure 3.23 *The forest before and after intervention.*

Rubber-Stamping a Nonaligned Clone

1. Select the **Eraser** tool, and erase the cloned star you just made. (Be sure that your background color is still white.) Leave the original star alone.

2. Double-click the **Rubber Stamp** icon and select **Clone (nonaligned)** from Rubber Stamp options.

3. Position the mouse on the original star. Press the **Option**(Mac)or **Alt**(PC) key and click the mouse button to begin sampling the star, as before.

4. Move the mouse to another location and begin painting. A star will appear, just as it did the first time. When the first star is finished, move the mouse to another location and try to paint a second one. In the nonaligned mode, you can do this. When you want to make multiple copies of one sampled object, this is the option to use (Figure 3.24).

Figure 3.24 Cloning with Rubber Stamp, nonaligned.

5. Erase the images or save the file.

Rubber-Stamping with a Pattern (Aligned)

1. Start with a white canvas, white background color, and black foreground color. Load the Assorted Brushes palette using the Brushes palette fly-out menu.

2. Select the **Paintbrush** tool from the Toolbox, and then select the concentric circles brush pattern from the palette. Click once in your window to paint one impression of this brush pattern. You will use this image as your pattern.

3. Choose the **Rectangular Marquee** tool from the Toolbox. Click and drag a small box around the concentric circles. Keep the box as close to the circle as you can, without touching the image (Figure 3.25).

Figure 3.25 Selecting an image to define as pattern for rubber-stamping.

4. Select **Define Pattern** from the Edit menu.

5. Open the Rubber Stamp Options box by double-clicking on the **Rubber Stamp** icon. Choose **Pattern (aligned)** as the option.

6. Erase the original concentric circle image from your window to give yourself space with the Eraser tool.

7. Start painting with the Rubber Stamp tool just as if you were using a paintbrush. This is an easy way to fill a space with a repeatable pattern. Whether or not you release the mouse button and press it again to continue painting, the *O*s stay in line because the pattern is aligned (Figure 3.26).

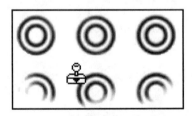

Figure 3.26 Rubber-stamping with aligned pattern.

Rubber-Stamping a Pattern (Nonaligned)

From your experience with cloning (nonaligned) you can probably anticipate what will happen when you stamp a nonaligned pattern.

When you release the mouse button and start painting again, the Rubber Stamp begins painting the image as if it was the first time. This is good for painting patterns like fish scales, stars, a field of grass, or abstract overlapping random textures when you're painting at less than 100% opacity (Figure 3.27). If you're painting at full opacity, of course, your overlying pattern will wipe out the underlying pattern.

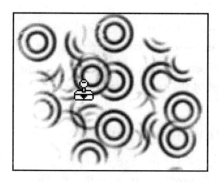

Figure 3.27 Rubber-stamping a nonaligned pattern.

The pattern you define doesn't have to be small. You can make it as large as you like, although very large patterns can be somewhat unwieldy.

N O T E

Rubber-Stamping from Snapshot

To practice rubber-stamping from Snapshot, you would need to use some Photoshop skills you haven't learned yet, so, for this example, an explanation will have to do.

Every image you create in Photoshop possesses a buffer area that is like an invisible holding zone where a copy of the image can be saved. To rubber-stamp from a snapshot:

1. Change your image in some way. You can colorize it or apply a filter, but it must be only one step that you can undo. For example, you can start with a gray drawing and colorize the picture by using the Hue/Saturation submenu from the **Adjust** command under the Image

menu. Check the **Colorize** box and, using the hue sliders, change all of the gray brush strokes to purple. Click **OK** to apply the change.

2. Select **Take Snapshot** from the Edit menu. This saves a copy of your artwork into the empty buffer.

3. Then press **Ctrl-Z** (PC) or **Command-Z** (Mac) to undo the colorization (this does not remove the colorized version, which still exists in the buffer).

4. With your original image back, double-click the **Rubber Stamp** tool and select **From Snapshot** from the drop-down Options list box.

5. Using the Rubber Stamp tool, paint over one aspect of the drawing, leaving the rest of the painting alone.

Rubber-Stamping from Saved

Let's say that you've saved a copy of your work on disk and then made changes to it. Perhaps you're happy with most but not all the changes you've made. The **Rubber Stamping from Saved** option allows you to repaint part of your disk-saved image over the image that you've changed. This allows you to undo many levels of changes:

1. Using a paintbrush and any-sized brush tip that you prefer, paint a simple image in a new file.

2. Save this image as **Rubber Stamp Saved Test**.

3. When the window comes back, change the image. You can paint over it with any of the tools, add colors, or do anything you like.

4. To recapture some of your original image, which you saved on disk, open the Rubber Stamp Options dialog box by double-clicking on the tool and then select **From Saved** from the drop-down Options list.

5. Use the Rubber Stamp to paint on any part of the image, and you will see the original picture reappear. For best results, use a brush shape that's appropriately sized for the part of the picture you're restoring—a small brush for a small shape, a large brush for a large area. There may be a slight delay as the computer "reads" the original image back from the hard disk.

Rubber-Stamping, Impressionist Style

The **Impressionist** option is quite similar to the **From Saved** option. However, instead of painting with the last saved version of a file exactly as it was saved, the Rubber Stamp paints with a texturized rendition of the saved file that resembles an impressionist painting.

Use this option in the same way that you use the **From Saved** option:

1. Save your image to your hard disk.
2. Double-click the **Rubber Stamp** tool and select the **From Saved** option in the Rubber Stamp Options drop-down list.
3. Paint with the Rubber Stamp as you would with any brush. Select the appropriate brush size for the detail you are going to paint.

USING THE LINE TOOL

Use the Line tool to draw straight lines of any length and width:

1. Start with a clean white screen.
2. Double-click on the **Line** tool from the Toolbox.
3. The Line Tool Options palette will open (Figure 3.28). Enter **6** pixels for the line width.

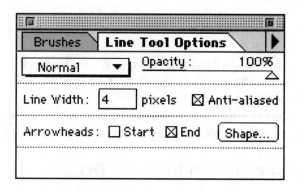

Figure 3.28 *Line Tool Options box.*

4. Open the Info palette.

5. Move the mouse pointer onto the screen. It will turn into a small set of cross-hairs. Holding down the **Shift** key, click and drag the mouse to draw a perfectly straight line (Figure 3.29).

Figure 3.29 Drawing a line with the Line tool.

Measuring Your Line as You Draw

Choose **Window:Show Info**. As you use the line tool, you will notice that the boxes in the Info box that usually give you RGB and CMYK information are instead filled with useful information about the line you are drawing. The box on the left measures the movement of the end of the Line tool with relationship to the starting point on the screen's *X, Y* grid.

The triangle to the left of the *X* and *Y* is the Greek symbol delta Δ, which represents change. As you drag the mouse, what you are measuring is the change in *X* and the change in *Y*. Because you held down the **Shift** key, you constrained the line to the *X* axis so that there was no change in *Y*. The same would happen if you held down the **Shift** key and drew a line straight up (there would be no change in *X*, only a change in *Y*).

In the second new box that appeared, the *A* represents the angle from the horizontal, and *D* represents distance, or the length, of the line you have drawn.

NOTE   Drawing a Line at a 45° Angle: To draw a line at a perfect 45° angle, press both the **Command**(Mac) or **Ctrl**(PC) key and the **Shift** key and drag the mouse in the desired angular direction. Remember that you must begin clicking and dragging before you hold down the **Command**(Mac) **or Ctrl**(PC) key, otherwise, you will have selected the Move Layer tool.

Using the Line Tool to Measure Distances

1. Double-click the **Line** tool to open the Line Tool Options box.

2. Enter **0** (zero) pixel width in the Option box.

3. Select a paintbrush and draw two dots a distance apart on your screen.

4. With the Info palette open, use the Line tool to measure the distance between the two points (Figure 3.30). Photoshop does not care whether the line you are painting has any thickness; it will give you the information just the same.

Figure 3.30 Using Line tool to measure distance.

Drawing Lines with Arrowheads

1. Double-click the **Line** tool to open the Line Tool Options palette.

2. Click on the **Shape** button. Type **20%** for the line width, and check the **Arrowheads at End** box.

3. Type **200** pixels for the arrowhead width and **900%** for the arrowhead length. Select **No concavity**. (*Concavity* is the amount of curvature of the sides of the arrowhead.) Click **OK**.

4. Click and drag the mouse on the screen. Release the mouse button when the line has reached the desired length.

5. Practice drawing lines of varying widths so that you understand which sizes and shapes of arrowheads are most aesthetically pleasing (Figure 3.31).

Figure 3.31 Arrowhead example from exercise.

Make your arrowhead wide enough for the pixel width of the line. If the arrowhead is out of proportion to the line, you may create a shape like Figure 3.32.

N O T E

Figure 3.32 Bad arrowhead.

USING THE ERASER

- Use the Eraser tool to erase part of an image. When you erase, you will always reveal the background color underneath (Figure 3.33).

Figure 3.33 Erasing screen to reveal background color.

- To erase the entire image on the screen, double-click the **Eraser** tool. This will bring up the Eraser Options palette and a button on the palette will ask if you want to erase the entire image or layer.
- Let's say that you've saved an image you've been working on. Then you make some changes to it, but you need to undo some of those changes. You can restore portions of the saved image with the **Magic Eraser** option:

1. Select the **Eraser** tool from the Toolbox.
2. Position the Eraser over the area you want to restore from the saved image on disk.

3. Press the **Option** key before pressing the mouse button and dragging the Eraser over the part of the image you want to restore. The Eraser turns into the Magic Eraser, a square with a page icon inside.

4. The original saved image will reappear in place of the changes you made.

5. The Magic Eraser performs a similar function to the **Rubber Stamp from Saved** option but with less flexibility and finesse.

If you want to erase something very small, it might make more sense to use a small brush or pencil (1 pixel in diameter) and to use it with the foreground color set to the color of the screen. The Eraser can be used to erase one pixel at a time but only if you are in a 16:1 enlargement of a file.

To restore the entire image from the last saved version on your hard disk, select **Revert** from the File menu.

You can set the Eraser to have "wet" edges or to mimic a Pencil, Block (normal eraser), Paintbrush, or Airbrush. Experiment with these effects to see how you can use them.

N O T E

SOME GENERAL THOUGHTS ABOUT PAINTING

- Pick the right tool for the job. If you don't have the right brush size or shape, make one. After all, this is Photoshop, not a one-trick pony.

- Think the task through before you start. Perhaps painting with 50% opacity in normal mode isn't your best choice. Maybe you should be painting in a hue-only or color-only mode, with variable stylus pressure.

- Experiment with different brushes and different effects. Watercolorists make color grids to test the interactions among different pigments. Photoshop artists must get to know their tools just as intimately.

- Go slowly for the best results. There is a decided lag time between mouse movement and screen display when you're painting with some brushes. If you draw a little more slowly, this lag will be less noticeable and less frustrating.

What You've Learned

Foreground and Background Color

- Select the foreground and background colors with the large color swatches on the Toolbox and on the Picker palette.
- Use the Eyedropper tool to select a color from the small color swatches or from the screen.
- Every tool turns into an Eyedropper when moved on top of the small swatches in the Picker palette.

Using Brushes

Creating and Managing Brushes

- The primary painting tools are the Paintbrush, the Airbrush, the Rubber Stamp, and the Pencil. Each has unique qualities and options for customizing the brush stroke.
- Double-clicking any tool in the Toolbox opens its respective Options box.
- The Brushes palette contains brush shapes that can be used by all the painting tools.
- Save, load, and append brushes by using the fly-out menu attached to the side of the Brushes palette.
- Create new brushes that can be used with any of the painting tools by selecting **New Brush** from the fly-out menu on the Brushes palette.
- Create a custom brush by dragging a Rectangular Marquee around a painted shape and selecting **Define Brush** from the Brushes palette fly-out menu.

Painting and Drawing with Brushes

- Draw straight lines with brushes by clicking once to start the line and then holding down the **Shift** key and clicking on the end point of the line.

- Draw continuous connected lines by continuing to hold down the **Shift** key while clicking on new end points.

- Paint lines of varying thickness, color, or opacity with the use of a digitizing pad and stylus.

- Set Fade to **Transparent** and **Background** in the Brush Options box of the Paintbrush, Airbrush, and Pencil tools.

- Change the Opacity slider to paint with more or less opaque paint. Use keyboard numbers as a shortcut to setting opacity percentages (in multiples of ten). (When the airbrush is active, this is called *pressure*.)

- Use painting modes like Normal, Lighten, Darken, Color Only, Hue, Saturation, Luminosity, Screen, Multiply, and Dissolve, Behind, Soft Light, Hard Light, and Overlay, for different creative effects. Select these modes from the fly-out menu on the front of the Brushes palette.

- Use the Rubber Stamp tool to clone an image or a pattern, aligned or nonaligned.

- Use the Rubber Stamp to paint from a snapshot or from the previously saved image on disk. Paint an impressionist image with the **Impressionist** option.

Using the Line Tool

- Use the Line tool to draw straight lines at any angle.

- Draw perfectly straight horizontal and vertical lines, or a line constrained to a 45° angle, by pressing the **Shift** key while drawing.

- Use the Line tool to measure the distance between two points by drawing a line of 0 pixel width. Set the pixel width of the line by double-clicking the **Line Tool Options** box.

- Create arrowheads at the start and/or the end of a line by using the Line Tool Options box.

Using the Eraser Tool

- Use the Eraser tool to erase any part of an image, revealing the background color behind it.

- Double-click the **Eraser** tool to erase the entire image, revealing the background color.

- Use the **Magic Eraser** option to replace a part of an image with the most recently saved version from the hard disk.

CHAPTER 4

Editing Tools

In this chapter...

- Sharpen and Blur tools
- Smudge tool
- Dodge, Burn, and Sponge tools

INTRODUCTION TO EDITING TOOLS

In Chapter 3, we talked about creating images using the standard painting and drawing tools and how to use the Eraser. In this chapter, you'll learn about five other tools that can be used to modify images: the Sharpen and Blur tools, the Smudge tool, and the Dodge and Burn tools.

How Editing Tools Are Like Painting Tools

Like the painting tools, the editing tools use the Brushes palette to determine the shape of their active areas. All the brush shapes are available, including those in the **Supplementary Brushes** folder provided by Adobe. The Mode pop-up menu on the Brushes palette also offers a choice of editing modes. There are no opacity choices but rather variations of exposure and pressure.

How Editing Tools Differ from Painting Tools

Editing tools manipulate only the image that exists already. They do not apply any additional paint to the screen (with the exception of the Smudge tool's **Fingerpaint** option). Editing tools, however, can blur, sharpen, lighten, and darken the pixels they interact with, thereby creating the effect of painting.

EXERCISE 4.1: USING THE EDITING TOOLS

The Smudge Tool

1. Create a new file in the default mode RGB, at least 4 inches x 4 inches, with white background and black foreground color.

2. Select a medium-sized hard paint brush and paint three colored lines fairly close to each other. In our example we made them purple, blue, and yellow. You will be smudging these lines together with the Smudge tool.

3. Select the **Zoom** tool (magnifying glass) from the Toolbox. Click and drag with the tool to select an area where the three colors meet. This area will be enlarged when you release the mouse button. This zooming shortcut is handy for getting a fast close-up view.

4. Select the **Smudge** tool (the pointing finger) from the Toolbox (Figure 4.1). You should be in the normal editing mode (Brushes palette).

Figure 4.1 Smudge tool icon.

5. Drag the Smudge tool across the three-colored areas. You'll see that the pixels seem to move by the action of the smudge. Actually, pixels cannot move, but the adjacent pixels take on color from the area in which the smudge begins.

6. Press **Ctrl-Z** (PC)or **Command-Z** (Mac) to undo the smudge.

7. Change the amount of pressure from the default 50% to **80%**.

8. Smudge the same area again. You'll see that the greater the pressure, the farther the smudge effect extends.

9. Undo the smudge again and change the editing mode to **Darken** by clicking on the pop-up menu on the Brushes palette.

10. Smudge the paint again. You'll notice that the smudged paint behaves the same way that applied paint did when you used the painting tools.

11. Continue experimenting with the modes and pressure settings.

12. Be sure to undo after each smudge so that you can reuse your lines.

Smudge Tool Options

1. Double-click on the **Smudge** tool to open the Smudge Tool Options box (Figure 4.2).

Figure 4.2 *Smudge Tool options.*

2. Check the **Finger Painting** box.

3. Select a different foreground color than the colors of the three lines.

4. Smudge with a medium-sized brush, 50% pressure. Notice that the stroke now begins with the foreground color before it smudges the other colors.

5. If you have a digitizing tablet, the two choices for stylus pressure allow you to vary the size and pressure (force) of the Smudge tool, depending upon how much pressure you apply to the stylus.

Uses for the Smudge Tool

The Smudge tool is good for creating soft, feathery effects:

- adding wisps of hair to a portrait
- adding subtle, realistic eyelashes
- creating cloud effects, soft textures, fabric folds
- blending colors together
- applying a special drawing technique for fine arts projects

The Smudge tool is not good for retouching sizable parts of a photograph because when used in large areas it can create an unnatural effect. To fix a blemish on a portrait, it's better to use the Rubber Stamp tool and clone a nearby sample of good skin over the imperfection.

The Blur and Sharpen Tools

The Blur and Sharpen tools are collectively known as the *Focus tools* and for good reason. You'll find them in the same square on the Toolbox. The tool that was used last will be the icon that is visible (Figures 4.3 and 4.4).

Figure 4.3 Blur tool icon.

Figure 4.4 Sharpen tool icon.

The Blur tool decreases the contrast between pixels in the area to which it is applied.

Using the Blur Tool

1. For this exercise, you can use the contrasting lines of color you created to practice with the Smudge tool, or you can draw some new lines.

2. Using the Zoom tool, enlarge an area where two strongly contrasting colors meet. Make sure you can clearly see the pixels (i.e., an enlargement of 10:1 or greater).

3. Double-click on the **Sharpen/Blur** tool in the Toolbox to see the Blur/Sharpen options (Figure 4.5).

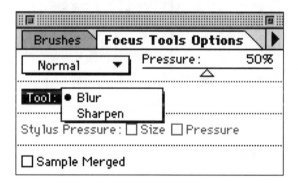

Figure 4.5 Blur/Sharpen Options palette.

4. If the Blur tool is not chosen, select it from the pop-up menu. The stylus pressure options are similar to those offered by other painting and editing tools. You can choose to vary the size and/or pressure of the stroke with the amount of pressure you put on the digitizing pad stylus.

5. Click and drag the mouse to apply the blur to the area where the two colors meet. You'll notice an immediate softening effect as the colors of adjacent pixels are averaged and the contrast between them is reduced.

6. Press **Ctrl-Z** (PC) or **Command-Z** (Mac) to undo the blur. You can continue pressing **Ctrl-Z** (PC) or **Command-Z** (Mac) to toggle back and forth between undoing and redoing the effect. This is a good way to compare options with any Photoshop function.

7. Experiment to see the effect of blurring in Normal, Darken, Lighten, Hue, Color, Saturation, and Luminosity modes. Set the mode using the drop-down Options list on the Brushes Options palette (Figure 4.6).

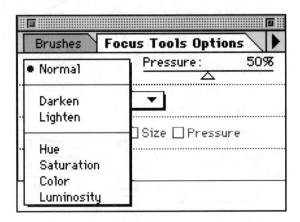

Figure 4.6 Editing modes for the Blur tool (Brushes palette).

Uses for the Blur Tool

- Softening areas of high contrast that might attract undesired attention in a photograph or painting.

- Subduing selected areas of the background. An alternate would be to apply the Blur filter, which we will learn about in a later chapter. However, the Blur tool offers you more manual control than you can accomplish with a filter.

- Smoothing of the hard transition that can occur when you paste one object into, on top of, or behind another.

Using the Sharpen Tool

1. Double-click on the **Blur** tool. Using the pop-up menu in the Sharpen/Blur Options box, choose the **Sharpen** tool.
2. Do not change the tool size on the Brushes menu.
3. Click and drag the Sharpen tool across the same area that you blurred.
4. The line becomes sharper again as the tool increases the contrast between the different colored pixels (Figure 4.7). Continue applying the tool and notice how much of the apparent sharpness comes back.

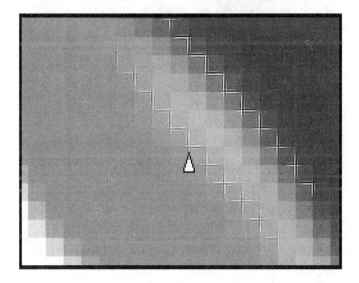

Figure 4.7 *Use the Sharpen tool to increase contrast between adjacent pixels.*

5. Just as you did with the Blur tool, try out the effects of sharpening in Normal, Darken, Lighten, Hue, Color, Saturation, and Luminosity editing modes.

Uses for the Sharpen Tool

The Sharpen tool increases the focus in selected areas of a photograph.

WARNING

This tool must be handled carefully because too much sharpening can create a pixellated look (Figure 4.8).

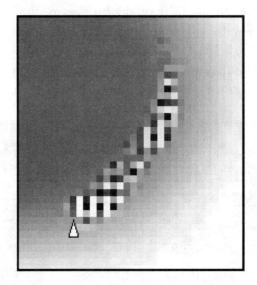

Figure 4.8 *Too much sharpening creates a pixellated look.*

SHORTCUT

Release the mouse button and press the **Option** (Mac) or **Alt** (PC) key while you're using the Sharpen tool to change immediately to the Blur tool and vice versa.

The Dodge/Burn Tools

The term *dodge and burn* refers to the way a photographer makes a portion of a print lighter or darker during the enlarging and printing processes.

Dodging prevents light from reaching the photosensitive paper, thereby keeping it lighter. Dodging is often done in shadow areas, so that they don't block up and lose detail. The Dodging tool is a disk mounted on a thin wire, which is moved between the light and the paper.

Burning is just the opposite of dodging. If a highlight area is overexposed in the negative, the photographer will give extra exposure to that area on the print so that details are brought out. The photographer may use his or her hands or a piece of cardboard to hold back light from the rest of the print so that only a selected area is burned or darkened.

When we use the Dodge and Burn tools in Photoshop, we are lightening or darkening the image without affecting the hue.

These two tools are grouped together in a single Toning Tools palette, which also includes a third tool, the Sponge, which can be used to "soak up" a particular color, either saturating the color to increase the amount of color in an area or desaturating it to dilute the color.

Using the Dodge Tool

1. Start with an empty white screen.
2. Select a large, soft brush and paint a fully saturated color of any hue. The third line of color swatches from the top of the Swatches palette provides many 100% saturated colors. For this experiment, the darker the color, the better.
3. Using the Zoom tool, click and drag to enlarge an area right in the middle of the saturated color you painted.
4. Select the **Dodge** tool from the Toolbox (the disk on a stick; see Figure 4.9). If only the Burn tool is visible (a curved hand; see Figure 4.10), double-click the icon to show the Toning Tool Options palette (Figure 4.11). Select a smaller brush size than the one you used to paint the color. Alternatively, Option-click to change brushes, or click and hold to access hidden options from the toolbar.

Figure 4.9 Dodge tool icon.

Figure 4.10 *Burn tool icon.*

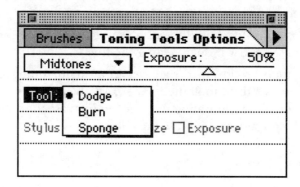

Figure 4.11 *Toning Tool options.*

5. Press the mouse button and move the Dodge tool in the darkest area of saturated color. Observe how it seems to lighten.

In Figure 4.12, the photo in the foreground has been dodged and burned in several modes for demonstration purposes. Is it better? Probably not this time, but it gives you a feel for what is possible.

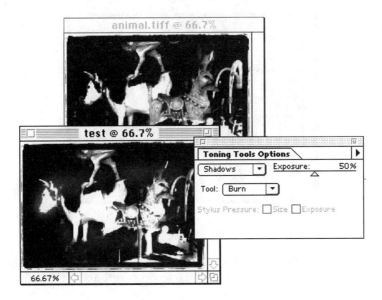

Figure 4.12 *Dodging and burning.*

Using the Burn Tool

1. Make sure that your background color is white, and then double-click on the **Eraser** to activate the eraser palette and erase the entire screen.

2. Select a light, less saturated color from the second row of the Colors palette. Paint a large area with a big, soft paintbrush and enlarge on it with the Zoom tool if you are not already in an enlarged screen view.

3. Double-click the **Dodge** icon and select the **Burn** tool from the drop-down menu in the Toning Tool Options palette.

4. Increase the exposure to **100%** on the Brushes palette. Use the Burn tool (small hand) in the same manner that you used the Dodge tool, moving it around in the colored area while pressing the mouse button. You'll observe an immediate darkening effect (Figure 4.13).

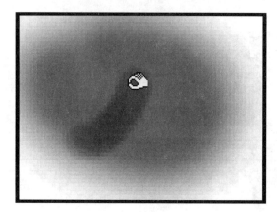

Figure 4.13 *Using the Burn tool to darken an area.*

5. Choose **Windows:Show Colors**, and then select the **Eyedropper** tool and run it over the lighter- and darker-colored areas to see how much the saturation and brightness have changed.

Release the mouse button and press the **Option** (Mac) or **Alt** (PC) key while you're using the Dodge tool to change immediately to the Burn tool and vice versa. This is called *toggling* between the two tools.

SHORTCUT

Exposure

The Exposure slider allows you to control the amount of lightening or darkening the Dodge or Burn tool will accomplish.

Shadows, Midtones, and Highlights

When the Dodge/Burn tools are active, the Toning Tool Options palette shows a different pop-up menu that allows you to control where the lightening or darkening effect occurs—in the Shadows, Midtones, or Highlights of an image (Figure 4.14).

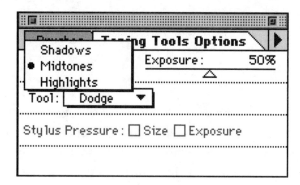

Figure 4.14 *Toning Tools palette with editing mode choices for the Dodge/Burn/Sponge tool.*

Using the Sponge Tool

The Sponge can be used to selectively increase the saturation of a particular area of your image, thus brightening it up, or to reduce the amount of saturation, thereby bringing an area into the CMYK gamut. Because of the limitations of the printing press, CMYK colors are generally not as bright and less vivid than the most saturated colors that can be produced with the RGB model.

Because it works only with color saturation, the Sponge cannot be used with indexed color (256-color) images or one-color (bitmapped, black-and-white) images.

Stylus Pressure

Like the other editing and painting tools you've explored, if you have a digitizing tablet with a pressure-sensitive stylus, you can set the stylus to vary the size of the brush stroke or the exposure as you vary the pressure. You'll find these settings in the Dodge/Burn Options box.

If you're working with a bitmapped (black and white, 1 bit) or an indexed color file you can't use the Smudge, Blur/Sharpen, or Dodge/Burn/Sponge Editing tools on the image.

What You've Learned

Editing Tools

- Use the Smudge tool to create the effect of smearing colors together.
- Use the **Finger Painting** option (Smudge Tool Options palette) to start the beginning of a smudge with the selected foreground color.
- Use the Blur tool to lower the contrast between pixels in a given area.
- Use the Sharpen tool to increase the contrast between pixels in a given area, creating the effect of sharper focus and more definition.
- Click and drag the Zoom tool to enlarge a small part of the image rapidly.
- Use the Dodge tool to lighten a part of an image.
- Use the Burn tool to darken a part of an image.
- The Sponge tool can be used to increase or decrease color saturation in portions of an image.

CHAPTER 5

Introduction to Selections

In this chapter...

- Using the selection tools
- Creating, altering, and saving paths
- Converting paths to selections and selections to paths
- Modifying selections
- Moving and copying selections
- Saving and loading selections

INTRODUCTION TO SELECTIONS

To change part of an image, Photoshop allows you to make selections. A *selection* is the part of the image inside the crawling selection border (called *marching ants* and various other names) when you define an area with one of the Selection tools (Figure 5.1). When you created oval shapes for the balloons with the Elliptical Marquee tool in the Balloon-A-Rama exercise in Chapter 1 you were making selections.

Figure 5.1 *Rectangular Marquee tool defines area on photograph.*

You can perform the following actions on selected areas:

- Paint or fill selected areas with color or pattern using all the Painting tools in any of the available modes.

- Edit a selected area using any of the editing tools in any of the available modes.

- Fill selections with the contents of other selected areas (e.g., pasting one image into another).

- Mask selected areas to prevent them from being changed.

- Apply a filter to a selected area.

- Edit a selection: scale its size, skew or distort its shape, change its perspective, flip it horizontally or vertically, rotate it, add to or subtract from it, and combine it with another selection.
- Save selections in channels or layers for later use.
- Convert selections to PostScript-defined paths.

When you create a selection in Photoshop, you are essentially doing what airbrush artists do when they cut masks out of film: you define an area in which painting (or another process) can take place. Photoshop allows you to make masks with three kinds of edges: anti-aliased, feathered, and non–anti-aliased (jagged edged). In addition, masks can be opaque, semitransparent, or graduated in transparency. (You will learn more about this when we work with channels.)

EXERCISE 5.1: SELECTION TOOLS

Making Rectangular and Square Selections

The easiest way to make rectangular and square selections is with the Rectangular Marquee (Figure 5.2). You can also make these shapes with the Lasso, but this marquee tool is easier and has added advantages.

Figure 5.2 Marquee icon.

Creating a Rectangle

1. Create a new window at least 5 inches x 5 inches.
2. Choose the **Rectangular Marquee** tool from the Toolbox. If the Elliptical Marquee tool is shown instead, toggle between the two by

pressing the **Option** (Mac) or **Alt** (PC) key as you click on the Toolbox, or by pressing the **M** key.

3. Position the mouse pointer in the window. Click and drag in a southeastern direction. You will be creating a rectangular selection (Figure 5.3).

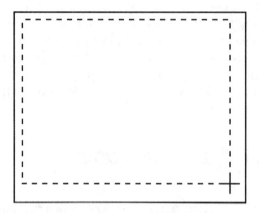

Figure 5.3 *Clicking and dragging to create a rectangle.*

To deselect any selection at any time, press **Command-D** (Mac) or **Ctrl-D** (PC), or click anywhere on the screen (with a selection tool) outside of the selection border. If you click outside the border with another tool, this shortcut will not work.

N O T E

Rectangular Marquee Options

Deselect the rectangle that you just made. To see other selection options, double-click on the **Rectangular Marquee** icon (Figure 5.4).

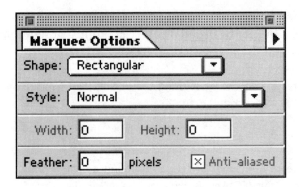

Figure 5.4 Rectangular Marquee option box.

The first mode in the drop-down Style list is **Normal**. This is the default option, which you will probably use most of the time when you want to draw rectangles of various shapes and sizes on the fly.

To Draw a Square

Constrained Aspect Ratio, the next option in the Style list, allows you to set a ratio that will limit the dimensions of the marquee. For example, setting a constrained ratio of 1:1 would force you to draw a square because for every inch you make on the *X* axis, you must drag an inch on the *Y* axis.

1. Click on the **Constrained Aspect Ratio** choice from the drop-down Style list.

2. Type **1** in both the Width and Height boxes.

3. Click and drag in the window just as you did before. You will be dragging out a square this time, and no matter how you move the mouse, you can't draw anything but a square (Figure 5.5).

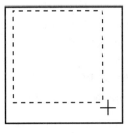

Figure 5.5 Clicking and dragging to select a square area.

The constrained aspect ratio could also be set to 1:2, 3:5, or any proportion that you select. This can be useful if you're creating a design that requires similarly proportioned shapes of varying sizes.

SHORTCUT

To create a square while using the default (Normal) Marquee setting, press **Shift** as you click and drag.

N O T E

To create a rectangular selection around a central point, press the **Option** (Mac) or **Alt** (PC) key as you drag the mouse. Press the **Option** (Mac) or **Alt** (PC) and **Shift** keys as you click and drag to make a square around a central point. (You can press just the **Option** (Mac) or **Alt** (PC) key if you have constrained the aspect ratio to square proportions in the Marquee Options box.) The square will grow symmetrically from your origin point (Figure 5.6). In this example, the cross-hairs were centered on the *X*. This centering technique also works with circles.

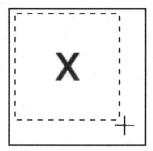

Figure 5.6 *Drawing a constrained shape around a central point.*

To create a rectangular selection of fixed size:

1. Deselect any active selections.

2. Reopen the Rectangular Marquee Options palette and select **Fixed Size** from the drop-down Style list. This option allows you to create a rectangular selection with a predetermined size. This is very handy if you're selecting images to fit presized boxes in a layout program.

3. Enter a width of **250** pixels and a height of **150** pixels. Click **OK**.

4. Place the mouse pointer in the window and click and drag to draw a marquee just as you did before. You'll see that the shape appears at its full size; it does not grow as the others did. You can move this shape around the window just by continuing to drag it. When you're done, deselect everything.

To create single-row and single-column selections:

1. Open the Rectangular Marquee Options palette again. The last two choices in the Shape drop-down list are **Single Row** and **Single Column**. Click on **Single Row**.

2. Position the mouse pointer in the window, and then click and drag. You will select a single line, which extends across the entire window. If you had chosen the **Single Column** option, you would have drawn a single vertical line. These lines, horizontal and vertical, have properties of selections and therefore can be filled with paint, rotated, and manipulated in many other ways.

FEATHERING A SELECTION

Feathering is a change that can be applied to a selection border to soften the transition between the inside of the border and the background. To demonstrate the difference between a feathered and nonfeathered selection:

1. Start with a clean white screen, white background color, black foreground color (default).

2. Enlarge the window to a 10:1 view, using the Zoom tool.

3. Double-click on the **Rectangular Marquee** to open the Options palette. The marquee mode should be Normal, and feathering by default should be left at a radius of 0 pixels.

4. Select a square shape and press **Option-Delete** (Mac) or **Alt-Delete** (PC)—or **Backspace** on some keyboards—to fill the shape with black. You'll notice that the black fill is solid all the way to the marching ants selection border (Figure 5.7).

Figure 5.7 *Close-up of selection filled with feather radius set to 0.*

5. Press **Command-Z** (Mac) or **Ctrl-Z** (PC) to undo the fill, and then press **Command-D** (Mac) or **Ctrl-D** (PC) to get rid of the selection.

6. Open the Rectangular Marquee Options palette and set the feather radius to **1** pixel.

7. Draw another square and fill it with black again. Press **Option-Delete** (Mac) or **Alt-Delete** (PC) or **Backspace** to fill the selection with black. You'll see that the black fill doesn't have a hard edge, but rather feathers softly from inside the border to outside (Figure 5.8). The higher the number you set for a pixel radius, the larger the zone of feathering and the softer, more blurred the effect. The zone of feathering is actually twice the pixel radius, as you saw in the enlargement. When you set a feather radius of **4** pixels, the border is actually feathered 4 pixels on the outside and 4 pixels on the inside for a total border width of 8 pixels.

Press **Command-D** (Mac) or **Ctrl-D** (PC) to deselect and then erase the entire image by double-clicking the **Eraser** icon to activate the Eraser palette. You can then click the **Erase Image** button in the palette.

Figure 5.8 Close-up of selection with feather radius of 1 pixel.

8. Return to a 1:1 window view. Change the feather option to **3** pixels in the Options box and then drag to describe another square.

9. Fill the feathered selection with black. In this normal view, you can see the results of the soft feathered edge (Figure 5.9). Repeat the preceding steps to create a rectangle with a 5-pixel feather (Figure 5.10) and even higher settings, if you wish (Figure 5.11).

Figure 5.9 Selection with 3-pixel feather.

Figure 5.10 *Selection with 5-pixel feather.*

Figure 5.11 *Selection with 10-pixel feather.*

MAKING ELLIPTICAL AND ROUND SELECTIONS

The Elliptical Marquee is used for selecting oval and circular shapes (Figure 5.12). The options are the same as comparable options introduced with the Rectangular Marquee tool.

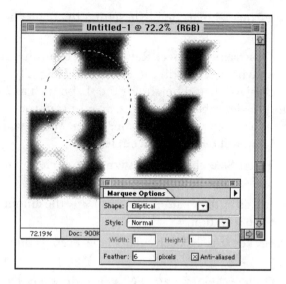

Figure 5.12 *Elliptical Marquee icon, at left, has also been used as a Fixed Size Marquee to turn the feathered boxes into hunks of Swiss cheese.*

Elliptical Marquee Options

• Double-click the **Elliptical Marquee** icon to open the Options palette (Figure 5.13).

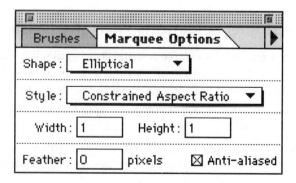

Figure 5.13 *The Marquee Options palette.*

- Choose the **Normal** marquee style setting to create an oval of any size and shape.

- Click the **Constrained Aspect Ratio** choice from the drop-down Style list and then type in a ratio in the Width and Height boxes to designate a proportional width and height for the shape such as **2:1**, **1:2**, **3:4**. Use this option to describe an oval with fixed proportions, although you may draw it as large or small as you prefer. When you set the aspect ratio at **1:1** you will be drawing a circle.

- Click the **Fixed Size** choice to designate a circle or oval of a specific height and width.

- Enter a number in the Feather box to specify the amount of feathering to apply to the selection.

- Use the **Shift** key to select a circular shape, even if you're in the Normal mode.

- Press the **Option** (Mac) or **Alt** (PC) key to draw a circle or an oval outward from a center point.

- Press the **Shift** and the **Option** (Mac) or **Alt** (PC) keys simultaneously to draw a circle outward from a central point.

If you have already constrained the selection to circular proportions using the **Fixed Size** option, you only have to press the **Option** (Mac) or **Alt** (PC) key.

N O T E

Making Freehand Selections with the Lasso Tool

You can use the Lasso tool to make freehand, irregular selections by hand. With the Lasso tool (Figure 5.14) you can make manual selections of part of an image. This duplicates the type of drop-out you would have done to a halftone image in traditional graphic arts (i.e., physically cutting away the bits you don't want or need).

We used the Lasso to outline a part of a person in this scene (Figure 5.15), an irregular shape that would have been difficult to describe with any other tool.

Figure 5.15 *Selecting with the Lasso tool—straight-edged mode.*

Lasso Features

To draw a freeform selection border:

- Select the **Lasso** tool.
- Drag the mouse pointer on the screen, holding down the mouse button (Figure 5.16).

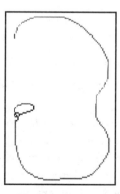

Figure 5.16 *Drawing a freeform shape with the Lasso tool.*

- Use this for selecting any kind of irregularly shaped area.
- You must keep the mouse button down the entire time you're dragging. As soon as you release the button, the beginning and ending points of the line connect, closing the selection.

To draw straight lines in a selection border:

- Hold down the **Option** (Mac) or **Alt** (PC) key and the mouse button as you touch key points along the perimeter of the object you're selecting. The Lasso will stretch and contract like a rubber band, allowing you to create a selection border with straight lines.
- Release the **Option** (Mac) or **Alt** (PC) key (but not the mouse button) to continue drawing a border in the freehand mode. Press the **Option** (Mac) or **Alt** (PC) key when you want to draw a straight line again. You can go back and forth like this, pressing and releasing the **Option** (Mac) or **Alt** (PC) key all around an object.
- When you release the **Option** (Mac) or **Alt** (PC) key and the mouse button, the selection will close, and the crawling border will appear.
- If you have not completed drawing the shape or release the button by accident, the beginning point and the ending point of the lasso line will self-connect. You cannot undo this operation and just go back a step. Pressing **Command-Z** (Mac) or **Ctrl-Z** (PC) will deselect the entire selection. (There are ways you can fix an incomplete or incorrect selection, as you'll soon learn.)

Lasso Options

- Double-click on the **Lasso** icon to show Lasso Options.
- Set the feather radius as you did with the Rectangular and Elliptical Marquees.
- If you don't want to feather the selection, but prefer a smooth edge, click the **Anti-aliased** check box. In a 6:1 enlargement, you'll see that anti-aliasing lightens some of the pixels along the edge of the selection (Figure 5.17), but it doesn't blur the image on both sides of the selection border as feathering does (Figure 5.18). If neither anti-aliasing nor feathering are applied, the border will have a jagged appearance.

(Figure 5.19) The selection border has been hidden in these images so that you can see the edge more clearly.

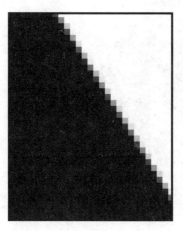

Figure 5.17 A 6:1 enlargement of the Lasso anti-aliased edge.

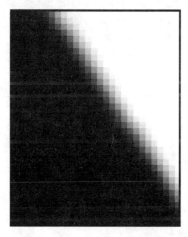

Figure 5.18 A 6:1 enlargement of the Lasso feathered edge, 1-pixel radius.

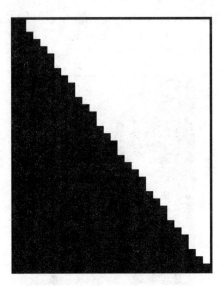

Figure 5.19 A 6:1 enlargement of the Lasso edge, no feathering, no anti-aliasing.

To hide the selection border at any time (while allowing it to remain active), press **Command-H** (Mac) or **Ctrl-H** (PC). Pressing this command a second time makes the border reappear.

N O T E

The Polygon Lasso

The Polygon Lasso tool works precisely in the same way as the Lasso tool, with the exception that it can be used to make straight-edged selections as well as freehand selections:

1. Choose the **Polygon Lasso** by selecting the straight-edged looking lasso from the Lasso Tool fly-out menu (Figure 15.20).

Figure 5.20 Polygon Lasso icon.

2. Define a feathered edge and enter a pixel value for the feathering, just as you did for the Lasso tool.

3. You may check **Anti-aliased** to turn off the default aliasing option.

4. Set a starting point for your selection by clicking within the image with the tool.

5. Click where you want the first straight segment to end. You can continue clicking end points for more straight segments.

6. You can draw a freehand segment with this tool by holding down **Option** (Mac) or **Alt** (PC) and dragging. Release the **Option** (Mac) or **Alt** (PC) button and continue making straight pieces.

7. Double-click within the image to close the selection border.

Making Selections by Color or Grayscale Value Using the Magic Wand

The Magic Wand (Figure 5.20) selects all touching pixels that are similar in hue and value to the pixel you first clicked on. You tell the wand how choosy to be by setting its tolerance. Based on the tolerance set, the wand extends the selection outward until it finds no more pixels with the color values you want. If the tolerance was set to **40** and you clicked with the wand on a pixel that had a color value of 100, the Magic Wand would select all pixels with values between 60 and 140. (Both hue and luminance are figured into a special equation as the wand decides which pixels it can and cannot select.) A high tolerance will select a wider range of pixels. A low tolerance will select a very narrow range of pixels.

Figure 5.21 *Magic Wand icon.*

If you want to select a wide range of a color, from bright to dark, set the tolerance higher than the default (32) and click the wand in the middle of the range of color values. If you click in an area of the color that is very dark or very light, you are giving the wand less latitude. (Remember, color component values can range from 0 to 255.)

CASE EXAMPLE

- A solid-color patch of color is a good example of the simplest kind of area you can select with a Magic Wand.
- We double-clicked on the **Magic Wand** tool to open the Magic Wand Options palette to check the tolerance. We left the tolerance at its default value of **32**.
- We clicked the **Anti-aliased** check box because we wanted the selection to be smooth edged.
- Returning to the window, we clicked the Magic Wand once in the center of the cherry. However, not all the pixels were selected, because the tolerance was set too low (Figure 5.22A).

A   B

Figure 5.22A and 5.22B *Selecting the cherry with the Magic Wand tool. In Figure 5.22A the tolerance was set to low, so not all the pixels were selected. The tolerance was reset in Figure 5.22B to make a better selection.*

- We reset the tolerance to **60** and clicked the cherry again. This time all the pixels were selected (Figure 5.22B).
- Because we wanted to see how far would be far enough, we reset the tolerance to **120**. As you can see, too much was selected in this case to be of much use to anyone.

Using the Magic Wand effectively requires some trial and error, as the tolerance required will depend very much on the object on which you're using the Wand.

MAKING SELECTIONS WITH THE PATHS PALETTE

If you have used an object-oriented illustration program or took serious drafting back in high school, you will recognize the Pen tool as a Bezier (Bez-ee-yay) curve–drawing device. With the Pen tool you can create lines and shapes that can be fine-tuned, saved as paths, filled with color or outlined (stroked), and used as the basis for selections. Conversely, you can change selections into paths and edit them with the tools on the Paths palette (Figure 5.23). While you see paths on screen, they contain no pixels and don't print with the image.

Figure 5.23 *The Paths palette—home of the Pen tool.*

The smallest part of a path is a *segment*: the line connecting two anchor points. Several segments, linked, make a *subpath*, and subpaths combine to form *paths*. A path can be a line or a closed shape or a series of lines, a series of shapes, or a combination of lines and shapes. You can stroke and fill subpaths as well as paths.

DRAWING STRAIGHT LINES WITH THE PEN TOOL

1. Start with a white screen, black foreground color, white background. Double-click on the **Pen** tool in the Toolbox to make the Pen palette active and select the **Pen** tool.

2. Make the Paths palette active by selecting **Windows:Show Paths** from the menu bar. Click in the window to set an anchor point. It is called an *anchor point* because it will anchor one end of a line. Release the mouse button. Click again a distance away to create a second anchor point, and a line will be drawn between the two (Figure 5.24).

Figure 5.24 Drawing a straight line by clicking to make two anchor points.

Notice that a new anchor point is darkened as it is created, indicating that it is selected. At the same time, the previous anchor point lightens, meaning that it is deselected. Release the mouse button.

3. Click to create a third anchor point and second line. Release the mouse button.

4. Move the pen on top of the first anchor point. A small loop appears to the side of the Pen tool, letting you know that clicking will close the path (Figure 5.25). Click on the first anchor point to close the triangle (Figure 5.26).

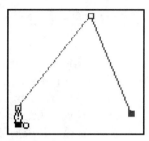

Figure 5.25 *Loop at side of pen indicates next click will close triangle.*

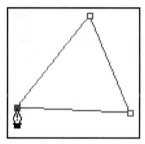

Figure 5.26 *Closing the triangle by clicking on the original anchor point.*

5. Be certain that you do not drag the mouse as you create any of these lines. If you do, you will create curved lines, not straight-edged ones. Press **Delete** twice to eliminate all lines before going on to the next part of the exercise.

NOTE   Hold down the **Shift** key to constrain the placement of an anchor point to a 45° angle or a multiple of 45°, such as a 90° angle. This also works to constrain the angle of a direction line to 45° or a multiple thereof. Both constraints are helpful for drawing some geometric shapes.

DRAWING CURVES WITH THE PEN TOOL

1. Click the Pen tool once in the window to create an anchor point and, holding down the mouse button, drag at an angle to form the first part of a curve. As soon as you begin dragging, the pen will turn into an arrow. The lines that emerge as you drag are called *direction lines.* The slope of the curve is the same as the slope of its direction lines, and the height of the direction lines determines the height of the curve. There are two dark dots at the end of each direction line. These are *direction points.* As soon as the direction lines are as long as the one in Figure 5.27, release the mouse button.

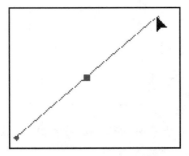

Figure 5.27 *Drawing the first part of a curve.*

2. Position the pen a short distance from the first point (Figure 5.28). Click, keeping the mouse button held down. A slightly curved line will form between the two anchor points.

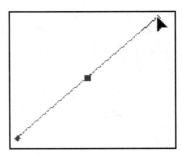

Figure 5.28 *Drawing the second part of a curve.*

3. Still keeping the mouse button down, drag in the direction away from the first anchor point. This action will shape the curve connecting the two anchor points, making it more exaggerated. Direction lines will emerge from the second anchor point, as seen in Figure 5.29.

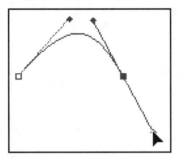

Figure 5.29 Shaping the curve.

4. Release the mouse button and click again, in line with the first two anchor points (Figure 5.30), and drag in the direction away from the second anchor point. Another curve is formed. You can continue in this way, building a gently curved line.

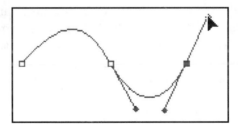

Figure 5.30 Adding another curve to the path.

5. When you've finished, click **Delete** once to eliminate the last anchor point, and click **Delete** twice to delete the path. Clicking **Delete** three times deletes all paths that have not been saved.

6. Again, position the Pen tool in the window and then click and drag to form your first anchor point and direction line. Click again to finish the curve, but this time drag back toward the first anchor point, instead of away from it (Figure 5.31). The shape that it describes is a curve with

two bumps, rather than one. To make only one bump between two anchor points, always drag in the direction away from the first anchor point as you're setting the second point.

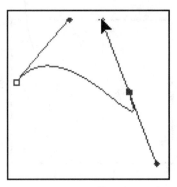

Figure 5.31 *Creating a curve with two bumps by dragging toward the first anchor point.*

USING THE RUBBER BAND OPTION

1. Before you add an anchor point, you may want to preview the curve it will be making. This is especially helpful when you're outlining an image. To use this Preview option, double-click the **Pen** tool icon, which will open the Pen Tool Options palette (Figure 5.32). Click on the **Rubber Band** check box.

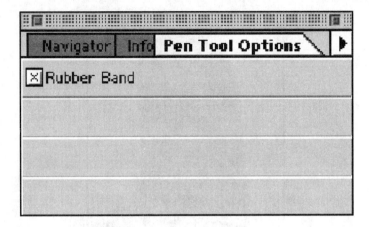

Figure 5.32 Pen Tool Options palette—***Rubber Band*** *option selected.*

2. Click and drag the pen to set an anchor point with two direction points. Release the mouse button but move the pen to set your second anchor point. A curved line will follow it. You can use this feature to assist you with anchor-point placement as you outline an object.

FINE-TUNING A PATH

It's very common to change the shape of a path after you create it. Working with paths is generally a practice of successive approximation until you create the shape or line just the way you want it. For example, after we outlined the arch of this bell tower with the Pen tool, we changed a few of the smooth points to corner points so that we could adjust the lines with more precision (Figure 5.33).

Figure 5.33 *Adjusting a path by moving a direction line.*

Moving an Anchor Point or Direction Point to Change the Shape of a Curve

1. Draw a simple path with the pen: one anchor point with direction lines, connected by a curve to a second anchor point.

2. Select the **Arrow** tool from the Pen toolbox, or toggle through the Pen tool by pressing the letter **P** until you reach the **Arrow** tool (Figure 5.34). Place the Arrow tool on the first anchor point. Click on the point and drag it. The shape of the curve will change as you do.

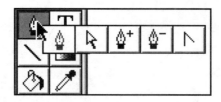

Figure 5.34 *The Arrow tool is second from the left in the fly-out Pen tool menu.*

3. Now place the arrow on one of the direction points (at the end of a direction line) and drag it back and forth. This is another way to change the shape of a curve.

When you select the pen again or toggle back through the pen options by pressing the **P** key, you can continue drawing from where you left off.

CHANGING A SMOOTH CURVE POINT TO A CORNER POINT

1. Create two curves, one over and one under, using three anchor points as we did in the previous exercise. When you use the arrow to move the direction point at one end of a direction line, the direction point at the other end of the direction line moves simultaneously. This happens only when the anchor point is a smooth point—the junction between two smooth curves. Moving the direction line changes the second half of the slope of the incoming curve and the first half of the slope of the outgoing curve (Figure 5.35).

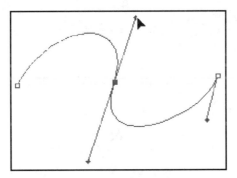

Figure 5.35 Moving direction lines changes the slope of the curve.

2. Smooth curves may not always be what you'd like. Let's say you'd like to draw a heart shape. To form the acute angle at the top of the heart, you would need to convert the central anchor point to a sharp corner point. Select the **Corner Point** tool from the Paths palette (Figure 5.36).

Figure 5.36 *Corner Point tool.*

3. Click on the center anchor point with the Corner Point tool, holding the mouse button down (Figure 5.37A). The curve will immediately change shape (Figure 5.37B). While continuing to press the mouse button, drag to create corner point direction lines. Unlike the smooth point direction lines that move in synchronization, corner-point direction lines can be manipulated separately.

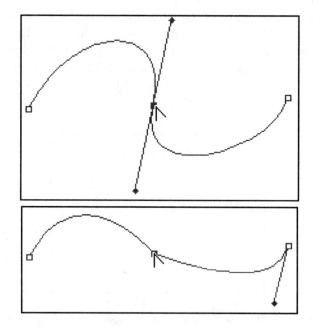

Figure 5.37A and B *The moments just before and just after changing a smooth anchor point to a corner point.*

4. Click and drag upward on the left direction point to change the direction of the curve (Figure 5.38).

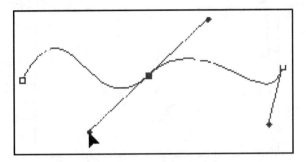

Figure 5.38 *Changing the direction of a curve.*

5. The third anchor point (far right) is still a smooth point. You can change the curve's shape just by moving the direction points on the direction lines with the arrow (Figure 5.39A). Continue tweaking the shapes of each of the curves. Your image should look like Figure 5.39B when you're done.

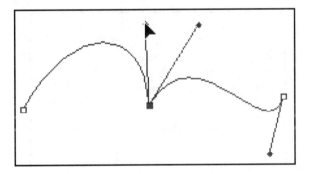

Figure 5.39A *Changing the shape of a curve by dragging on the direction point.*

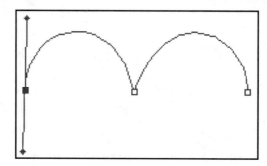

Figure 5.39B *The finished shape: two curves connected at a corner point.*

6. Click with the Pen tool on the third anchor point (the last one you drew). Click to add two more points (one at the apex of the heart, the other on top of the first anchor point to close the shape). Then, using the Arrow tool, adjust the shape with the direction lines until you like it (Figure 5.40).

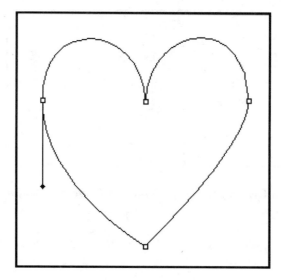

Figure 5.40 *The completed heart path.*

7. Save the path. Press the arrow on the right side of the Paths palette to reveal the pop-up menu. Choose **Save Path** (Figure 5.41) and type **Heart** in the text box. Click **OK**. Then save the entire Photoshop file

using the **Save** command under the File menu. Name the file **Heart** and leave the Photoshop 4 file format (pop-up menu) as the default. Click **Save**. The name of the path will appear in the Paths palette (Figure 5.42).

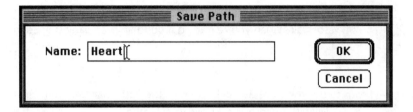

Figure 5.41 *Save Path dialog box.*

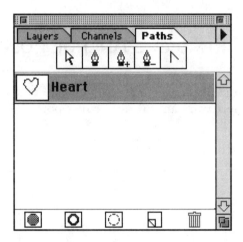

Figure 5.42 *Paths palette with saved path.*

The first time you click on a smooth point with the Corner Point tool, it converts it to a corner point. Clicking again converts it back to a smooth point.

N O T E

SHORTCUT

Press the **Ctrl** (PC) or **Command** (Mac) key to display the arrow pointer whenever the Pen tool is in use.

N O T E

Using fewer anchor points to define a curve usually gives better results. More is not necessarily better. However, there are times when you'll need to add points, especially when you're tracing around an irregularly shaped image.

SHORTCUT

Learn to use the icons at the bottom of the Paths palette. From left to right, they are Fill with foreground, Stroke with foreground, Load as selection, Make work path from selection, Create new path, and Delete path.

ADDING AND REMOVING ANCHOR POINTS

1. To add an anchor point to a line, select the **Pen** tool with the plus sign and click where you want to add the new point (Figure 5.43).

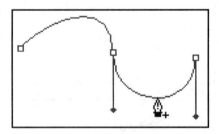

Figure 5.43 Adding an anchor point.

2. To remove an anchor point, use the Pen tool with the minus sign to click on an existing point (Figure 5.44).

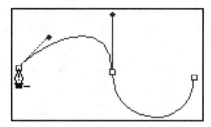

Figure 5.44 *Removing an anchor point.*

MOVING A PATH

Use the following steps to move a path:

1. Select the path in the Paths palette.
2. Select the **Arrow** in the Pen toolbox.
3. Option- or Alt-click the path to select it.
4. Drag the path to the place where you'd like it to be.

MANAGING PATHS

Saving, Loading, and Creating New Paths and Deleting Paths

- You have already saved one path, Heart, which shows up selected in your Paths palette.

- If you create more shapes and lines while a path is selected, they will be saved with that path, automatically. You do not have to save the path again.

- To create a new path you must first deactivate the active path. Do this by clicking the arrow on any area outside of your saved path, but still within the Paths palette. The saved Path's box becomes inactive, and the path is hidden, although still saved. You can then begin drawing a new path on the blank screen. You'll note that as soon as you begin to draw, a new box labeled *Work Path* appears in the Path palette (figure 5.45), and you can see your new path begin to take shape there.

WARNING

You must save the new path by name before viewing the old path again, or your new work will be lost.

To view a saved path, click on the appropriately labeled box to activate it.

With your Heart deactivated, create a new path. Don't get fancy because we're going to delete the path in a moment.

Save the path as **Throwaway Path**. It will appear checked in the palette window.

Select **Delete Path…** from the Path palette or drag the path name to the Trash Can icon at the bottom of the palette, and the path instantly disappears. Only saved and activated paths can be deleted in this way. An active path can also be deleted by pressing **Delete** on the keyboard.

FILLING AND STROKING PATHS

In this exercise you will create a shape, fill it with the foreground color, and apply a contrasting color to the outline of the path.

1. Create a closed parallelogram shape using the Pen tool. Click to make its corner points; do not drag. Hold down the **Shift** key to constrain the corner angles to 45° or multiples thereof.

2. To select all the object's anchor points, drag a marquee around the parallelogram and release the mouse button.

3. Name the path Parallelogram using the **Save Path…** option in the Path palette. The anchor points are hidden now.

4. Select a bright gold for your foreground color.

5. Select **Fill Path** from the pop-up menu (Figure 5.46). The Fill Path dialog box will appear (Figure 5.47). For this example, select **Foreground Color**, **Blending at 100% Opacity**, and **Normal** mode with the **Anti-aliased** box activated. Click **OK**, and the path will fill with gold. Next, we'll create a border for the shape. Alternately, using these same nor-

mal criteria, you can elect to click on the **Fill Path** and **Stroke Path** icons at the bottom of the Paths palette.

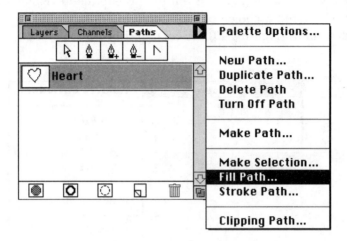

Figure 5.46 *Fill Path submenu command.*

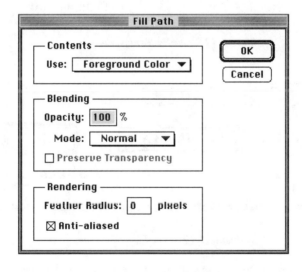

Figure 5.47 *Fill Path dialog box.*

6. Change the foreground color to a vivid blue. Select a medium-sized brush from the Brushes palette.

7. If you select **Stroke Path...** from the pop-up menu (Figure 5.48), you will be offered a choice of tools from a drop-down list in the Stroke Path window (Figure 5.49). Select the **Airbrush** tool.

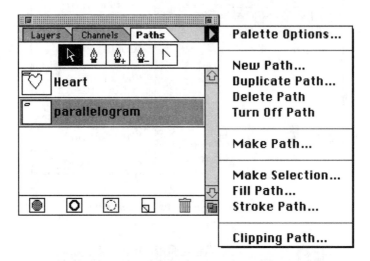

Figure 5.48 *Stroke Path submenu command.*

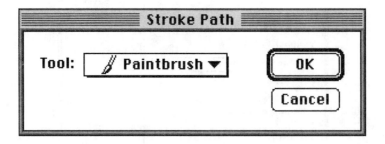

Figure 5.49 *Stroke Path dialog box.*

8. The border of the shape will be stroked with the foreground color, and the width of the stroke will be the width of the brush you use. The path will be visible through the stroked color but will not appear in the art-

work. Deactivate **Parallelogram** on the Paths palette to see this effect; then check it again.

9. Undo the stroke by pressing **Command-Z** (Mac) or **Ctrl-Z** (PC). Change to a large, soft brush and select **Stroke Path...** again. This time, choose the **Pencil** and click **OK.** The stroke will be applied.

10. You can also stroke the path with one of the specialty brushes. Double-click in the image window to erase the filled and stroked parallelogram. Notice that erasing has no effect upon the Parallelogram path. It is still selected in the Paths palette. Deselect the **Parallelogram** path on the menu in preparation for making a new path.

11. Create a new path by dragging with the Pen tool. It's a simple over and under curve with three anchor points. (See Figure 5.30.) Save the path as **Goose Flight**.

12. Select **Append Brushes** from the Brushes palette fly-out menu and choose **Assorted Brushes...** the file with all the interesting shapes.

13. Select the image of the Canadian goose. Double-click on the icon and when the Brush Options window appears, change the Spacing to **130%.** Click **OK.**

14. Choose **Stroke Path** from the pop-up menu. Paint the image with the Paintbrush tool when given a choice of tools in the Stroke Path dialog box.

15. The path will fill with a line of evenly spaced geese (Figure 5.50). When you're finished, undo the image; then delete the goose flight path in the Paths palette.

Figure 5.50 Stroking path with custom brush shape.

You can fill and stroke subpaths the same way that you learned to fill and stroke paths.

Fill Path and **Stroke Path** are powerful tools for creating precisely filled and outlined shapes. Of course, you can use them with all the painting and editing tools, in modes appropriate for those tools. Pen tool paths behave very much like selection borders. In fact, you can use a path to create a selection border. You will not be irreversibly converting the path into a selection; you will be using the path as a template from which to make a selection.

MAKING A SELECTION BORDER FROM A PEN TOOL PATH

1. Click in the Paths palette to select the parallelogram path once more.

2. Choose **Make Selection...** from the fly-out menu (Figure 5.51).

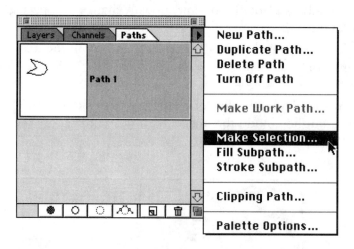

Figure 5.51 *Make Selection pop-up menu.*

3. In the Make Selection dialog box (Figure 5.52) you can set the feather radius for the selection border (leave it blank now) and you can choose the **Anti-aliased** option if you wish.

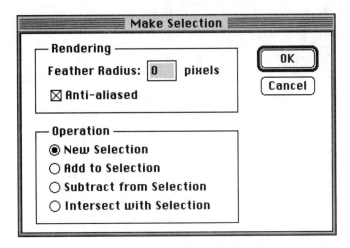

Figure 5.52 *Make Selection dialog box.*

4. The parallelogram shape becomes an active selection border (Figure 5.53).

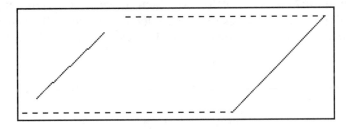

Figure 5.53 *Parallelogram path becomes selection.*

CREATING A PATH BASED ON A SELECTION

Just as you can take a path and make a selection border, you can also take a selection border and create a path, which can then be modified with the Pen tool.

1. Deactivate all paths in the Paths palette.

2. Select the **Lasso** tool from the Toolbox and drag to form a freeform shape (Figure 5.54).

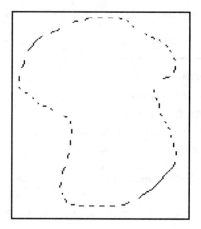

Figure 5.54 *Shape drawn with Lasso tool before conversion to path.*

3. Select **Make Path...** from the Paths palette submenu (Figure 5.55). When the Make Path dialog box opens leave the tolerance at its default setting, 2.0 pixels. Click **OK**. The selection border will be changed into a path. Click on the path with the Arrow tool to make the anchor points visible (Figure 5.56).

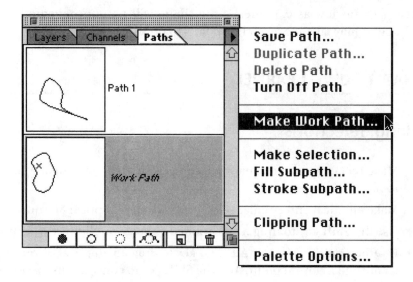

Figure 5.55 Make Paths command from Paths palette submenu.

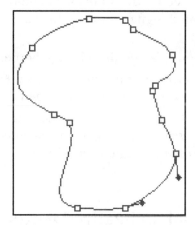

Figure 5.56 Lasso-drawn shape after conversion to path.

This tolerance is different from the tolerance used with the Magic Wand tool. Setting the Make Path tolerance tells the computer how closely you want the path to follow the original shape of the selection. A higher tolerance (up to 10) provides smoother curves but doesn't hug the shape as well. A lower tolerance path (as low as 0.5) means the shape will be approximated more closely, but it may take more anchor points to do so.

WHAT YOU'VE LEARNED

Making Selections

- Make rectangular and square selections with the Rectangular Marquee tool.
- Make elliptical and circular selections with the Elliptical Marquee tool.
- Use the **Shift** key to drag a constrained circular or elliptical selection.
- Use the **Option** (Mac) or **Alt** (PC) key to drag an elliptical or rectangular around a central point. Add the **Shift** key to constrain its size to a circular or square shape.
- Create ellipses and rectangles of fixed size using choices in their respective Marquee Options boxes. Single-row and single-column selections can be designated in the Rectangular Marquee Options palette.
- Feather a selection to soften the selection border.
- Make freehand selections with the Lasso tool. Hold down the **Option** (Mac) or **Alt** (PC) key to make straight-edged Lasso lines.
- Use the Magic Wand to make a selection based on pixel color (or grayscale value, if selecting in a grayscale document). Choose the **Anti-aliased** option from the Magic Wand Options box for a smooth-edged selection.

Using the Pen Tool and Paths Palette

- Make straight-line and curved paths with the Pen tool in the Paths palette.
- Modify the curve using the arrow and the Corner Point tools.
- Add and subtract anchor points with the Pen Plus tool and the Pen Minus tool.

- Move a path by selecting all the anchor points in a path and then dragging on any one of the anchor points.

- Save, load, and delete paths by using the submenu commands on the Paths palette (i.e., **Save Path…**, **Load Path…**, **Delete Path**).

- Fill paths and stroke paths with any of the painting tools using Paths palette submenu commands **Fill Path…** and **Stroke Path…**.

- Create a selection border from a path (**Make Selection**).

- Create a path from a selection border (**Make Selection**).

CHAPTER 6

More About Selections

In this chapter…

- Modifying selections
- Adding and subtracting from selections
- Moving and copying selections

MODIFYING SELECTIONS

In Chapter 5, we looked at some of the basics of making selections. In this chapter, we'll learn how to add to and subtract from selection borders using the Toolbox tools. We'll also learn how to move, copy, save, and load selections.

ADDING AND SUBTRACTING FROM SELECTIONS

To add to any selection or to add multiple selections using the Lasso, Marquee or Magic Wand tools:

- Hold down the **Shift** key, and click in the area to be added. If you are using the Magic Wand, the tolerance can be adjusted to limit or expand its range before doing this. You can do this as many times as you wish—just remember to hold down **Shift** before each additional click (Figure 6.1).

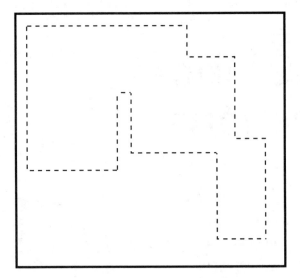

Figure 6.1 *The Marquee tool has been used to add and subtract several rectangle shapes.*

- When using the Lasso tool, drag to encompass the additional area to be added. You can release the mouse button and move the mouse to encompass multiple noncontiguous areas as long as you hold down the **Shift** key while making the selections.

- Holding the **Shift** key down, drag a Rectangular or Elliptical Marquee tool around the area to be added.
- As long as you remember to press the **Shift** key before making each additional selection, you can even switch selection tools.

To subtract from any selection or to subtract multiple selections:

- Hold down the **Option** (Mac) or **Alt** key (PC) to subtract from your selection. Again, remember to hold the key down before each additional click.
- If you are using the Magic Wand tool, hold down the key and click in the area to be subtracted. (Reset the tolerance if necessary.)
- If you are using the Lasso tool, hold down the key and drag to encompass the area to be subtracted.
- If you are using the Rectangular or Elliptical Marquee tool, hold down the key and drag a marquee around the area to be subtracted.
- You can switch tools if you remember to hold down the **Alt** or **Option** key before making each subsequent subtraction.

You can switch between adding and subtracting from selections—just switch between keys when you do.

CREATING A SELECTION USING MULTIPLE TOOLS

1. Using the Rectangular Marquee tool, draw a square.
2. Hold down the **Shift** key and drag a similarly shaped box that slightly overlaps the first. Notice how the two boxes flow together to become one irregular shape(Figure 6.2).
3. Select the **Lasso** tool from the toolbox.
4. Hold down the **Shift** key once again, and draw a roughly circular shape that overlaps your flowing boxes (Figure 6.3). Again, the boxes flow together, creating an interesting selected shape.

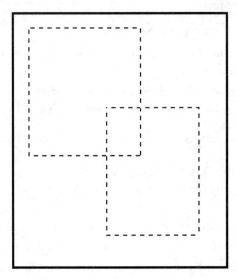

Figure 6.2 *Two squares have become one selection using the Marquee tool and the* **Shift** *key.*

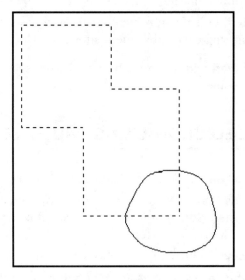

Figure 6.3 *Adding a roughly drawn Lasso shape.*

5. Experiment by adding and subtracting from your selection using the Magic Wand, Lasso tool, and various Marquee shapes.

Remember that **Shift** adds and **Alt** (PC) or **Option** (Mac) subtracts.

NOTE

CASE EXAMPLE: THE CALLA LILIES ARE IN BLOOM

We selected the calla lilies photo so that we could drop the background away and work with the lilies by themselves. We chose the **Magic Wand** tool and played around with the tolerance until we found the one that worked best for this range of tonality. In this particular case, it was 120. We clicked in the middle of the bottom lily and kept selecting and deselecting, all the while fiddling with the tolerances, until the Magic Wand chose all of the bottom lily, something we knew could be accomplished because the extreme white of the lily contrasts sharply with the very dark background (Figure 6.4).

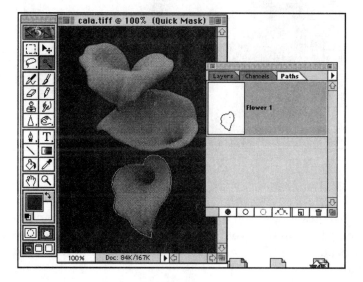

Figure 6.4 The lilies have been selected and masked using the Quick Mask icon at the bottom left of the toolbox.

Selecting the Paths palette, we chose **Make Work Path** from the fly-out menu and a Path was neatly made around the lily. To test the appearance of our work, we dropped a quick mask over the work to see how precisely the lily had been selected. We then removed the quick mask, using the corresponding icon (Edit in Normal Mode) at the bottom of the toolbox.

Once again selecting the **Magic Wand** tool, we chose an area of consistent white tones within the center lily. Some experimenting with the tool and a few deselections gave us an area just slightly larger than the two lilies. Using **Option** (Mac) or **Alt** (PC) on the selected area outside of the lilies gave us a snapping hard line around both of the top flowers (Figure 6.5). At this point, we could use the Pen tools to tighten up the paths, but we didn't feel the need in this instance.

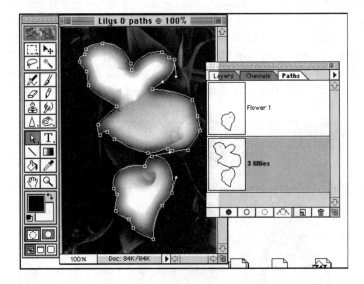

Figure 6.5 *The Magic Wand tool helps to create a snapping hard line around the flowers.*

In Figure 6.5, just to give you a hint of what can be done at this point, we've stroked the path with foreground color using the Airbrush tool. While there is no practical reason to do this, it does make for an interesting combination of visual textures.

MORE CHOICES UNDER THE SELECT MENU

The Select menu offers even more ways to modify selections (Figure 6.6).

Figure 6.6 *The Select menu.*

Selecting All and None of an Image

Selecting all (**Command-A** on the Mac or **Ctrl-A** on the PC) selects everything in the document window right out to the edge.

Selecting none (**Command-D** on the Mac or **Ctrl-D** on the PC) deselects all selections, as does clicking with any selection tool (except the Magic Wand tool) anywhere outside a selection border or borders, if there are multiple, noncontinuous active selections.

Inversing the Selection Border

Inverse reverses what is selected and not selected in the document window. In the case of our lilies, we made our path of three a selection on the Paths menu, then inversed the selection to select only the lilies. We then chose the **Gradient** tool and chose to fill with a very striking background that would reproduce nicely in black and white (Figure 6.7).

Figure 6.7 *Inversing a selection allows you to manipulate everything outside the area you selected.*

This is an extremely handy technique for drawing on both the inside and out-side of a selection border. Try this:

1. Select an oval shape with the Elliptical tool.
2. Choose an airbrush. Select a large, soft brush size. Paint around the selection border with a robin's egg blue color, just to suggest the shape. You can only paint inside the selection border as shown in Figure 6.8.

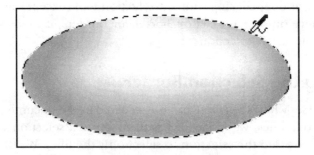

Figure 6.8 *Painting inside the selection border.*

3. Inverse the selection, change the airbrush to gray, and paint a shadow below the shape. You can still only paint inside the selection border, but by selecting the **Inverse** command, you've made the inside become the outside, as shown in Figure 6.9. Hide the selection border (**Command-H** on the Mac or **Ctrl-H** on the PC) if you wish.

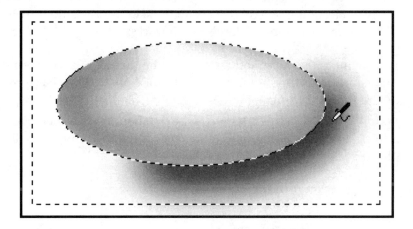

Figure 6.9 Painting inside the inverted selection border.

4. Inverse the selection again, change the color back to blue, and increase the pressure. Paint another soft stroke to further define the shape, as shown in Figure 6.10. You can continue inversing the selection in this way to build up color and tone. Don't confuse the **Inverse** command with the **Invert** command under the **Image:Map:Adjust** menu, which inverts the color values in a document.

Figure 6.10 The finished shape, created by inversing the selection borders.

When painting with the large Airbrush tool, you can paint completely outside of the selection border, and the edge of the overspray may give you just the degree of softness you want inside the selection border.

The **Grow** command (**Command-G** on the Mac or **Ctrl-G** on the PC) enlarges the extent of a selection based on pixel color. It takes its instructions from the Magic Wand's tolerance setting. Here's how it works:

1. Paint a line with a large soft airbrush in the middle of a white window. In the Airbrush Options toolbox, set the fade-out to **30**, to **background**, to give yourself a range of values.

2. With the Magic Wand's tolerance set low (about 20, anti-aliased), click in the middle of the line where the color is darkest. Only a small area of pixels will be chosen (Figure 6.11).

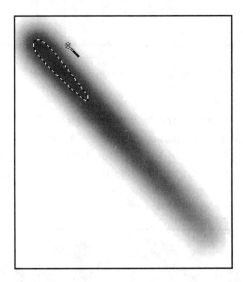

Figure 6.11 *Pixels chosen by the Magic Wand.*

3. Select **Grow** from the Select menu. The range of the selection will be extended, but not by very much (Figure 6.12).

4. Double-click on the **Magic Wand** icon to bring up the Magic Wand Options box. Change the tolerance to **70**, again anti-aliased. This time, the selection grows to a much greater extent (Figure 6.13).

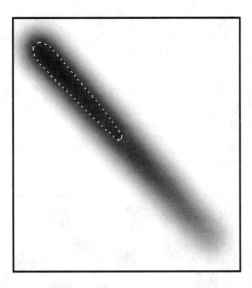

Figure 6.12 *Selection extended by the **Grow** command with the same Magic Wand tolerance setting.*

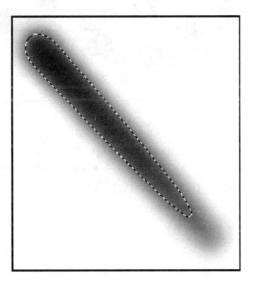

Figure 6.13 *Selection extended by the **Grow** command with the Magic Wand tolerance increased.*

The **Similar** command enlarges the selection to find all colors that are the same as the Magic Wand's target color, no matter where they may be throughout the image. Here's how it works:

1. Select a large paintbrush (45-pixel radius). Double-click on the brush shape to open it and set the spacing to **200%**. Draw a series of dots on a solid colored background of any color.

2. Click the **Magic Wand** in any one of the dots. Leave the wand at its default tolerance of 32 (Figure 6.14).

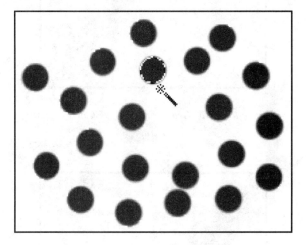

Figure 6.14 *Select one colored dot with the Magic Wand tool.*

3. Choose **Similar** from the Select menu. All the dots will now be selected, even though they are separated (Figure 6.15). You can't overestimate the value of this simple command. For example, you can use it to select all the blue sky in a photograph, even tiny spaces between the branches of trees.

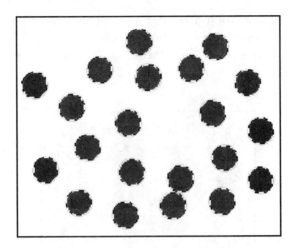

*Figure 6.15 Use the **Similar** command to select all the dots.*

 The **Grow** and **Similar** commands do not work on bitmapped images because the Magic Wand is not functional in those files.

NOTE

MODIFYING THE BORDERS OF SELECTIONS

The Select menu offers several ways to manipulate selections.

The **Feather...** command is used to feather the edges of any selection, even if the selection was not feathered with a tool when it was created.

The Magic Wand tool, for example, does not have a **Feathered Radius** option, but you can feather a selection made with the Magic Wand using the **Feather...** command.

The **Border** command allows you to select a bordering area around a selection border:

1. Make a rectangular shape with the Rectangular Marquee tool. Fill it with a solid color by pressing **Option-Delete** (Mac) or **Alt-Delete** (PC).

2. Choose **Select:Modify:Border...**. Set the border width to **8** pixels. Click **OK.**

3. You will have chosen a border around the inner rectangle (Figure 6.16.) The border extends both inside and outside of the previous selection border line. The **Border** command can be applied to any selection border around an object of any shape.

Figure 6.16 *Selecting a border around an image.*

NOTE

From the **Select:Modify** fly-out menu, you can choose to place a border around a selection, smooth a selection border, or expand and contract it. These actions can have interesting uses in special projects, as we'll see in later chapters.

The **Select:Modify:Contract** command allows you to remove edge pixels from the border of a selection. Sometimes when you cut an anti-aliased image from one background and paste it into another, you'll see traces of the old background around the very edge of the selection. The **Contract** command replaces those offensive pixels with pixels that don't contain the background color.

The **Select:Modify** submenu also includes **Smooth** and **Expand** commands. **Smooth** gets rid of the rough edges of a selection, while **Expand** is the opposite of contract: it adds pixels to the edge of a selection.

HIDING SELECTION BORDERS

When you want to preview a selection without those pesky marching ants, you can choose to hide the selection:

1. Select a rectangle with the Marquee tool.
2. Fill it with color.
3. Choose **View:Hide Edges** to preview your image.
4. Choose **View:Show Edges** to continue working normally.

SHORTCUT

You can toggle the **Hide** and **Show Edges** commands by using **Command-H** (Mac) or **Ctrl-H** (PC).

COPYING SELECTIONS

You can copy a selection in several ways. The simplest way is to press **Command-C** (Mac) or **Ctrl-C** (PC) and then **Command-V** (Mac) or **Ctrl-V** (PC). In this case, the copy of the image would be pasted directly on top of the copied image, but in a new layer.

You can also make a copy of a selection by dragging it:

1. Create a simple rectangle using the Marquee tool.
2. Fill the selection with color, leaving the selection border active.
3. Select the **Move** tool.
4. Hold down the **Option** (Mac) or **Alt** (PC) key and drag the rectangle.
5. Continue dragging and copying until you get a feel for it.

COPYING BETWEEN PHOTOSHOP FILES

You can use the **Edit:Copy** and **Edit:Paste** commands to move selections between Photoshop documents. It's a better use of both system resources and your own time to simply drag a selection from one open file and drop it into another. Photoshop 4 creates a new layer for the dropped selection. Here's how it works:

1. Open two new files.

2. Reshape the window so that both files are visible on your screen.

3. In one box, select a loose rectangle with the Marquee tool. Fill it with color.

4. With the marching ants still visible, select the **Move** tool and drag the box to the other open file as though you were simply dragging it to a new location.

5. Position the box in the new file and drop it.

6. Notice that a new layer is created on the Layers palette (Figure 6.17). This would also happen if you had a multilayered file open as well.

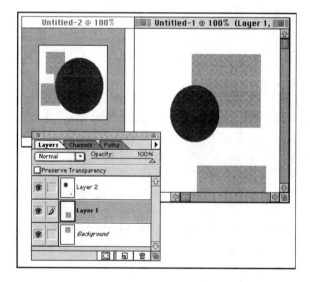

Figure 6.17 *Copying images between files.*

WHAT YOU'VE LEARNED

Modifying Selections

- Add to selections by holding down the **Shift** key as you make each new selection with the Rectangular or Elliptical Marquee, Lasso, or Magic Wand tools.

- Subtract from selections by holding down the **Shift** or **Ctrl** key as you make each new selection with the Rectangular or Elliptical Marquee, Lasso, or Magic Wand tools.

More Selection Choices from the Select Menu

- Select all of the document by pressing **Command-A** (Mac) or **Ctrl-A** (PC).
- Select none (i.e., deselect everything) by pressing **Command-D** (Mac) or **Ctrl-D** (PC).
- Inverse the selection border (i.e., select everything that wasn't selected before) by choosing **Inverse** from the Select menu.
- Grow a selection size (**Command-G** on the Mac or **Ctrl-G** on the PC) based on the tolerance set in the Magic Wand Options box.
- Choose all pixels similar to the one targeted by the Magic Wand by selecting **Similar** from the Select menu.
- Select a border area around an active selection (**Select:Border** menu).
- Soften the border of any selection with the **Feather** command (from the Select menu). Many tools have built-in feathering capabilities that allow you to feather as you select. Use this option to feather a selection after the fact or to increase feathering on a lightly feathered selection.
- Defringe a floating selection (i.e., change edge pixels that have part of the background color still attached to them) so that the selection looks better when you paste it onto another background using the **Select:Modify:Contract** command.

Moving and Copying Selections

- Copy a selection by pressing the **Option** (Mac) or **Alt** (PC) key while dragging it with a selection tool.
- Use **Copy** and **Paste** to copy and paste any selection.
- Copy by dragging and dropping between open documents.

CHAPTER 7

Copying, Cutting, and Pasting, and Applying Selection Effects

In this chapter…

In earlier chapters, we've mostly looked at mastering some of the basics of Photoshop, the skills you need to unlock some of the magic of this powerful program. After covering a few more basics at the beginning of this chapter, we'll be ready to use those skills to have some real fun.

INTRODUCTION TO COPYING, CUTTING, AND PASTING

The Clipboard

The Clipboard is the area where information is held when it is cut or copied out of a document. The Clipboard can hold only one item at a time; every time you cut or copy again, the contents of the Clipboard are replaced. The Clipboard even makes it possible for you to copy a picture from Photoshop and paste it into another document if the **Export Clipboard** box is checked in the General Preferences dialog box under the File menu. If this box is not checked, you will not be able to paste a picture from Photoshop into a document in another program, and the current contents of the Clipboard will be lost when you close Photoshop. If you don't plan to paste an image from Photoshop into a document in another program, turn this option off to save processing time.

Floating and Defloating Selections

We introduced floating selections in earlier chapters, but we'll review it briefly here because it is an important concept to keep in mind when cutting, copying, and pasting.

There are essentially two types of selections in Photoshop: floating and nonfloating. When you make a selection using a selection tool, you have created a nonfloating selection. If you move or delete a nonfloating selection, you are essentially moving or deleting that portion of the layer.

The floating selection is one that has been moved or otherwise manipulated but not deselected (Figure 7.1). A floating selection shows up on the Layers palette, but it is actually a temporary layer. You can move and adjust the selection in any way, provided you don't deselect it.

When taking these selections to more advanced stages (i.e., complex editing and filters, etc.), it's best to convert your floating selection into a layer (Figure 7.2). You'll then be able to manipulate the floating selection with impunity, something you can't do once you've defloated a floating selection that is not on a layer of its own.

Figure 7.1 *A floating selection.*

Figure 7.2 *The floating selection has been created as a layer to make it possible to manipulate all layers to maximum effect.*

The somewhat complex concepts involved with layers is important to real success with Photoshop.

A Closer Look at Floating Selections

A floating selection "floats" above the pixels of the image. If a floating selection is cut or deleted, it disappears. (This is why you can't fill a floating selection with the background color by pressing **Delete**.) There are three types of floating selections: a selection that is pasted in from another program, a piece of type that has just been created with the Type tool, and a selection that has been made to float by pressing **Command-J** (Mac) or **Ctrl-J** (PC). Floating a selection essentially makes a copy of the image and pastes it back on top of itself so that if the floating selection is eliminated, the original image is untouched.

Copying a Selection

To copy part of an image, simply select it and choose **Copy** from the Edit menu. This places a copy of the image on the Clipboard. From there, it can be pasted into the same document or into another document.

Alternately, as discussed in earlier chapters, you can drag the selection into another open Photoshop document.

Cutting and Deleting a Selection

- Use the **Cut** command from the Edit menu to cut a selection and place it on the Clipboard.
- Cutting a floating selection removes the selection border and the pixels within it. After the cut, the selection border is gone.
- Cutting a nonfloating selection exposes the background color underneath the selection. Again, after you cut, the selection border disappears.
- Pressing the **Delete** or **Backspace** key or selecting **Clear** from the Edit menu completely removes a floating selection. If a selection is not floating, pressing **Delete** removes the selected pixels to expose the background color, but the selection border remains. When you delete a

selection, it is not copied to the Clipboard and therefore cannot be pasted elsewhere.

EXERCISE 7.1: PASTING A SELECTION

Before you paste anything in a Photoshop document, you must have copied or cut the item you want to paste. Photoshop provides a standard **Paste** command under the Edit menu and two special options—**Paste Inside** and **Paste Behind**—which greatly expand your creative options.

The Paste Command

With a selection copied or cut to the Clipboard, select **Paste** from the Edit menu to paste the selection into the active window. When there is an active selection border in the destination window, the cut or copied image will be pasted automatically on top of that active selection. When there is no active selection in the destination window, the cut or copied image will be pasted in the exact center of the window.

The Paste Into Command

You can also paste one selection into another, which gives you still further control of pasting possibilities:

1. Create two documents, one with a white background, the other with an image you like.

2. In the white document, create a square selection border. Apply a 2-pixel, green stroke to the outside of this border using the **Stroke...** command. Do not deselect the square.

3. In the second document, use the Marquee tool to create a selection quite a bit larger than the green box in the first document. Copy this selection (Figure 7.3).

Figure 7.3 Use the Marquee tool to select an area larger than the one you'll be pasting into.

4. Return to the first document (Figure 7.4), where the green-bordered square is still an active selection.

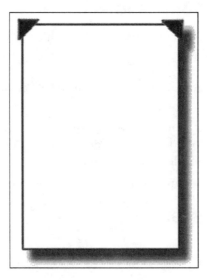

Figure 7.4 For better visualization, I opted to use an empty frame for this demonstration. Using the Magic Wand tool, I selected an active area inside of the frame.

5. Select **Paste Into** from the Edit menu. Your copied selection centers itself inside the green square (Figure 7.5). At this point, it is possible to use the Move tool to manipulate the pasted selection within its new confines.

Figure 7.5 *Using the* **Paste Into** *command, you can define exactly where you'd like your selection to go in the new document.*

The Paste Behind Command

Not only can you paste one selection into another, you can also paste one selection behind another using the **Paste Behind** command from the Edit menu. For example, this is very useful for placing a new sunset behind a city skyline or a moon behind a pyramid or a different background behind a portrait.

While a selection that has been pasted behind is active, it can be scaled, rotated, flipped, painted, or filled, just like other active selections. If the source selection, when pasted behind the target image, is completely obscured, use the mouse pointer to reposition it until it's the way you like it. As a floating selection, it can be removed at any time just by cutting or deleting.

TRANSFORMATIONS AND ROTATIONS

Transform and **Free Transform** are two basic Photoshop commands that you'll find yourself using again and again. Both offer varying degrees of control in terms of your image's dimension and perspective. In this section, you'll learn how to manipulate the size, shape, and orientation of a selected area or areas and you'll gain an understanding of how those changes affect image quality.

You can flop and flip the entire image by choosing the **Rotate Canvas** options from the Image menu (Figure 7.6).

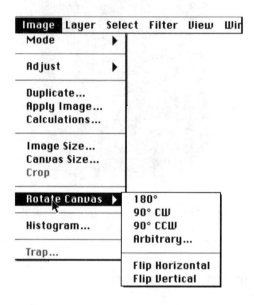

Figure 7.6 *Flip options from the Image menu.*

EXERCISE 7.2: FLIPPING AN IMAGE

1. Select an image that you want to flip (Figure 7.7).
2. Choose **Flip Horizontal** (Figure 7.8) or **Flip Vertical**.

Figure 7.7 *The original image.*

Figure 7.8 *The image flipped horizontally.*

From the same menu location, you can also choose to flip the image 180° and by any number of degrees clockwise (CW) or counterclockwise (CCW). The **Arbitrary** command lets you select how many degrees you'd like to move the canvas (Figure 7.9).

Figure 7.9 *The canvas flipped an arbitrarily selected 25° clockwise.*

TRANSFORM AND FREE TRANSFORM

Photoshop gives you the flexibility to rotate, scale, skew, distort, or alter the perspective of a selection or even an entire layer using the **Transform** command (Figure 7.10). **Free Transform** lets you do all or any of these things in one operation.

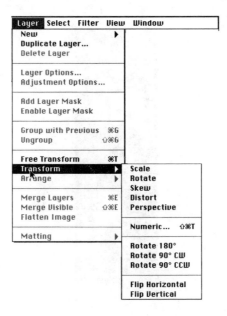

Figure 7.10 Using the Transform and Free Transform commands.

EXERCISE 7.3: TRANSFORM

In a single exercise, let's go quickly through each of the basic **Transform** commands to get a feel for what they can do for your artwork and what place they will play in your creations:

1. In a large new window, use the Line tool to create an arrow pointing to the 12 o'clock position. Using the Rectangular Marquee tool, drag a rectangle around the entire arrow, selecting it as the area to be rotated. Once you have completed your arrow, save the file. We'll be using this image again later in this chapter.

2. Try each of the following operations on your selection. Choose **Undo** after each move to return the arrow to its original position.

3. Using the **Scale** command adds handles to your selection box. This lets you push, pull, and drag your selection into the size and shape you desire (Figure 7.11). Practice altering the perspective in this way, remembering to choose **Undo** after each single operation.

Figure 7.11 *The Scale command.*

4. You can specify a rotation either with the **Layer:Transform:Rotate** command, which once again gives you a handled box to turn and twist at will, or you can choose **Layer:Transform:Rotate 90 degrees** (or 180 degrees, either CW or CCW) to get a precise rotation in the direction you desire.

5. Choosing **Layer:Transform:Skew** (Figure 7.12) gives you more handles. This time you can squeeze part of an image to get the desired effect. Practice with this, remembering again to choose **Undo** after each single operation.

6. Choosing **Layer:Transform:Distort** (Figure 7.13) lets you alter perspective from two or more sides. In all of these examples, while the size and shape of the box may change, all of the contents of the original selections are still intact, although now they might—depending on how far you skew—look wildly different.

7. Choosing **Layer:Transform:Perspective** (Figure 7.14) gives you full control of the view, as it were. Have fun altering your image in a number of ways, remembering (of course) to choose **Undo** after each go at the perspective.

Figure 7.12 *The **Skew** command allows you to distort perspective from a single side.*

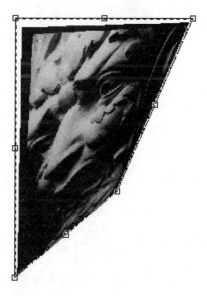

Figure 7.13 *The **Distort** command lets you alter perspective from two or more sides.*

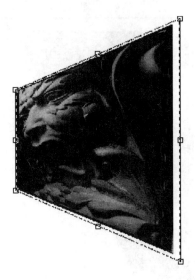

Figure 7.14 *The **Perspective** command gives you full control of the view.*

Numeric Perspective

The **Layer:Transform:Numeric** command brings up a dialog box (Figure 7.15) that lets you perform all of the previous transformations in a single, predetermined operation:

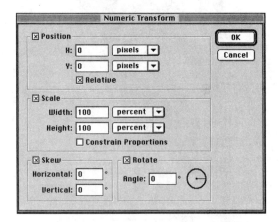

Figure 7.15 *The Numeric Perspective dialog box.*

1. Use your arrow, once again. Draw a rectangular Marquee around the arrow to indicate the area you wish to transform.

2. Choose **Layer:Transform:Numeric**.

3. The *X* and *Y* values refer to moving the selection. These can be specified in the measurement system you desire (i.e., picas, pixels, inches, etc.). Type **10** in the *X* box and **15** in the *Y*.

4. The next two boxes allow you to choose the scale of the selection by percentage. Type **90** for the width and **140** for the height.

5. To skew the selection, specify angles of the slant by degrees. Type **10** in the Horizontal box and **15** in the Vertical box.

6. The last box lets you rotate the entire selection by degrees. Type **5** in this final box.

7. Press **OK** to watch your transformations take shape (Figure 7.16).

*Figure 7.16 The **Transform:Numeric** command allows you to do several operations with a single command by specifying a combination of effects numerically.*

Because you performed several operations in a single move by using the **Numeric** command, it is possible to undo all of these effects at once.

NOTE

FREE TRANSFORM

The **Free Transform** command lets you scale, rotate, skew, distort, and adjust perspective in a freehand way and with a single set of concatenated operations. This means that placement of the transformation is easier. Also, because the data is resampled in one pass, you can expect better image quality. In Figure 7.17, all of the possibilities of the **Free Transform** command have been executed on our image. Because it is *free* transform, it was done on-screen while we tweaked it, and because it was done in a single operation, it can be easily undone:

Figure 7.17 *Using the **Free Transform** command.*

1. Get out the arrow file we created earlier.

2. Select an area with the rectangular Marquee tool.

3. Select **Layer:Free Transform**. We will practice doing all of the possibilities of **Free Transform** to help get a feel for it.

4. Drag a handle to scale. To scale proportionately, press **Shift** as you drag.

5. To rotate, move the pointer outside of the selection area until it turns into a curved double-headed arrow. Now simply drag. Pressing **Shift** while dragging constrains the rotation to 15° increments.

6. To freely distort the image, press **Command** (Mac) or **Ctrl** (PC) and drag a handle.

7. To symmetrically distort the image, press **Option** (Mac) or **Alt** (PC) and drag a handle.

8. To skew the image, press **Command-Shift** (Mac) or **Ctrl-Shift** (PC) and drag a handle. You'll see that the pointer turns into a white arrowhead with a small double arrow while it is active and over a side handle.

9. Here's where you start wishing for more fingers. For perspective, press **Command-Option-Shift** (Mac) or **Ctrl-Alt-Shift** (PC) and drag a corner handle.

10. To apply your transformations, press **Return** or **Enter**. If you'd like to cancel this set of transformations, press the **Esc** key.

NOTE   While using the **Free Transform** command to apply a number of transformations, you'll note that not all of the transformations show up on-screen right away. If you'd like to see your progress at any time, press **Return** or **Enter**. Remember, though, that doing this causes the operation to complete, and beyond this new point it will not be possible to undo any of the steps. As always, saving frequently is a good idea.

EFFECTS AND IMAGE RESOLUTION

When you're working on-screen, just for your own pleasure, delight, and learning, image resolution is not much of a consideration, and, in many ways, almost everything looks pretty swell in the glowing, colored light of the modern additive-light computer monitor.

Resolution becomes an issue when we begin to prepare files that will be seen by the world outside of our own computer e.g., files to be output or printed or those to be used electronically in mediums like the World Wide Web).

The goal is to have our creations look just as tough and strong when they're presented to the rest of the world as they do on our monitors. While this is possible and restricted only by the quality of the output medium, it also takes some basic—and growing!—knowledge to choose the right combination of circumstances in which to create files.

N O T E

Making decisions about image resolution is important because it affects both file size and quality of output. Basically, higher is better but bigger. That is, the higher the resolution, the more pixels it consists of, the better the output, the more disk space the file will take, and the longer it will take for the computer to perform operations on the file. Therefore, making a decision about image resolution will usually factor in several of these things.

INTERPOLATION

When the size of an image is changed in any way (through scaling, stretching, rotation, distortion, or resizing), Photoshop recalculates the pixel values. If a selected area is enlarged, for example, from 200 x 200 pixels to 400 x 400 pixels, new pixels have to be added and their color defined. Photoshop decides what color those added pixels should be through a process called *interpolation*. Three choices are available: bicubic interpolation, bilinear interpolation, and nearest neighbor interpolation. These options are specified in the General Preferences dialog box (Figure 7.18).

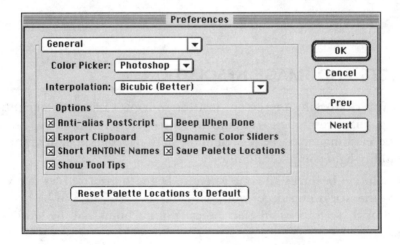

Figure 7.18 The methods of interpolation is chosen in the General Preferences dialog box.

The choice of interpolation method affects the quality and speed of the resulting image. If you've looked at the General Preferences, the default interpolation method is bicubic. Bicubic is the slowest method, but its results are the best. It is generally the method that should be used because it is the most accurate for continuous tone images.

What You've Learned

Copying, Cutting, and Pasting

Use the Clipboard to cut or copy images out of a document. You can use the Clipboard to quickly export images into another program.

Floating and Non-Floating Selections

There are two types of selections in Photoshop: floating and non-floating. For complex editing, it's best to convert a floating selection into a layer of its own. Pressing **Delete** or **Backspace** or selecting **Clear** from the Edit menu completely removes a floating selection.

Pasting

You can select Paste to add an image from your clipboard to your currently active file. Paste Into does the same, but it pastes the image into an active selection. Paste Behind lets you paste the item in your clipboard behind other items in the file.

Transformations and Rotations

You can use various Transform and Rotate commands to control an image's dimension and perspective. The entire contents of a file can be rotated by choosing **Rotate Canvas** from the image menu.

Free Transform lets you perform a combination of perspective altering commands in one operation.

Numeric Perspective lets you alter your image in several ways at once.

Effects and Resolution

When the size of an image is changed, Photoshop recalculates the pixel values. Re-sizing can add extra pixels. Photoshop decides what color the new pixels will be through a process called interpolation. Bicubic interpolation is the slowest method, but is the most accurate for continuous tone images.

CHAPTER 8

Working with Type

In this chapter...

- Creating type in Photoshop
- Importing type from an object-oriented application

Adobe Photoshop gives you the opportunity to add bitmap type to images. Using Photoshop as a typesetting tool can be frustrating, and if you're looking to add a fair amount of concisely set type, you are usually better off first setting the type in an object-oriented program like Illustrator or FreeHand and then importing it into Photoshop.

There are times, however, when a small amount of type can be satisfactorily and more easily created in Photoshop. We'll look at both methods of working with type in this chapter.

ADDING TYPE TO YOUR DOCUMENT

Creating Type

1. Open a new document with the default black foreground and white background.
2. Select the **Type** tool from the Toolbox and click in the center of the screen.
3. The Type Tool dialog box will open (Figure 8.1).

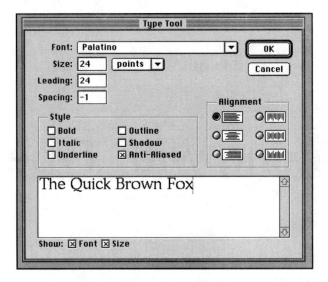

Figure 8.1 *Type Tool dialog box.*

4. Select the font from the pop-up menu. Choose any font you like for this exercise. There's nothing worse than spending a lot of time looking at a font you don't care for. The font (sometimes called the *typeface*) is the name of type you will use, such as Times, Garamond, or Optima. Some of the fonts will already have styles embedded in them, like bold, italic, or bold italic. If you have many fonts in your System Folder, this list may be longer than the screen. Choose the font you want by scrolling through the list.

5. Select a font size of **32 points**. The font size is expressed in points or picas, either of which you can choose from the pop-up menu. A point (pt) is a typographic unit of measurement, equivalent to 1/72 inch. A pica (p) is six times the size of a point. There are 12 points to a pica, and 6 picas to an inch. You can use the **Tab** key to move to the next boxes.

6. Choose a number for the leading. Use the default leading of 0 (no number entered). *Leading* is the distance from the base of one line of type to the base of the adjacent line (Figure 8.2). The term comes from the old days of typography in which lines of type were spaced out by inserting a row of lead between them. Most fonts have leading automatically built into them, and the amount of leading exceeds the size of the type by one to two points. For example, 12-point type may have 14 points of leading as a default. Photoshop gives you the opportunity to change the leading in this dialog box to suit your taste. For example, to achieve a creative effect, you might want four or five letters in a column, with a great deal of space between each one. You can do this by adjusting the leading.

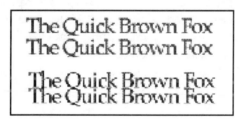

Figure 8.2 *Measuring the leading between two lines of type. In this example, the top two lines are set "tight," i.e., 24 point type over 24 point leading. The bottom two lines were set 24/18, i.e., 24 point type over 18 point leading. Note how much closer to each other the second set is.*

7. Select the letter spacing. Type **–1** in the Spacing option box. Each font has built-in instructions that tell Photoshop how closely adjacent letters should be placed when you set a line of type. Because you may want to change this default, spacing the letters more closely or farther apart, Photoshop provides the Spacing option, called *kerning* in the typographic trade (Figure 8.3). Selecting a negative number from -99.9 to -0.1 moves the letters closer together, and selecting a positive number

from 0.1 to 999.9 moves the letters farther apart. The number entered applies to either points or pixels, according to your choice.

The Quick Brown Fox

The Quick Brown Fox

Figure 8.3 Tighter spacing is set to –1; looser spacing is set to 10.

8. Apply a style to the type. Just as in word processing programs, Photoshop lets you change the style of the type with these check boxes.

9. Select the **Anti-aliased** option. Anti-aliasing changes the values of some of the pixels at the very edges of the selection so that type blends into its background. You must have Adobe Type Manager (ATM) installed or you must use TrueType fonts to take advantage of this. Adobe Type Manager (which was automatically installed if you used Photoshop's **Easy Install** option) uses the outlines of PostScript Type 1 fonts to create anti-aliased type in any point size. Unless you're going for a deliberately jagged look or working with extremely small point sizes, you'll want to keep this box checked all the time.

10. Set the alignment. Choose **Center**, which is represented by a series of centered lines in the Alignment box shown in Figure 8.1. You can set type to appear to the right of where you click the **Type** tool (left aligned), to the left of where you clicked the tool (right aligned), or centered on the tool (centered). The right column shows the similar vertical alignment options, also represented by lines that graphically illustrate how your text will be arranged.

11. Type the text. Type **Roses are red** in the Text box. Press **Enter** and type **Violets are blue**. If you make an error, press **Delete** or **Backspace** to correct it, or select an entire phrase by dragging over it with the Type tool and then **Backspace** to eliminate the words and start over. Click **OK** when you're finished.

NOTE

Unlike other dialog boxes, you cannot activate the **OK** button with the **Enter** key because that is used for text entry.

You can enter up to 32,000 characters of text, or as much as the Windows text box holds. The text will wrap in this area, but not in the document. To get the type to break at the end of the line, you need to press **Enter**.

12. Your type will appear, floating, in its own layer (Figure 8.4). Because it is currently a floating selection, you can move it with the Move tool or with the left, right, up, and down arrows. If you press **Delete**, the type will disappear. (Press **Undo** immediately if you do this.) You could also use **Command-X** (Mac) or **Ctrl-X** (PC) to cut the type, and it would be saved on the Clipboard for you to paste in again if you like. Don't cut, delete, or deselect the type because we're going to use it in the next part of this exercise. If you accidentally remove the type and can't undo your deletion, click the Type tool in the document again—all the previous settings and type will be "remembered" in the Type Tool dialog box.

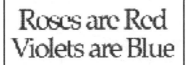

Figure 8.4 *Floating type.*

Warning to PC Users: incompatibilities with some video drivers may cause TrueType fonts to behave incorrectly or not show up at all. To work with this problem, set the type larger than you need it (e.g., 120 pt type when you need 32 pt), and then scale it to the required size using the **Scale** command.

BIG DATA

If you've accidentally specified type that overflows your canvas (Figure 8.5), don't worry. Photoshop 4 makes sure that the edges of your type (or other data) won't get clipped. Simply manipulate the type into position using the Move tool or arrow keys, or select **Undo** from the File menu to clear the screen to start over.

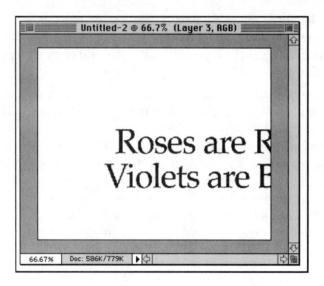

Figure 8.5 Type that overflows the canvas won't be clipped.

ADDING COLOR TO TYPE

1. Still using the type you created in the previous exercise, select a bright red from the color palette.

2. Press **Option-Delete** (Mac) or **Alt-Delete** (PC) to fill the floating type selection with the color.

3. Select a blue from the color palette and a choose a large brush. Set the Opacity to **100%**. Use the brush to paint on the words *Violets are blue*.

4. Click twice on the **Gradient** tool. Select **Spectrum** from the Gradients Options box. Drag the Gradient tool from the left of the type toward the right of the screen. The type fills with rainbow colors (Figure 8.6).

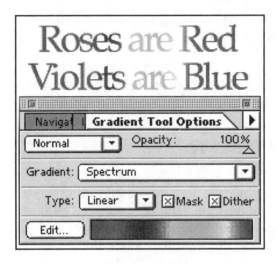

Figure 8.6 Gradient tool options.

You can fill type with any color or blend of colors using any Paint or Gradient tool.

APPLYING EFFECTS TO TYPE

1. Select **Layer:Transform:Perspective** from the Layer menu. Drag the handles to create the perspective (Figure 8.7).

Figure 8.7 Perspective added to type.

2. When you like the preview, press **Enter** or **Return** to approve the selection. Save the file or erase the image when you're done.

Because type is a floating selection, you can apply any effect that you might apply to a selection—flip it, rotate it, scale it, skew it, add perspective, or distort it.

MORE TYPE IDEAS TO TRY

- Deselect floating type just as you would any other floating selection, by holding down the **Command** key (Mac) or **Ctrl** key (PC) and using any selection tool to encompass the letter, letters, or word to be eliminated. You can also use this technique to remove just part of a letter. To deselect the entire letter, set the Magic Wand tool to a high tolerance (e.g., 250) and click inside a floating letter's selection border while holding down the **Command** key (Mac) or **Ctrl** key (PC). This can be much tidier than trying to drag around the letter with a Lasso.

- Create mixed fonts of white type in a black (mask) channel and then load all the type as one selection to be manipulated any way you'd like. We'll have an exercise on this technique in a later chapter.

- Using channel options, filters, feathering, and the **Paste Behind** and **Paste Into** commands, you can create glowing type, neon-bordered type, and type with soft offset drop shadows (Figure 8.8). Spending a lot of time applying filters and effects to letters is a good way to prevent yourself from getting any work done ever.

Figure 8.8 *The same type used in Figure 8.7 but with several different filters used on selected letters as well as the entire set of letters.*

CREATING TYPE FOR IMAGES

In most cases, when you're creating type in Photoshop it is with the idea of using it within some larger piece.

Creating type while working on an image file in Photoshop adds the type to a new layer, so that you can work with the type independently of the various layers that might be involved with the image:

1. Open an image file. If you don't have one, select one you like from the Photoshop 4 tutorial folder.

2. Select gray as your background color. Position the Type tool where you'd like the type.

3. In the Type dialog box, input something you think would make a catchy headline on a single line. I used 48-point type for my example.

4. From the Filters menu, select **Blur:Gaussian**. When you see the Blur dialog box, crank the slider to the extreme right for maximum blur. Press **Enter** (Figure 8.9).

Figure 8.9 *Gray type has been blurred over the image.*

5. Select a color that contrasts with the dominant background color of your image. Once again, select the **Type** tool and click in the screen in the approximate area where you would like to place your type.

6. When the dialog box pops up, all of the information you used to select the first whack of type will still be in place and intact. Without changing anything, press **Enter**. This will automatically create yet another layer with only your new type in it (Figure 8.10).

7. Select the **Move** tool, and position the new type slightly below and to the right (or above and to the left, if you prefer the look) of the first block of type (Figure 8.11). This creates a very simple drop-shadowed type over an image.

Figure 8.10 Your second type selection will most likely be slightly askew of the first.

8. At this point, if you wanted to, you could link the two type layers together on the Layers palette and move and manipulate them together (Figure 8.12). If you open the flowers image on the CD (located in the Exercises folder within your respective platform folder), you will see the file shown in Figure 8.12 and the way in which the layers are linked.

Figure 8.11 *A slight, hand-built, drop shadow adds depth and character to your document.*

Figure 8.12 *The finished file as included on the Teach Yourself Photoshop 4 CD.*

WHEN NOT TO CREATE TYPE IN PHOTOSHOP

Keep one essential point in mind when you're considering adding type to a Photoshop document: the type that you create in Photoshop will not print out as cleanly and crisply as the type created in an illustration program or in a layout program such as QuarkXPress or Adobe PageMaker, even though these programs work with the same PostScript Type 1 or TrueType fonts.

The type you create in an illustration program is sent directly to the imagesetter where the PostScript type instructions are interpreted and printed as smooth curves. The type you create in Photoshop comes into your document as a floating selection based on the PostScript outlines, but it is rasterized (i.e., turned into pixels) so it can be integrated into the image. A close-up view of two letters shows the difference (Figure 8.13). If you want razor-sharp type overlaid on an image (such as a title on a magazine cover) you need to export the image to a layout or illustration program and add the type there as the finishing touch.

Figure 8.13 *Type created in Photoshop (left) and in QuarkXPress (right).*

WHAT YOU'VE LEARNED

Working with Type

- Use the **Flip** commands to flip a selection or an entire unselected image across its horizontal or vertical axis.

- Use the **Fixed Rotation** commands to rotate a selection or an entire unselected image. Choices include 90° clockwise, 90° counterclockwise, and 180°.

- Use the **Arbitrary Rotate** command to rotate a selection from −359° to 359° clockwise or counterclockwise.

- Use the **Free Rotate** command to rotate a selection by clicking and dragging on handles.

- Use the **Scale** command to change the size of a selection nonproportionately or proportionately (by holding down the **Shift** key).

- Use the **Skew** command to slant a selection.

- Use the **Perspective** command to give a vanishing point perspective to a selection.

- Use the **Distort** command to change the shape of a selection. Each corner handle can be moved independently.

Working with Type

Add type to an image with the type tool:

1. Choose **Font** to select the name of the typeface from the pop-up menu.
2. Choose **Size** to determine the height of the type in points or picas.
3. Enter a number for leading to determine line spacing.
4. Enter a positive or negative number for spacing to set letter spacing.
5. Choose **Style** to apply styles to the type.
6. Select **Anti-aliased** to give smoother edges to the type.
7. Choose **Alignment** to set the type to the left, right, or centered on the pointer.
8. Enter up to 256 characters of text in the Text box.

Apply Effects to Type

- Type is created as a floating selection and can be manipulated like other floating selections. It can be painted, filled, rotated, flipped, and treated with other Effects options from the Image menu.

CHAPTER 9

Introduction to Channels, Masks, and Actions

In this chapter…

- Channel concepts
- Navigating between channels
- Grayscale (mask) channels
- Channel palette submenus
- Demonstration: kerning type using channels
- Using Quick Masks
- Introduction to Actions

CHANNEL AND MASK CONCEPTS

It is entirely possible to have been a computer user or an artist for years without ever encountering the concept of channels and masks in quite the way Photoshop looks at them. On first glance, Photoshop's channels and masks may look a little intimidating to new users. In many ways, they should! These are, after all, sophisticated concepts that have changed the digital world in so many ways. That's scary stuff.

On first take, it can look easier to bypass the whole issue of channels and masks and party on with the Rubber Stamp and Smudge tools. If you're tempted in this way, take a deep breath and jump in. Are they complicated concepts? Yes, at first, they are. Are they difficult to master? A world that seems to be filled with geeks who delight in putting three breasts on Heather Locklear and their own heads on Sly Stallone's body doesn't make it look that way.

Channels are the means by which you can save and load masks so that you can edit your images. In this chapter, you'll learn more about masks and channels and how to use them. The concepts introduced here will come in handy in later chapters as we continue to explore the Layers capabilities of Photoshop.

Every document is composed of channels, with an RGB image composed of three color channels (one each for red, green, and blue) and a composite channel (Figure 9.1). The CMYK channel is composed of four color channels. A document can have a total of 24 channels. Those extra channels, often called *alpha* or *mask* channels, are 8-bit grayscale images in which selections (masks) are stored. Each of these additional channels adds to the size of your overall file. Each channel is in perfect registration with every other channel, and all channels have the same size and resolution.

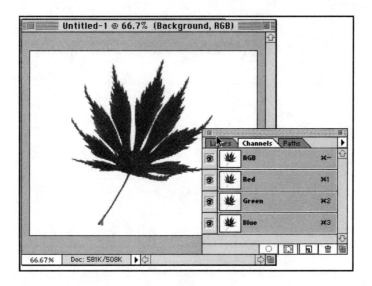

Figure 9.1 *Displaying the channels of a simple color document.*

- A masked area is one that you cannot paint on, edit, filter, or manipulate in any way. A masked area is protected by a mask, which, by default, is represented by the black area in the channel. Think about the way that a rubylith overlay is used in traditional graphic arts.

- A selected area is an area that you can paint on, edit, fill, filter, flip, or rotate or to which you can apply effects. A selection by default is represented by the white area in the channel.

A visible channel is one in which the Eye icon is turned on (Figure 9.2).

An editable channel is one in which the Paintbrush icon is turned on.

Figure 9.2 *The Eye icon indicates that the channel is visible. The Paintbrush icon indicates that the channel is editable.*

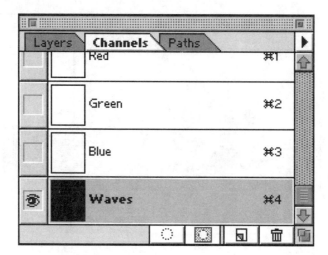

Figure 9.3 *The target channel—in this case called Waves—has been selected for editing.*

The Target channel is the one you have selected for editing. You create a channel as a Target channel when you click on it and it becomes highlighted (Figure 9.3).

N O T E Photoshop has the ability to display thumbnails representing the images contained in each channel. You can turn this display off to speed operation on slower computers or modify the size of the thumbnails by choosing **Palette Options** and then selecting a size or clicking on the **Off** button. If you'd rather display channels in tones of gray rather than representative colors, choose **File:Preferences:General** and uncheck the **Color Channels in Color** option.

N O T E Photoshop automatically creates the color channels appropriate to your file based on the color method chosen. You will not be able to alter these channels in any real way beyond turning the Eye icon off and on to view your work in progress. Any additional channels you create, also known as *mask* or *alpha* channels, are your storage pockets for graphic information in this specific file. You may reshuffle and delete at will.

MANIPULATING CHANNELS

Channels aren't static. At various times, you will want to move, duplicate, or otherwise manipulate them to enhance your document.

Changing Channel Order

You may not move the color information channels that Photoshop creates automatically. However, you can easily change the order of any mask channels you might have created:

1. Open a multicolor document. Choosing one from the TYPS disc will be fine.
2. Open the Channels palette by selecting **Window:Show Channels**.
3. Using the mouse, grab a channel and simply move it up or down. When the channel appears in the desired position, release the mouse button.

Channel Duplications

Sometimes it's a good idea to create a duplicate of a channel you will be changing as a backup just in case your calculations slip. All won't be lost, as you can just delete the botched channel and continue working with the duplicate as though you'd never messed up at all.

It can also be a good idea to duplicate channels into a new file. This allows you to keep a database of channels in another file where their presence won't bog down your work file. These duplicated channels can be loaded into the desired document at your leisure:

1. Highlight a channel you wish to duplicate (Figure 9.4).

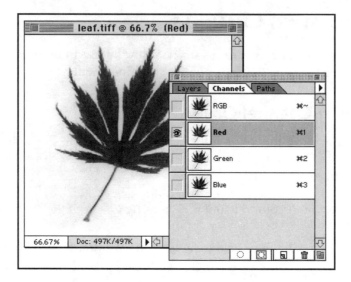

Figure 9.4 *The red channel is highlighted and ready for duplication.*

2. Select **Duplicate Channel** from the Channels palette.

3. Name the duplicate channel in the dialog box and select a target file. At this point, you can choose to duplicate the channel directly into your current work file, into an existing file, or into one you create at this stage. If you choose to create a new file, Photoshop creates a single channeled grayscale image.

SHORTCUT

To create a duplicate channel within the same file, simply drag the old channel into the Create New Channel icon (Figure 9.5) at the bottom of the Channels palette.

Figure 9.5 *The Create New Channel icon.*

Deleting a Channel

At times, you may create channels that you do not want to save with a document. Although you would not want to delete the component channels of an RGB or CMYK image, you may want to delete a grayscale channel you have created:

1. Create a new channel by selecting **New Channel** from the Channels palette.

2. Name the channel **Throw This Away**.

3. Activate the RGB image and its three channels.

4. Click on the **Eye** icon by Throw This Away. When you open the Channels palette fly-out submenu, you'll notice that the **Delete Channel** command is grayed out, meaning it is not a choice at the moment.

5. Turn off the Eye icons for the R, G, and B channels. Now you can delete the channel named Throw This Away by selecting **Delete Channel** from the submenu. The channel disappears from the Channels palette. Alternately, you can drag the unwanted channel into the trash can at the bottom of the Channels palette.

N O T E If you delete a channel in the middle of the list, the higher-numbered channels will all move up, while retaining the names you've given them. It is not necessary, by the way, to name a channel. It is only for your convenience when working with complex images with many masks. When you have at least one mask channel, you can turn off all the Eye icons for the R, G, and B channels (or the C, M, Y, and K channels) by clicking the **Eye** icon for the composite image.

Splitting Channels

Photoshop allows you to simply split channels into separate files by using the **Split Channels** command (Figure 9.6). Choosing this command closes the original file and opens a separate window for each channel, each named accordingly (Figure 9.7).

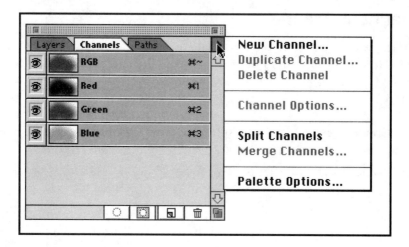

Figure 9.6 The ***Split Channels*** *command from the fly-out menu in the Channels palette.*

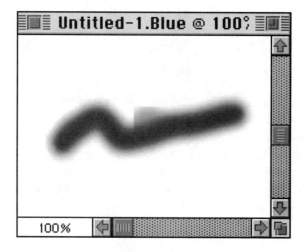

Figure 9.7 *Splitting channels causes an appropriately named file to be created for each channel.*

Images that are composites of channels, such as RGB and CMYK, may be split into their components with this technique. You can do this if a file is too large to be manipulated as a whole. Split channels can be merged back into one document when you've finished processing each one.

To split a channel:

1. Open the document that you wish to split.

2. Choose **Split Channels** from the Channels palette fly-out menu. Each channel will be placed into its own document and the original document will be closed, but not destroyed. The RGB documents produce three files, the CMYK documents produce four, and the multichannel documents produce as many files as there were channels in the original document.

3. If you plan to split channels, be sure to save your original document first.

Merging Channels into a Single Document

Several documents may be merged into one, provided that they are the same size, although the resolution of the files can be different. To merge several channels:

1. Open the files you want to merge. These files must be grayscale. Each file will be a channel in the new merged document. You cannot merge an RGB file and a grayscale file because by definition the RGB image is already three channels.

2. Select **Merge Channels** from the Channels palette pop-up menu. There are either three or four mode choices, depending upon how many files you have open. If you have four files open, you can create a CMYK document. With only three files, you can create an RGB, Lab, or Multichannel (grayscale) document.

3. Set the mode with the pop-up menu. The number of appropriate channels will appear automatically in the box. If you selected **Multichannel**, enter the number of grayscale channels you wish to merge.

4. If you decide to merge RGB color or lab color, you will be asked to specify the files you want for each of the red, green, and blue channels (RGB Color) or for the Lightness a and b channels (Lab Color). If you select **Multichannel**, you will be prompted to select a file for each channel. Click **OK** when you are done.

5. A new document will appear as each of the component documents is closed.

USING MASK CHANNELS TO KERN TYPE

Here's a way that you can tighten up letters and create more attractive spacing using the Magic Wand tool and the **Mask Channels** command:

1. Create a new RGB document, 640 pixels x 480 pixels.

2. Create a new mask channel and name it **Type**. Fill the channel with the foreground color, black, by pressing **Command-A** (Mac) or **Ctrl-A** (PC) to select all. Then press **Option-Delete** (Mac) or **Shift-Delete** (PC) to fill the space. Deselect everything.

3. Reverse the default colors by clicking on the double-headed arrow by the toolbox color swatches, making the foreground white and the background black. Use the Type tool to create the word *AWARE* in 70-point bold type, anti-aliased, all caps, centered, with the spacing option left blank. Deselect the word.

4. Using the Magic Wand tool set to a very high tolerance (210), click inside the white part of the *W* to select it. This will grab all the white in the *W*, plus the gray anti-aliasing around the edges. Nudge the *W* to the left with the keyboard arrows, then deselect it. Repeat the selecting and repositioning processes with the *A* to its right and then with the rest of the letters (Figure 9.8).

Figure 9.8 Type in the Mask channel before and after kerning.

5. Activate the RGB image in the Channels palette. Select the **Gradient Blend** tool and drag it from the bottom of the screen to the top to fill the image with a blend from white to black. Load the type as a selection, fill it with black foreground color, and fill it again with the white foreground color. Offset the selection slightly using the keyboard

arrows. The reason the type was created in a channel and placed against a graduated background was to dramatize the usefulness of mask channels for kerning—and the virtual impossibility of doing it without them.

6. Another solution to the kerning dilemma is to create and kern the type in Adobe Illustrator or another program with superlative typographic capabilities and bring it into Photoshop using the **Place** command.

USING QUICK MASKS

Sometimes you may want to use a mask on an image, even though you don't want to go to the trouble of using a Lasso or other tool to create a selection. In Photoshop, Quick Masks simplify the mask-making process. If you want to make changes to only a small part of a file or image, you have several ways in which you can select only this area:

- Use the Lasso tool to select the area to work on. Drag around all of it, using the **Shift** and **Command** keys to add to and subtract from the selection.

- Use the Magic Wand tool to select the area by color.

- Use the Pen tool to click points around the edge of the item to be changed and then convert that path to a selection.

- Use the **Quick Mask** option to paint an area that will be converted to a selection.

In the Quick Mask mode, you draw a mask in a transparent mask channel that lays on top of the color or grayscale image. A Quick Mask is just like other mask channels in that it contains only eight-bit grayscale information: the pixels can be only black, white, or one of 254 levels of gray.

As with other channels, you can use white, black, and gray paint to edit a mask. However, neither the black nor white paint appears when you're in the mask mode. By default, the mask appears as a transparent red color and indicates the area to be protected. Painting with black adds to the colored overlay, and painting with white erases the colored overlay. This overlay can represent either the masked (write-protected) area or the selected (unprotected) area, depending upon what you indicate in the Mask Options dialog box.

How to Make a Quick Mask

1. Click the **Quick Mask** icon to switch to Quick Mask mode (Figure 9.9). Only the highlighted mask channel is editable. The others are write-protected.

Figure 9.9 *The Quick Mask icon.*

2. To paint an area to be selected, double-click on the **Quick Mask** icon to open the Mask Options dialog box and choose **Color Indicates:Selected Areas**. We had to change this because by default the colored area indicates protected, not selected, areas. Click **OK**.

3. As we paint the mask, it appears as a transparent red overlay.

When you select the **Quick Mask**, the foreground and background colors reset automatically to their default values (black is foreground, white is background).

To summarize:

*   The white circle on black background icon is the **Masked Areas** option. The mask color-protects an area from being edited (Figure 9.10).

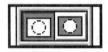

Figure 9.10 *Quick Mask mode:* ***Selected Areas*** *option.*

*   The black circle on the white background icon is the **Selected Areas** option. The mask color selects an area to be edited (Figure 9.10).

*   Change these options in the Mask Options dialog box.

*   Exiting the Quick Mask mode by clicking on the **Normal Mode** icon converts the mask into a selection border. You can now save this selection in a mask channel by choosing **Save Selection** from the Select menu.

How to Modify Quick Mask Options

WARNING

Be flexible. Photoshop supplies you with a wealth of tools so that you can have more image-editing flexibility. Don't become dependent on one tool to do everything. Experiment with different combinations until you become skilled with all of them.

SHORTCUT

You can save a selection to a channel that already exists by dragging the Selection icon to the channel on the Channels palette. Holding down the **Shift** key adds this new selection to the current selection in the channel; holding down the **Command** (Mac) or **Ctrl** (PC) key subtracts the new selection from the current selection; and holding down the **Shift** and **Command** (Mac) or **Ctrl** (PC) keys together selects only the portion that intersects the old and new selections in that channel.

Introduction to Actions

Actions are the high-octane macros of the Photoshop environment. Most simply, Actions allow you to record a series of editing steps in an Action List that you can later apply to another selection, file, or many files in a batch operation.

One use you might have for Actions is to record the steps taken to achieve a multifaceted effect you find yourself repeating in your work.

At the high-level end of the Action command's duties, you might find a service bureau executing the same Actions List on several—or several hundred—files located in the same folder via the **Batch** command.

While the **Actions** command is very powerful, it is not without some fairly obvious limitations. You can't, for example, record the use of tools, nor can you use it to make selections.

The Actions Palette

The Actions palette is set up in a way that is reminiscent of a tape recorder (Figure 9.11). The commands will look familiar: stop, start, play, and record. The fly-out menu (Figure 9.12) accessible from the right-arrow on the Actions palette gives more complete access to the quick commands available via the icons on the bottom of the palette itself.

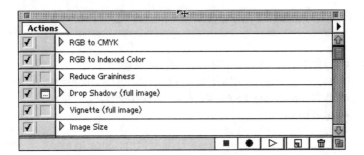

Figure 9.11 *The Actions palette.*

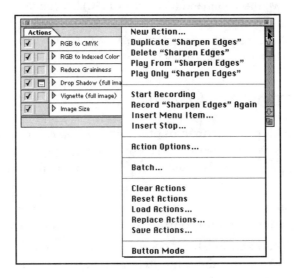

Figure 9.12 *The Action palette's fly-out menu.*

USING ACTIONS

We'll create a simple Actions List just to get a feel for the possibilities and how easy Actions are to use:

1. Open a new file. Make it 640 pixels x 480 pixels, RGB, with a screen resolution of 72 pixels per inch (ppi).

2. Using the Pen tool, create a simple shape. Choose **Make Selection** from the Paths palette to render your shape as an active selection.

3. Choose **New Action** from the Actions palette fly-out menu. Name it **New Action Duplicate** in the New Actions dialog box. Leave the other settings at default.

4. Choose **Start Recording** from the fly-out menu in the Actions palette.

5. Choose **Copy** and then **Paste** from the Edit menu to copy the selection.

6. Tap your right and down arrows three times each to slightly move the selection.

7. Select **Stop Recording** from the fly-out menu in the Actions palette.

You have created an Actions List that will perform a simple duplication of an active selection. Note that while **Record** was activated, everything you did to the file was recorded by the program. If you made an error along the way, it's a simple matter to delete portions of the Actions List by highlighting that portion of the list and dragging it to the trash can at the bottom of the Actions palette.

While Actions are most useful for people who have large quantities of repetitive image editing to perform (e.g., batch preparation of files to be exported to a Web page) it is also easy enough to use that anyone can prepare simple macros for use within their files.

WHAT YOU'VE LEARNED

The Channels Palette

- Use the Channels palette to manage the various channels of your document.

- Make a channel viewable by clicking on its **Eye** icon or anywhere in the channel area.

- View and edit any channel by pressing **Command** (Mac) or **Ctrl** (PC) and its channel number.

- Create a new channel with the **New Channel** option on the submenu.

- Delete a channel with the **Delete Channel** option on the submenu.

- Using the Channels Option dialog box, indicate whether the colored area will represent masked (protected/noneditable) or selected (nonprotected/editable) areas. Change the color used to describe a masked or selected area with the Color Picker.

- Merge several grayscale documents into one RGB Color, CMYK Color, Lab Color, or Multichannel document using the **Merge Channels** command.

Using Masks and Quick Masks

- Store masks in channels to use whenever needed.
- You can do anything to an 8-bit mask that you can do to an RGB or CMYK image: edit masks with any of the painting and editing tools; paint using black, white plus 254 shades of gray; apply fills and gradient blends; and feather selections. The choices are practically endless. You can even paste a grayscale photograph into a mask channel.
- Use masks to select specific parts of an image, which you can then edit using all the painting and editing tools as well as filters and other special effects.
- Use masks to kern type or modify other shapes before bringing them forward to the color or grayscale image.
- Use the Quick Mask mode to create a mask or edit a selection without necessarily saving it in a mask channel.
- Change mask options with the Mask Options dialog box. Double-click the **Quick Mask** icon to open this.

INTRODUCTION TO ACTIONS

- Use Actions to save lists of repetitive commands.
- Use Batch Actions to perform repetitive commands on many Photoshop files in a folder.
- The Actions palette is as simple to use as a tape recorder, and the commands are similar.
- Create a simple Actions List to automate a task.

CHAPTER 10

Introduction to Layers

In this chapter…

- Layer concepts
- Creating and editing new layers
- Working with layers
- Layer shortcuts

LAYER CONCEPTS

Layers and Adjustment Layers provide some of Photoshop's basic power simply because they give you full control of all of the aspects of the images you create. Everything you have already learned about channels and masks will help you understand layers. Many of the same techniques and concepts apply, but where channels relate to a single color aspect of the entire image, layers relate to each aspect of the image individually. It's powerful stuff.

To understand layers, it helps to think about how a basic document image is arranged. When you open a blank document with the **New** command, you might think of it as being empty, just a plain white canvas ready for your manipulations. In truth, the document is already filled with something: an opaque white background—as long as the default **White** button is checked in the Contents box of the New dialog box. You also could have specified the current background color as the contents of the new document or checked the **Transparent** option.

It's hard to show "transparent" or, at least, to differentiate it from white, so Photoshop represents it with a translucent checkerboard pattern (Figure 10.1) that can be modified by selecting **File:Preferences:Transparency & Gamut…**.

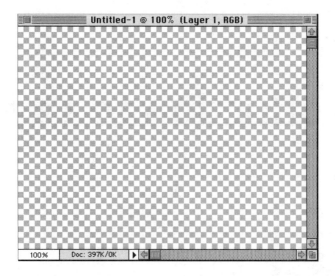

Figure 10.1 *The translucent checkerboard that, in Photoshop, means transparent.*

Prior to Photoshop 3.0, all Photoshop documents had only this background layer and nothing more. If you are working with an image that was created in an earlier version, you will need to save them in a later format of Photoshop.

NOTE

In Photoshop's layers, each is a complete full-color image of its own. You could paste a picture of a yellow taxi in one layer, a stout tree with lush green foliage in a second layer, and then combine them in flexible ways. Each layer is in many ways like a separate document, with color channels of its own. If you can think of layers as a kind of full-color channel with many of the properties of the channels you already have used, you'll be halfway to understanding this feature.

The other concept you need to understand is transparency. Layers are not like separate documents because they aren't automatically filled with opaque white. Layers are transparent until you place something on them. Think of a white art board as the base, or background, of your document. You create that white art board background when you open the document using the **File:New** command.

Layers, then, are like transparent sheets of acetate that you lay on top of the background. When you draw something or paste an image on one of those transparent sheets, it covers up or obscures part of what lies underneath, either completely or partially, depending on whether the new image is fully opaque or transparent. When you create yet another new layer, it goes in front of the background and first transparent layer, perhaps obscuring part of what exists behind.

The order of individual layers is the third concept you need to understand. As you work with layers, you may need to change the order in which layers are arranged so that some objects are in front of or behind others. Fortunately, this is easy to do.

Photoshop lets you work with layers individually, save documents with the layers preserved, and even print individual layers if you desire. When you are finished working with a document, you "flatten" the layers together, merging them into a final, background-only image that is your finished work. Of course, there is nothing to keep you from saving the final version under a new name, keeping the layered document for additional manipulations later on.

Adjustment Layers allow you to manipulate a layer or series of layers without actually changing the image (Figure 10.2). An Adjustment Layer acts like a layer mask, but the changes you make are stored within the Adjustment Layer itself.

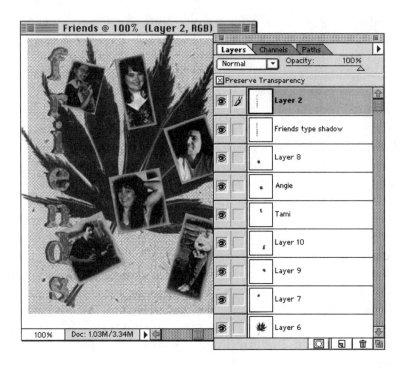

Figure 10.2 *Layers in action. Note that each element has an accompanying layer indicated on the Layers palette.*

You can follow along with the next exercise to learn about the basic features of the Layers palette. If you like, use some of the files on the diskette that accompanied this book.

Exercise 10.1: Creating and Editing New Layers

1. Open a new file. Make it 640 pixels x 480 pixels, RGB, with a screen resolution of 72 ppi. Save this new file as **FLOWERS**.

2. Load the Amaryllis image from the Chapter 10 folder on the CD-ROM.

3. Select only the flower itself using the **Color Range** command from the Select menu. You'll see a dialog box like the one shown in Figure 10.3. From the Select dropdown list, choose **Reds**. Click **OK**. Photoshop chooses pixels based on color similarity, rather than just brightness similarity, as the Magic Wand tool does.

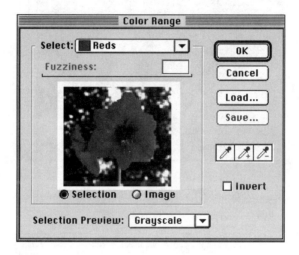

Figure 10.3 *Color Range dialog box.*

4. Use the Lasso to snare within the flower any pixels that haven't been selected using the Color Range function. You should experiment with the Color Range capabilities further. You can select portions of images based on a series of different color selections, using the Eyedropper tool in the Color Range dialog box to add or subtract additional areas, based on color samples that you draw from the preview image in the box.

5. Your selection will look like Figure 10.4. Copy the selection and switch to your ncw, cmpty filc.

6. You can create a new layer in either of two ways. By pasting the selection directly into your new file, you will note that a new, unnamed layer is created automatically (Figure 10.5).

Figure 10.4 *The flower has been selected.*

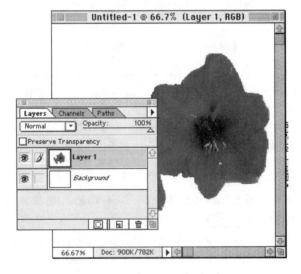

Figure 10.5 *Creating a new layer.*

7. Alternately, from the Layers palette, choose **New Layer...** and name it **Amaryllis** (Figure 10.6). Paste the flower that you've copied to the Clipboard from the other file to the new, blank layer.

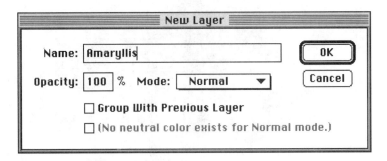

Figure 10.6 Name the layer Amaryllis.

N O T E By default, the Layers palette thumbnails will be turned on. This is an element of Photoshop operations where there is room for both personal preference and operating system demands. It's nice to see large thumbnails of elements of your work in progress, but making thumbnails smaller or turning them off entirely can save disk space and improve overall performance. Layers thumbnails can be turned on and off just like Channels icons, using the **Palette Options** choice from the fly-out menu. Experiment with what works best for you and your system.

8. Repeat steps 2–7 using the Hibiscus file within the Chapter 10 folder ont he CD. Select, copy, create a new layer (named Hibiscus), and paste. If you opt simply to paste without first creating a new layer, you'll note that a new unnamed layer is created automatically, containing only your pasted information (Figure 10.7).

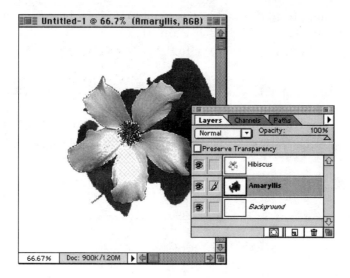

Figure 10.7 *Images pasted into layers.*

9. Turn off the white background layer by clicking on the **Eye** icon until the icon vanishes. Do the same with the Amaryllis layer. With only the Hibiscus layer visible, you should see something like Figure 10.8. Note that the checkerboard pattern that represents transparent areas of the image is visible.

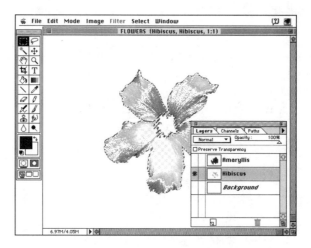

Figure 10.8 *Only the Hibiscus layer is visible.*

Working with Layers

Now we can practice working with individual layers as separate entities. You'll quickly see how this capability gives you a great deal more flexibility in working with the components that make up an image.

Exercise 10.2: Layer Manipulation

Using the same image we worked with in the preceding section, follow these steps:

1. Switch to the hibiscus layer. The hibiscus should still be selected. If not, set the Magic Wand tool to 255 (the maximum setting) and reselect it. You can use **Select:Save Selection** at this point to preserve the selection in case you lose it for some reason. It can be easy to get mixed up when working with multiple layers.

2. Since the Hibiscus is a dull white color, let's brighten it up a bit. Choose two related colors from the Color Control panel of the toolbox. Select one dark and one light hue of the same value. We selected purple and ochre.

3. Double-click on the **Gradient** tool to bring up the Gradient Tool Options palette. Set Opacity for **40%**, Style to **Foreground to Background**, and Type as **Radial**.

4. Add the gradient effect to the hibiscus by placing the cursor in the center of the flower and dragging out to the edges. You'll see an effect like that shown in Figure 10.9.

5. Reposition the hibiscus by deselecting it, but keeping the Hibiscus layer selected and dragging it to the upper left of the window using the Move tool. Then turn on the Amaryllis and Background layers by clicking on the box next to the layer name. Reposition the Amaryllis by selecting the Amaryllis layer and dragging the image into the desired position. Your new image with all layers showing should look like Figure 10.10.

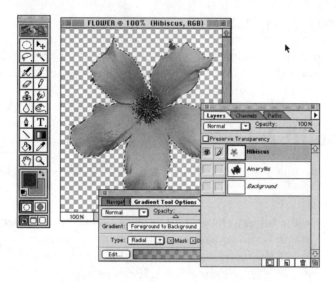

Figure 10.9 *Gradient added to the hibiscus.*

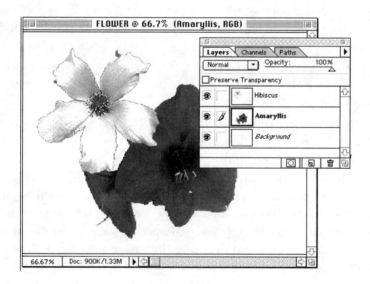

Figure 10.10 *Image with all layers showing.*

6. To see that the layers are indeed still separate, drag the Hibiscus layer within the Layers palette to the top of the list. That places it in front of the amaryllis. You can see the petals of the hibiscus in front of the amaryllis in Figure 10.11.

Figure 10.11 Hibiscus moved in front of the Amaryllis layer.

7. Use the Type tool to add the word *Flowers* to the layer (Figure 10.12). You'll note that a new layer is created automatically. To name this layer for easier access, double-click on that layer and name it **Flowers Type**. I created my type in 140-point Treefrog with a bright ochre foreground color. Then I stroked it lightly with a deep purple to make the type jump out from the flowers. You don't need to go to these extra lengths if you don't want to.

8. Move the Flowers layer around in the Layers palette to see what different stacking orders do. Figure 10.13 shows the type layer between the two blossoms.

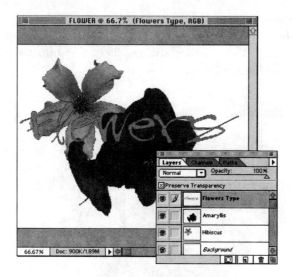

Figure 10.12 *Add the word Flowers to the image.*

Figure 10.13 *Type between flower layers.*

Adding a Background

1. Create one more layer and name it **Sun**. Select a sky blue as your foreground color and white as your background color. Then fill the layer with clouds using **Filter:Render:Clouds**.

2. Select an elliptical area of the Sun layer, fill it with yellow, and insert a flare using **Filter:Render:Lens Flare**. With the Eye icons not selected on the other layers, your Sun layer should look something like Figure 10.14.

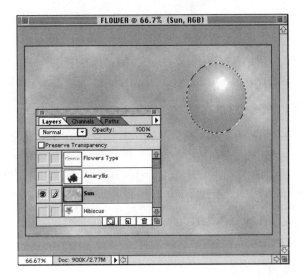

Figure 10.14 *Sun layer with clouds and lens flare added.*

3. Click on the **Eye** icon in all of the layers in the Layers palette to view the image with all the pieces in place. Your final image should look something like Figure 10.15.

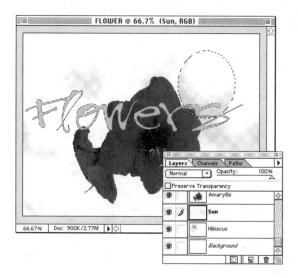

Figure 10.15 Layers palette and the finished Flowers image.

4. Save a "separated" version in the Photoshop format to your hard disk before proceeding. Then, combine them into one image by selecting **Flatten Image** from the fly-out menu in the Layers palette. Save this image as **Flowers Flattened**, and use it in any program that accepts the file format you selected (e.g., PICT, TIFF) The layers have been removed and combined into a single image.

LAYER SHORTCUTS

- As with channels, you can copy, move, or duplicate layers within a document or between documents by dragging and dropping from one window to another.
- Delete a layer by dragging it to the Trashcan icon at the bottom of the Layers palette.
- Add a new layer by clicking on the **New** icon at the bottom of the Layers palette.

- Layers can be used to create clipping groups as we did earlier in this book, just by defining a selection in one layer as a mask for layers in front. Use the Layer Options dialog box to group these layers together. When grouped, the bottom layer controls the mode and transparency of the others in the group.

- You can nudge the contents of a layer in one-pixel increments press your keyboard's arrow keys in the direction you'd like the move. To nudge in 10-pixel increments, press **Shift** and an arrow key.

WHAT YOU'VE LEARNED

Layer Concepts

- Layers are a kind of "super channel," with many more capabilities and options.

- The chief limitation of a channel is that it is essentially a grayscale image. You can modify the brightness and contrast or other grayscale characteristics of a channel, but you cannot add or remove any color to the channel itself.

- Each of Photoshop's layers, in contrast, can be a complete full-color image of its own. Layers are transparent until you place something on them. They are transparent sheets of acetate that you lay on top of the background.

- As you work with layers, you may need to change the order in which layers are arranged so that some objects are in front of or behind others.

- As with channels, you can copy, move, or duplicate layers within a document or between documents by dragging and dropping from one window to another, or delete a layer by dragging it to the Trashcan icon at the bottom of the Layer's palette.

CHAPTER 11

Working with Layers and Adjustment Layers

In this chapter...

- More thoughts on layers
- The Layer Mask
- Creating a Layer Mask
- Introduction to Adjustment Layers
- Working with Adjustment Layers

MORE THOUGHTS ON LAYERS

You hear lots of analogies for Photoshop's layers, but the more you think about it, the less they're open to analogy. The painter's canvas is one-dimensional, and if you pile more paint on top of what is already there, you cover that which has gone before. End of story. A stack of photo transparencies? Well, that's closer, but it's still not there. Transparencies are called transparencies for a reason: they're transparent, and they stay that way. Photoshop's layers can be manipulated to not only be either transparent or opaque, but also an almost infinite number of permutations in between. And not just this saturation can be affected. We can manipulate each of those layers individually to invert them, throw them out, copy them to other documents, and just generally party to our creativity's content.

Forget analogies, then; let's deal with straight facts. Photoshop lets you create up to 100 layers per image. Each of these layers is almost like a little document in itself, as it incorporates its own blending mode and opacity.

Ideally, you compose your document so that each new element has its very own layer. In this way, mistakes become true learning experiences and not headaches because it's so easy to just grab the offensive layer and turf it.

WARNING

If you create a new document with the **Transparent** option, it is created without a background layer. Images without a background layer can only be saved in the Photoshop format.

THE LAYER MASK

You can modify how a layer is combined with other layers by creating a separate mask. The layer mask lets you control how various elements on a layer are hidden and how they are revealed. You can make changes to the layer mask and apply special effects to it without actually affecting the layer's pixels. Once you apply the mask, the changes become permanent. If you don't like what you've done, you can remove the mask without applying it.

On-screen, Layer Masks look just like an extra thumbnail to the right of the layer thumbnail to be affected (Figure 11.1). Black portions indicate stuff that is hidden, and white indicates what is revealed. You can add a layer mask for each layer of a document.

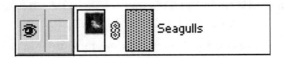

Figure 11.1 *A layer mask.*

N O T E

Adding a layer mask is easy. Simply choose the **Add Layer Mask...** icon from the toolbar at the bottom of the palette (Figure 11.2). An additional thumbnail representing this layer will appear in the Falling Shadow's layer's listing in the palette. The currently active portion of the layer (the mask or the layer itself) is surrounded by a black outline. To select an inverted Layer Mask, **Option**-click (Mac) or **Alt**-click (PC) on the Layer Mask icon. Alternatively, choose **Add Layer Mask** from the Layer menu.

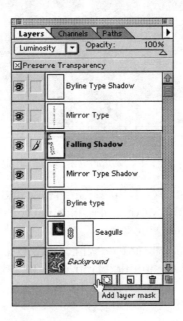

Figure 11.2 *Adding a layer mask.*

EXERCISE 11.1: CREATING A LAYER MASK

1. Open the file **IMG0040.PCD** from the CD-ROM, choosing a resolution of **256 x 384** from the Kodak CD dialog box.

2. With the dog's photo still open, open a new file. Make it 4 inches by 4 inches with a white background.

3. Go back to the open dog file. With the rectangular marquee tool, select an area tightly around the dog's head as indicated in Figure 11.3.

Figure 11.3 *Selecting an area to work with.*

4. Use the Move tool to grab the selected area and drag it to the new and untitled file. Use the Move tool to position the dog roughly in the middle of the square file you created.

5. Your unnamed file should now have two layers: a plain white background layer and the untitled layer that the dog is on. Save the file as **DAWG**.

6. The white background layer could get kind of boring, so let's change it. Highlight the background layer as shown in Figure 11.4, so that you can work with just that layer. Choose a color for your background. I decided to pick up some of the dog's own color and used the Eyedropper tool to select a rich gold from the top of his head. Then press or **Option-Delete** (Mac) or **Alt-Delete** (PC) to fill the background with your color of choice.

Figure 11.4 *Filling the background layer.*

7. Click on the dog layer to make it active. Create a Layer Mask for that layer by clicking once on the **Add Layer Mask** icon (Figure 11.5) at the bottom of the Layers palette. Another box with a link icon appears to the right of the dog thumbnail (Figure 11.6). This is your Layer Mask. If you click once on the left icon, the Dog Layer is active. If you click directly on the Layer Mask, the Layer Mask becomes active, and a black box additionally highlights that area. Make sure you have the **Layer Mask** selected before you proceed.

Figure 11.5 *Adding a layer mask to an open file.*

Figure 11.6 *The Layer Mask icon appears to the right of the Layer icon.*

8. Before we begin manipulating the Layer Mask, remember that if you want to hide the mask, you paint it with black. To subtract from the

mask and show what's underneath, you paint it with white, and to change the opacity of the mask, you paint with gray. Select a large, soft Paintbrush and use black to paint a soft vignette quite closely around our cute canine's face. Note that although you are painting with black on the Mask, it shows up on-screen as though you were using the same color as the background. Note also that while you work, the Layer Mask icon in the Layers palette begins to reflect your work on the screen.

9. Although everything is going well, we've gotten a little too close to the dog's face (Figure 11.7), and we need to open it up a bit. Still using a large, soft brush, select **white** as your foreground color and "paint" away the bits of the vignetting that are too close in. You'll note that everything is the same as before, but now the paint is disappearing as you work, leaving a clean area under your brush (Figure 11.8). Keep working until you are happy with the result. If you take too much away, it's a simple matter to flip back to black and add a bit more. You'll note also that if you get too close to the edge of the image, the hard edge between the photo and the background will become apparent. Work over this to soften it up.

Figure 11.7 We've painted too closely to the dog's head and must take away some of the paint by using white.

Figure 11.8 *Painting the Layer Mask with white leaves a clear area under your brush.*

10. Now select a **medium gray**. Using a medium-sized soft brush, describe a soft edge for your vignette. If you experiment with different grays from the Color Swatches, you'll see that the level of gray you use will determine the amount of opacity you get, with a light gray giving you the least amount of coverage.

11. To get a feel for what we've done, turn off the background mask by clicking on the **Eye** icon in that layer (Figure 11.9). You can see that the dog is perfectly vignetted and even ghosted at the edges where we used the gray. You can begin to see the possibilities.

12. We've been working in Normal blending mode throughout this exercise, but all other modes are possible to each layer. Experiment with these possibilities. For instance, using the Dissolve mode on the Dog Layer provides a pleasing, speckled finish (Figure 11.10).

Figure 11.9 Previewing your work with the background mask turned off.

Figure 11.10 Experimenting with possibilities.

13. If you want to view your handiwork unimpeded by anything else, **Option**-click (Mac) or **Alt**-click (PC) click or on the **Layer Mask** icon (Figure 11.11). To bring back your normal view, click an eye icon in the Layers palette.

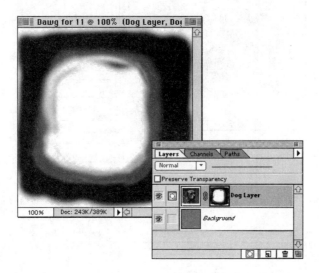

Figure 11.11 Looking at the Layer Mask alone.

14. When you are satisfied with your work, you will want to apply the Layer Mask and discard it because Layer Masks, like alpha channels of any sort, most often take more storage space than a file without them. Select **Remove Layer Mask** from the Layers menu. A dialog box will appear asking if you would like to apply the Layer Mask or discard it. Select **Apply** (Figure 11.12). Figure 11.13 shows the final result.

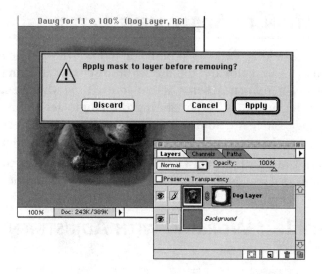

Figure 11.12 *Discarding the Layer Mask.*

Figure 11.13 *The finished artwork with the Layer Mask applied and removed.*

INTRODUCTION TO ADJUSTMENT LAYERS

Adjustment layers add an extra level of magic to Photoshop. The Adjustment Layer lets you play with color and tonality without actually affecting the image. What this means in a practical sense is that you can see what a change might do without having to worry about causing difficult-to-get-out-of changes to your entire image. Since the Adjustment Layer affects all the layers beneath it, you can insert your layer for adjustments between any layers you like.

Adjustment layers have built-in Layer Masks. That means that you can easily mask out an area that you don't want affected to be by the Adjustment Layer.

EXERCISE 11.2: WORKING WITH ADJUSTMENT LAYERS

1. Open the file **Book Cover** in the Chapter 11 folder of the CD (Figure 11.14). As you can see, it is an eight-layered cover for a fictional work of fiction. The two images—the seagulls and the flower—are from the Hyogen-sha Royalty Free photo collection and are included on the CD-ROM, although both have been manipulated from their original versions. The other elements were created entirely in Photoshop. Although we like the overall composition, some elements will benefit from Adjustment Layers.

2. With the uppermost thumbnail in the Layers Palette active, select **New Adjustment Layer**. Do this either from the fly-out menu in the Adjustment palette, or by selecting **Layer:New:Adjustment Palette**.

3. The New Adjustment Layer dialog box will present several options. You will see there are several types of adjustment layers to choose from. In fact, almost all of the options from **Image:Adjust** are here (Figure 11.15). For our first Adjustment Layer, choose Selective Color (Figure 11.16). Leave the default name **Selective Color**. For now, we'll leave the defaults of 100% Opacity and Normal Mode where they are, and leave the Group box unchecked.

4. The Selective Color dialog box appears (Figure 11.17) and is handled exactly the way it was in Chapter 15, Working with Color. Choosing to work with the neutrals from the fly out menu, adjust cyan to –21%, magenta to –26, yellow to –42 and black to +20. The colors overall are richer and stronger, but the poor birds are beginning to look a bit blue.

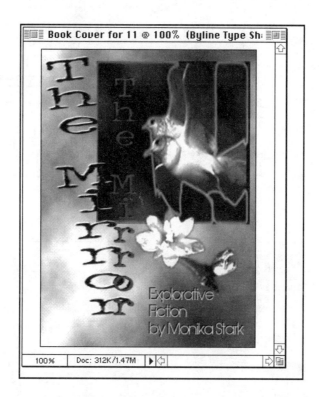

Figure 11.14 *The Book Cover image from the CD-ROM.*

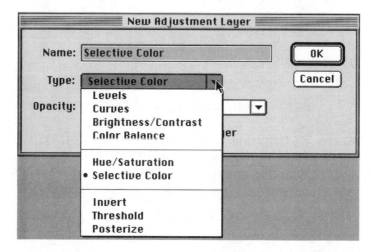

Figure 11.15 *New Adjustment Layer dialog box showing with*
the Type dropdown menu shows size.

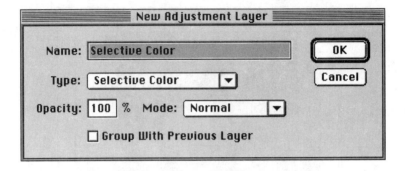

Figure 11.16 *Selective color is chosen.*

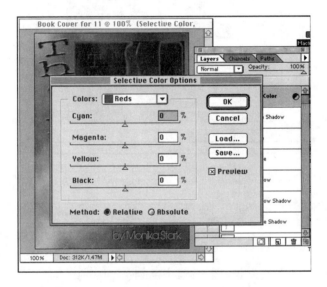

Figure 11.17 *The Selective Color Options dialog box.*

5. Grab the Selective Color Adjustment Layer, and drag it all the way down to just above the Background Layer. Notice how all the colors appear to readjust to where they were before, with the exception of the Background Layer, which is still affected by the Adjustment Layer.

6. Make the top thumbnail in the Layers palette active again by clicking on it once. Create another adjustment layer, this time choosing **Hue/Saturation** (Figure 11.18). Click in the **Colorize** box, then set the hue to –81, saturation to 64, and lightness to +17. If you have checked the **Preview** box, you'll notice that the image overall becomes a rich purple. Click **OK**.

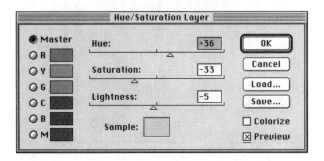

Figure 11.18 *The Hue/Saturation Layer dialog box.*

7. Now we have this incredibly purple book cover, and that won't do at all; it's just too much of a good thing. Grab the Hue/Saturation thumbnail in the Layers palette, and drag it between the Mirrors Type Shadow and Flowers thumbnails.

8. Now the type on the image is the same color it was before, but it's still too much of a good thing. Who ever heard of purple seagulls? Choose a medium-fine paintbrush and, with **black** selected, paint over areas of the image you'd like to clear of the purple inflicted by the Adjustment Layer. You can take away as much or as little of the Adjustment Layer as you want, just like a Layer Mask. Like the Layer Mask, if you take away too much, you can add to the mask again by painting in white. Painting in gray will take away only part of the adjustment effects in the areas you specify.

The finished image is shown in Figure 11.19.

Figure 11.19 *Our finished book cover.*

 To edit the Adjustment Layer Mask, use any of the editing tools to remove, add, or change the opacity of an effect.

N O T E

- Painting in black removes the adjustment effect.
- Painting in white displays the full effect.
- Painting in gray removes the adjustment effect only partially.

WHAT YOU'VE LEARNED

Layers

- You can create up to 100 layers per file.
- Layered documents reduce the margin for error.
- Images created without a background layer can only be saved in Photoshop format.

Layer Masks

- The Layer Mask controls how a layer's elements are hidden and revealed.
- Add a Layer Mask by choosing the **Add Layer Mask** icon from the Layers palette.
- Applying the mask makes it permanent.
- To hide desired portions of the Layer Mask, paint it with black.
- To subtract from the mask, paint with white.
- To alter the opacity of the mask, paint with gray.
- To view the mask alone, **Option**-click (Mac) or **Alt**-click (PC) on the **Layer Mask** icon. To bring back the normal view, click any **Eye** icon in the Layers palette.

Adjustment Layers

- Adjustment Layers let you manipulate the image without actually changing the pixels.
- Adjustment Layers affect all the layers beneath it, so you can move the Adjustment Layer to any location on the Layers palette.
- Adjustment Layers have built-in Layer Masks, so you can choose to edit out areas you don't want affected by the Adjustment Layer.
- Create a new Adjustment Layer by selecting **New Adjustment Layer** from the fly-out menu on the Layers palette.

CHAPTER 12

Introduction to Scanning and Printing

In this chapter…

- About scanning
- About printing
- Setting printing options in Page Setup
- Setting halftone screens

GETTING STUFF IN AND OUT OF PHOTOSHOP

By this time you'll be concerned with two important aspects of Photoshop: how to get things in via the scanner and how to get stuff out via your own printer. This chapter looks at both of these important functions.

ABOUT SCANNING

Photoshop will work with any scanner that ships with a Photoshop-compatible scanning plug-in module or that supports the TWAIN interface. If you are unsure if your scanner is Photoshop compatible, check with the manufacturer. Most recent-generation scanners, however, are compatible with Photoshop. Again, the scanner's manufacturer will have the latest information on getting their scanner to work with your hardware configuration.

NOTE   If your scanner doesn't ship with a Photoshop-compatible scanner driver, all is not lost. You can still scan your images in the software provided with the scanner, save the images as TIFF, BMP, or PICT files and then open them in Photoshop. When using stand-alone scanning software, the scanned images need to be saved to disk and then opened in Photoshop using the **Open** command under the File menu.

SCANNING WHILE YOU'RE USING PHOTOSHOP

If your scanner shipped with a Photoshop-compatible plug-in module, you can scan images while you're running Photoshop. The plug-in module must be placed in the plug-ins folder that you created when you installed Photoshop. You must restart Photoshop for the module to appear under the Import command under the File menu (Figure 12.1). The plug-ins folder is also where you stash Photoshop filters and filters sold by third-party vendors. All of these plug-ins add functionality to Photoshop. To install additional plug-in modules, drag them into your plug-ins folder or follow the manufacturer's instructions. Most scanner-provided software allows you to crop images, adjust image brightness and contrast, and do some basic color correction as the image is scanned.

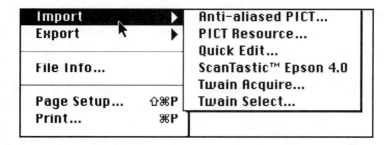

Figure 12.1 *Accessing a scanner while using Photoshop.*

SUGGESTIONS FOR GOOD SCANS

When scanning with a flatbed scanner:

- Make sure both the scanner's glass surface and the image you wish to scan is clean: free of dirt, dust, fingerprints, and cat hair.
- Warm up the scanner before you do your first scan.
- Place the print in the middle of the scanning area. If you place it too close to the top, it might become overexposed because the light tube takes a moment to begin moving.
- Identify whether the scan is to be in color, grayscale, or line-art mode.
- Prescan the image so that you can limit the area you'll want to scan, thereby reducing file size.
- Set the resolution and dimensions of the scan. At this point, you can adjust brightness, darkness, and color balance if you wish, but don't go overboard trying to perfect the scan with the scanning software. After all, that's what Photoshop is for.

ABOUT PRINTING

You've gotten things in to Photoshop and learned a lot about the program and how it works. The next thing you'll want to know is how to get things out: printing your final work as well as proof copies during the design process.

To prepare an image for reproduction, it must first be output on paper or on film as a positive or negative. From this intermediate output stage, the image is turned into a plate, which is used on a printing press.

Continuous tone images must first be screened (i.e., converted into a pattern of tiny dots) before they can be printed. This process is variously called *screening*, *halftone screening*, or *halftoning*. The density, shape, and size of the dots determines the look of the final printed image.

To create a grayscale image, the image is screened to create dots of varying size, which will be printed with black ink. For color images, four halftone screens are used (cyan, magenta, yellow, and black), and each of the resulting plates is printed with the appropriate color ink. Photoshop creates screen patterns automatically based on the printing options you select. Always check with your printer to determine the halftone screen resolution for the finished printed piece before you begin work on a project.

SETTING PRINTING OPTIONS

Open the Page Setup dialog box (Figure 12.2). This box will look somewhat different on your system, depending upon your platform and kind of printer you own, but the content will be similar. The top of the box contains the usual settings for paper size, reduction and enlargement of image, paper orientation, and printer effects: settings that you'll find for almost every application. For more information on these, check the manual that came with your desktop printer.

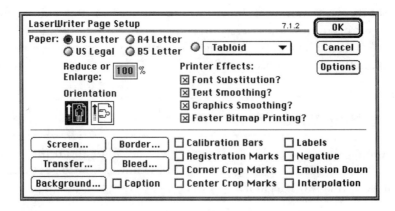

Figure 12.2 *Page Setup dialog box.*

Below the line are settings that are specific to Photoshop output, which will be discussed in detail in the following section.

PRINTING INFORMATION ON THE IMAGE

- *Labels.* Clicking the **Labels** box prints the document name and channel name on the image.

- *Crop marks.* Clicking the **Crop Marks** box prints crop marks on the image, at the corners or bottom as specified. This tells you and others involved in the process where trimming should take place.

- *Calibration bars.* Selecting this option prints an 11-step grayscale, which you can use to calibrate your monitor. Black is 0, white is 100, and there are 9 intervening steps. Collectively, they represent density gradations in 10% steps.

- *Registration marks.* Registration marks are used when you are printing with multiple plates, such as those used in four-color or duotone processes. These marks help keep the plates aligned so that the image is printed properly.

- *Caption.* To include a caption on a printout, click the **Caption...** button to bring up the dialog box. Enter the caption text, and click **OK**.

- *Border.* You can print a black border around an image in any width from 0 to 10 points, millimeters, or inches. Decimal values are acceptable.

- *Bleed.* Establishes that you are designing an image that will bleed and allows you to print crop marks inside the live area. A dialog box lets you specify the width of the bleed.

FILM OPTIONS

- *Negative.* When you are printing an image on paper, you will usually want a positive image, in which case you should not check the Negative box. However, if you are printing the image on film (as in the case of printing color separations), your printer will probably request a negative. To print a film positive, do not check this box.

- *Emulsion down.* The side of a film or photographic print paper that is light-sensitive is called the *emulsion side.* You must specify emulsion side up or emulsion side down for film output. Emulsion down is the most common film output choice, although some publications may request emulsion up. The default is emulsion up (Emulsion Down box not checked).

OTHER PRINTING OPTIONS

- *Background.* The area surrounding the printed image is called the *background,* not to be confused with the background color on Photoshop's Colors palette. You can change this color from the default (white) to any other color. Clicking the **Background...** button brings up the Color Picker. Change the color as you have learned to do. Black is often the best background choice if you are printing slides on a film recorder.

- *Interpolation.* This option applies only to PostScript Level 2 printers, which can resample a low-resolution image to reduce a jagged appearance. Ignore this option if your printer lacks this capability.

- *Transfer functions.* Use the Transfer dialog box to adjust transfer functions. Transfer functions and their relationship to dot gain and loss will be discussed in later chapters.

HALFTONE SCREENS

When you click the **Screen...** button in the Page Setup dialog box, you'll see the Halftone Screens dialog box (Figure 12.3).

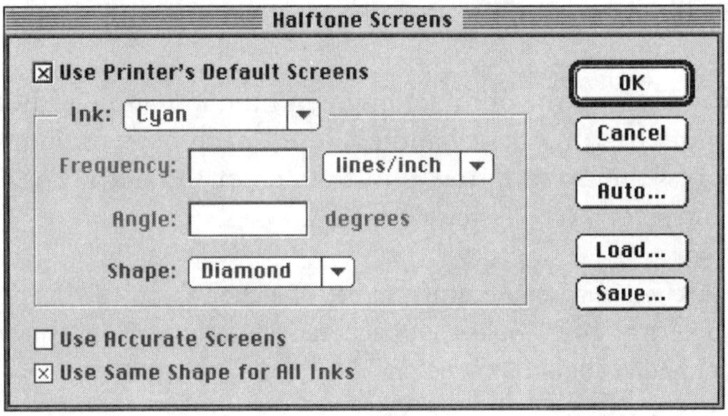

Figure 12.3 *Halftone Screens dialog box—CMYK image.*

Halftone Settings for Grayscale Images

Although the printer's default screen is most often best for the beginner's purposes, this is one area you might want to play with.

For a grayscale image, the value for the frequency (expressed as lines per inch or lines per centimeter) can be anywhere from 1 to 999.999. The screen angle can be plus or minus 180°. However, a 45° screen rotation is customary for grayscale (black-and-white) images. Finally, select the dot shape from the pop-up menu.

Halftone Settings for Color Images

When printing halftones for a color separation:

1. Select the color of the screen from the Ink pop-up menu. This will be cyan, magenta, yellow, or black, each of which corresponds to the four channels in the image.

2. Enter the screen frequency and screen angle for each of the four screens based on information provided by your printer. Each halftone screen will be printed at a different angle. If these angles are not placed correctly, an unattractive patterned effect, called *moiré*, can occur when the image is printed. You've seen moiré when you look at your daily newspaper and a badly printed color photograph begins to give you a

headache. As a rule, the default angle settings will produce the best result.

3. You can also use the automatic screen function and let Photoshop calculate the best frequency and angle for each of the ink colors. To do this, press the **Auto** button, and then enter the output printer resolution and screen frequency. Click **OK**.

WARNING

Only check the **Use Accurate Screens** function if you have a PostScript Level 2 printer or an Emerald controller. See Photoshop documentation for more information about this function.

4. Finally, select the dot shape from the pop-up menu. Click the **Use Same Shape for All Inks** box if you want each ink to be printed with the same dot shape.

SAVING HALFTONE SCREEN SETTINGS

Once you've made halftone screen settings for one image, you can save them to use later with other images. Use the Save and Load options in the Halftone Screens dialog box. If you want to save these new settings as a default, hold down the **Option** (Mac) or **Alt** (PC) key and click the right pointing arrow. To return to the original Photoshop defaults, press the **Option** (Mac) or **Alt** (PC) key and click the left-pointing arrow.

OPTIONS IN THE PRINT DIALOG BOX

More print options are available when you choose **Print** from the File menu (Figure 12.4).

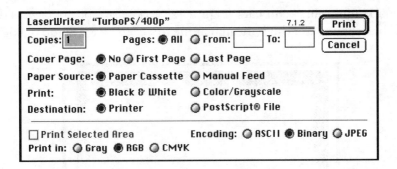

Figure 12.4 Print dialog box.

In addition to standard print choices, you'll see:

- *Print selected area.* Use this option to print just part of an image. The selection must be made with the Rectangular Marquee tool, not one of the other selection tools.

- *Print in CMYK.* If you have an RGB image and want to print a CMYK version of it, click **Print in CMYK**. This box will not appear if you have a CMYK image. You must have entered correct settings in the Printing Inks Setup dialog box for this choice to execute properly (see Chapter 20).

- *Print separations.* Click **Print Separations** to print four individual color separations, one for each channel—instead of one CMYK image. This box will not appear if you are printing an RGB image. It is visible only when you are printing an image that is in the CMYK mode.

- *Encoding.* If you are using a printer or a network that doesn't support Binary encoding, you can transfer the document in ASCII format instead.

PREVIEWING WHAT YOU PRINT

To see how your image will print on paper, move the mouse pointer to the lower-left-hand corner of your active Photoshop screen (where the file size box is) and press and hold the mouse button. A window will pop up showing the placement of the file on the printed page, complete with registration and crop marks and calibration bars (Figure 12.5). The size of the page is determined by the page size you indicated at the top of the Page Setup dialog box.

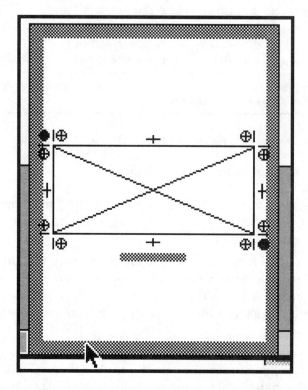

Figure 12.5 *Previewing a page before printing.*

WHAT YOU'VE LEARNED

- You can scan using plug-ins within Photoshop or using stand-alone scanning software.

- If you're not sure whether your scanner will work with Photoshop, contact the company that made your scanner.

- Use the Page Setup dialog box to add labels, crop marks, calibration bars, borders, captions, registration marks, and to specify bleed area to your printed output.

- Select **Background** to place your printed image on a colored background.

- Use the Page Setup dialog box to designate whether the image should be output as a positive or negative, emulsion up or emulsion down.

- Select the Screen dialog box to set correct halftone screens for grayscale and color images.

- Use additional options in the Print dialog box to print just a selected area, to print a CMYK version of an RGB image, to print CMYK separations, or to switch from Binary to ASCII encoding.

- To see a preview of the printed image on the page, click the mouse in the lower-left-hand corner of the image where the file size is displayed.

CHAPTER 13

Adding Fills and Gradients

In this chapter...

- Using keyboard shortcuts
- Using the Paint Bucket tool
- Using the **Fill...** command
- Using the **Stroke...** command
- Filling with patterns
- Linear and gradient fills

FILLS AND GRADIENTS

Working with fills and gradients is such a fun and integral part of Photoshop that we've been sneaking their use into exercises throughout the book. Like many other aspects of Photoshop, fills and gradients are easy to use once you get the hang of it, and they can add finish and polish to your work as well as structure to your basic designs.

We've already gone over the finer points of creating selections using the selection tools and how to save these selections using channels. In this chapter you'll use those selection skills to fill selections with color, patterns, and gradient blends, and to fill a border on a selection.

There are several ways to create fills in Photoshop:

- Use keyboard shortcuts to fill an area with either the foreground or background color.
- Use the Paint Bucket tool to create anti-aliased or non–anti-aliased solid or patterned fills.
- Use the **Fill...** command to fill a selection with a solid color or pattern.
- Use the Gradient tool to create a variety of graduations on tone and/or color.

EXERCISE 13.1: FILLING SELECTION USING KEYBOARD SHORTCUTS

To fill with the foreground color, press **Option-Delete** (Mac) or **Alt-Backspace** or **Delete** (PC). You can change the foreground color by selecting a new color from the Colors palette with the Eyedropper tool or by using the Eyedropper to sample a color from the document you're working on:

1. Reset the colors to the default (i.e., black foreground, white background).
2. In a new file, use the Elliptical Marquee tool to create an oval selection.
3. Press **Option-Delete** (Mac) or **Alt-Backspace** or **Delete** (PC) to fill the selection with black.

4. Enlarge the selection to 1600% to see the curved edge of the selection where the anti-aliasing is apparent (Figure 13.1). This effect occurs by default, even when the elliptical selection is not feathered.

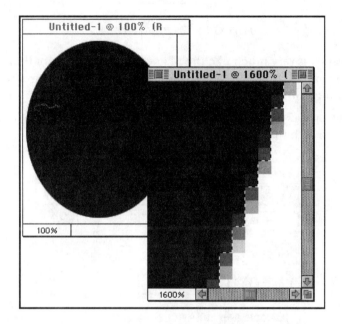

Figure 13.1 *Our elliptical masterpiece at 100% and enlarged to 1600%. Note that the larger view shows the anti-aliasing.*

4. Press **Command-Z** (Mac) **Ctrl-Z** (PC) to undo the fill and keep the view enlarged.

If you want more control over what you're filling with, display the Fill dialog box by pressing **Shift-Delete** (Mac) or **Shift-Backspace** (PC).

SHORTCUT

EXERCISE 13.2: FILLING WITH THE PAINT BUCKET TOOL

The innocuous-looking Paint Bucket tool (Figure 13.2) can actually be very helpful—even powerful—in certain situations.

Figure 13.2 *The Paint Bucket tool.*

In some ways it is very much like the Magic Wand tool, except that it fills adjacent pixels that are similar in color and allows you to fill them with a color of your choosing, rather than creating a selection.

You select the pixels to be affected by determining the pixel tolerance, just as you do with the Magic Wand tool (Figure 13.3).

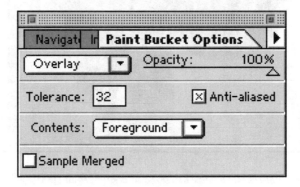

Figure 13.3 *Pixel tolerance.*

 The Paint Bucket tool will not work with images in the bitmap or indexed color mode. To use it with images saved in this way, simply convert them to an acceptable format, such as RGB, by using the **Image:Mode** command.

WARNING

Use the Paint Bucket tool to fill either a selection or a solid-colored area with no pixels selected.

Exercise 13.3: Filling with the Paint Bucket Tool

We'll learn how to use the Paint Bucket tool by colorizing a black and white photograph with a lot of tonally well-defined areas.

You'll notice that the Paint Bucket tool is a little tricky to use precisely. For instance, where you click the point of the Paint Bucket's drip will sometimes get you an entirely different reading of areas that are quite close together. Be prepared to play a bit to get just the right combination of tolerance levels and where to click the drip. After a while, you get a feel for it and the whole process goes much more quickly:

1. Open the Calas file within the Chapter 13 folder on the CD-ROM (Figure 13.4).

Figure 13.4 *The Calas image from the CD-ROM.*

2. Double-click on the **Paint Bucket** icon to display the Paint Bucket options.

3. To color the photograph, you can choose whatever colors you like. We chose a deep purple for the flowers and a dark green for the foliage.

Choose both colors you'll be using now, so that the foliage color is the foreground color.

4. Set the blending mode to **Color** and the tolerance to **130**, to start. Click in the center of one of the top two flowers. Because they are touching, you'll see the paint overflow into both top flowers. Still at tolerance 130, click in the lower flower. Not that the part of the flower closest to the stem doesn't fill with purple.

5. Switch the foliage color to be the background color. Reset the tolerance to 45 and click on some medium-toned area of foliage. Note that the color flows into all of the background area and does not encroach on the flowers in any way with the exception of the area already mentioned. This is because that part of the flower in tonally closer to the foliage to the flowers because it is in shadow.

6. To color the green part of the flower, we selected a small paintbrush, set the blending mode to color, and with the area enlarged with the Zoom tool, hand-colored that area over the Paint Bucket's green, which gives it a very natural look. Alternately, you could create a selection in that area using any of the selection tools and color that area with the Paint Bucket tool as you did the unselected areas.

7. Revert to the saved Calas image and experiment with different tolerances and colors. You rapidly get a feel for what works and what doesn't with regard to tolerances.

HOW ANTI-ALIASED IS ANTI-ALIASED?

1. Using the file we created with the filled oval back in Exercise 13.1, take a big, soft paintbrush, make sure the blending mode is normal, and paint a white diagonal line across the gray oval.

2. Change the foreground color to black and with the Paint Bucket tolerance set to 32, click once in the top half of the oval (Figure 13.5).

3. The gray area will fill with black, but when you enlarge on the border, you'll notice that the line is quite jagged. Undo the fill.

4. Next, take the Magic Wand tool with the tolerance set to 32 and click in the same area. Feather the selection 1 pixel and press **Option-Delete** (Mac) or **Alt-Backspace** (PC) to fill with black. The fill is still jagged, but the edge is softer. Undo the fill, but leave the selection.

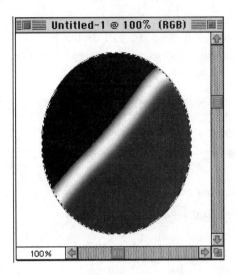

Figure 13.5 Top area filled black with Paint Bucket alone, tolerance 32, anti-aliased.

5. With the selection still active, choose **Make Path** from the fly-out sub-menu on the Paths palette. Set the tolerance to 5 pixels (a smaller number would create a line with too many convolutions). When the path is created, select **Fill Path**. Zoom in to examine it close-up, if you like.

From this demonstration, it is evident that all fills are not equal and that there are usually at least a couple of correct ways to do any one thing in Photoshop. Experimentation and practice will help you to understand the differences and see which one works best for you.

EXERCISE 13.4: USING THE FILL AND STROKE COMMANDS

Filling a Selection

Use the **Fill...** command from the Edit menu to fill any selection with the foreground color:

1. Create a rectangular selection on a white background.

2. Change the foreground color to the color of your choice. Select **Fill...** from the Edit menu, and the Fill dialog box will open (Figure 13.6). Leave the default settings as they are. Click **OK** or press **Enter**. The selection will fill with color.

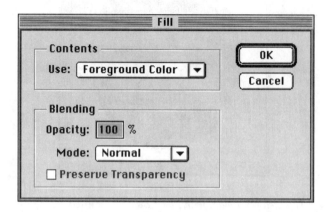

Figure 13.6 *The Fill dialog box.*

Changing the Settings in the Fill Dialog Box

1. Choose to fill with the foreground color or with a pattern that you create.

2. Set the opacity from 1 to 100%. The higher the percentage, the more opaque the fill. The lower the percentage, the more transparent the fill.

3. Set the fill blending mode to designate how the fill will affect the pixels it covers. These modes are the same as the painting modes discussed in another chapter.

Using Fill Patterns

You can create your own pattern to use as a fill or use one of the Adobe Illustrator PostScript patterns that ship with Photoshop.

To create a pattern:

1. Create a new document and fill it with solid blue. Set the background color to gold.

2. Using the rectangular marquee tool, drag to create a small rectangular selection.

3. Press **Option-Delete** (Mac) or **Alt-Backspace** (PC) to fill the rectangle with gold. Deselect everything.

4. Using the Rectangular Marquee tool, drag to enclose the gold rectangle and some of the surrounding blue.

5. From the Edit menu, select **Define Pattern**.

6. Open a new document.

7. Select **Fill…** from the Edit menu. Choose **Pattern** for the choice of contents. Make the opacity 100% and the mode Normal.

8. The window will fill with your newly created pattern (Figure 13.7).

Figure 13.7 *Filling with a pattern you create.*

N O T E   Each time you define a new pattern, the old pattern is replaced. To save a pattern, copy the selection as soon as you select the area to be defined. Open a new document and paste the selection inside. The size of the document will be the exact size of your selection. Then, with the sample still selected, choose **Define Pattern**. If you like the result of the fill, save the document. As an alternative, you can save many small patterns in one large document, but you must save a selection border for each one.

Applying a Stroke to a Selection

Use the **Stroke** command in the Edit menu to apply a filled border to a selection. This is different from the border you created using the **Border** command under the Select menu. The **Stroke** command creates a colored border of a defined pixel width and places it inside, outside, or centered on the selection border. The **Border** command creates a selected border area, which you can fill using a variety of techniques.

To apply a stroke to a selection:

1. Create an oval selection using the Elliptical Marquee tool.
2. Select **Stroke...** from the Edit menu (Figure 13.8). Set the stroke width to 8 pixels, centered, 100% opacity, normal mode. Click **OK**.

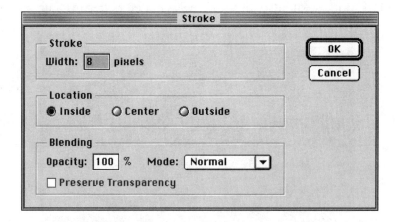

Figure 13.8 The Stroke dialog box in front of the previously stroked object.

3. The stroke will be applied to both sides of the selection border.

THE GRADIENT TOOL

The Gradient tool is used to create a smooth transitional fill between two or more colors. If there is a selection, the selected area will be filled. If there is no selection, the fill will be made to the entire layer. You can choose one of the gradient fills in the Tool Options palette, or you can create your own. Either way, filling with gradients can be fun and satisfying.

A few of the uses of gradients include:

- Soft sunset and dawn effects
- Three-dimensional shading on objects and type
- Backgrounds for multimedia and videographics
- Grayscale gradients saved as selections. When the selections are loaded, they can be used to apply effects, color corrections, and filters in a selective and graduated way.

Figure 13.9 The Gradient tool icon.

Basically, there are two types of gradients (Figure 13.10):

- *Linear fills* are applied in a straight line from the beginning point to ending point, no matter what the shape of the selection may be.
- *Radial fills* radiate out from the beginning point to the ending point, like the glow radiating from the sun.

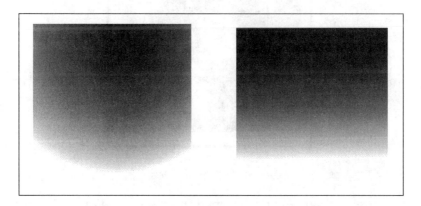

Figure 13.10 The radial fill (left) radiates out from the beginning point. The linear fill (right) is applied in a straight line.

EXERCISE 13.5: PLAYING WITH GRADIENT FILLS

The many fills that Photoshop provides and the immeasurable combinations of color and style of fill is what make the Gradient tool really fun. In addition, because you are in control of the level of fill any selection receives, the effects of even the precise same specification can be wildly different.

The best way to get to know the Gradient tool is to give yourself some space to play with it. That's what this exercise is all about:

1. Using the Rectangular Marquee tool, drag to create a rectangular area to fill.

2. Double-click the **Gradient** tool to open the Gradient Tool Options dialog box. For now, leave all the options at their default.

3. With the foreground and background colors reset to their default black and white, place the Gradient tool at the left side of the rectangle and then click and drag horizontally to indicate the direction of the fill. Release the mouse button. Your rectangle will fill with an even, linear graduation from left to right (Figure 13.11). Undo the fill.

Figure 13.11 A simple linear fill.

4. Choose **Orange, Yellow, Orange** from the Gradient Selection pull-down menu, and then click and drag the Gradient tool horizontally as you did in step 3. Your rectangle fills with a lovely glowing orange gradation. Undo the fill.

5. Choose **Radial** from the Fill Type pull-down menu in the Gradient toolbox and then click and drag the Gradient tool horizontally as you did before. A sunburst erupts from your rectangle (Figure 13.12). Undo the fill.

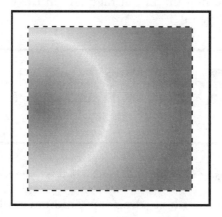

Figure 13.12.*A simple radiant file.*

6. Continue experimenting with combinations of fill types and gradations until you get an understanding for how the tool works. Try dragging from the top-left corner or from bottom to top and watch how each permutation alters the effect you end up with.

FILLING TYPE WITH GRADIENT FILLS

Type is, of course, just another selection, but some of the effects you can get by simply using the Gradient tool can be startling:

1. Click on the **Type** tool and click an area on a clean file.

2. When the Type dialog box presents itself, type a phrase—your own name can be fun to play with—and choose a nice, fat typeface so you can really see the results of the gradient fills. I used 40-point American Typewriter Bold with –2 spacing in my examples.

3. Double-click on the **Gradient** tool icon to bring up the Gradient Tool palette.

4. Select **Normal**, **Linear blend**, with **100% opacity**, and **Chrome** as the gradient type.

5. Select an area slightly above the type and drag down until you're just below the lowest characters. Release the mouse button (Figure 13.13). Note that your type has filled with a rough visual approximation of chrome, including the bright highlight at the center of the area you chose. Undo the fill.

Figure 13.13 Type filled with a chrome linear blend.

6. With the same settings, drag the Gradient tool from left to right. Release the mouse button. You'll note that the type of fill you get depends on how far you drag the mouse button and from where. If you dragged only a little way, the fill will go only as far as you did. On the other hand, if you dragged beyond, you'll get higher highlights toward the middle.

7. Undo the fill and experiment with dragging different lengths: sometimes only part way through the type, sometimes all the way, and sometimes at an angle. Remember to undo each time.

8. Choose the **Violet, Orange** gradient type from the pull-down menu and experiment with dragging in different directions, undoing after each try. You'll notice that this fill has a slightly different characteristic from the chrome. Where the chrome ends abruptly where your mouse stopped, the Violet, Orange will continue to fill unspecified letters with the last color selected. You'll find that the nature of the gradient determines whether or not this is the case. Again, experimentation will bring the best results here.

9. Once again experiment with combinations of different gradients and fill types as well as applying them with varying strokes and from different directions. Remember to choose **Undo** after each experiment.

GRADIENT FILL CREATION AND EDITING

Sometimes the effect you're looking for can't be found with the existing gradient fills. Photoshop lets you create and edit your own fills easily right from the Gradient Fill palette.

Creating a New Gradient

1. Double-click the **Gradient** tool to display the Gradient palette.
2. Click **Edit** to bring up the Gradient Editor (Figure 13.14).

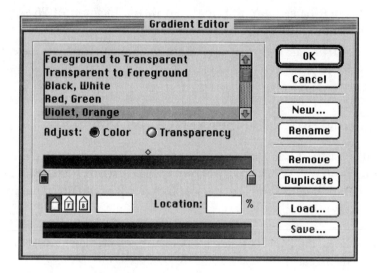

Figure 13.14 The Gradient Editor.

3. Click **Color** for the adjustment mode, then click **New**. When prompted to name your new gradient, you may type in a name or use the default name, **Gradient 1**. Click **OK**.

4. To define the color of your new gradient, click the left square under the gradient bar. When the triangle above this square turns black, it indicates that the beginning color is being edited.

5. To choose a color, click on the color swatch underneath the gradient bar and choose a color from the Color Picker. Press **OK**.

6. Click the right square underneath the gradient bar to define the ending color. When this triangle turns black, once again click on the color swatch and pick a color. Click **OK**.

7. To set the starting and ending point of the gradient, either drag the boxes directly below the gradient bar to the desired location, or you can specify the starting and ending location by entering the desired value in the Locations box. 0% places the starting point at the far left, while 100% places it at the far right. For now, enter **25%** and watch where the boxes—and the colors—end up.

8. You can also determine the midpoint of the blend. Grad the diamond directly above the gradient bar and drag into the desired position: either left or right. You'll note that with a location of 25% specified, you can drag the midpoint only so far.

9. Click **OK** to add your new gradient to the list. You now have a brand new fill to use. Go try it out if you like, and edit at will.

THE GRADIENT TRANSPARENCY MASK

The opacity of the fill at different locations on the gradient is controlled by the Transparency mask. The Transparency mask is set to 100% by default, but you can manipulate the transparency to have it fill gradually, blending into a color with less opacity.

Turn off the Gradient Transparency mask by deselecting **Mask** in the Gradient Options palette.

N O T E

WHAT YOU'VE LEARNED

Fills

- Use **Option-Delete** (Mac) or **Alt-Backspace** or **Delete**(PC) to fill a selected area with the foreground color.

- Use the Paint Bucket tool to fill an area with foreground color or a pattern.
- Set Paint Bucket mode on the Paint Bucket Options palette.
- Fill a selection with the foreground color or a pattern using the **Fill** command from the Edit menu.
- Change the Fill opacity and mode settings in the Fill dialog box.

Patterns

- Define a pattern by selecting an area with a Rectangular Marquee tool and choosing **Define Pattern** from the Edit menu.

Stroke

- Apply a stroke to a selection using the **Stroke** command from the Edit menu.

Gradient Fills

- Create linear and radial blends with the Gradient tool.
- Change the midpoint of the gradient, and edit and create gradients from the Gradient Editor within the Gradient palette.
- Fill type and other selections with gradation with the Gradient tool.

CHAPTER 14

Image Resolution and Importing Files

In this chapter…

- Resizing and resampling images
- Cropping images
- Opening documents
- Acquiring images and importing files
- Saving documents in different formats
- Exporting documents

In this chapter you will learn how to resize and resample images and how to crop them using the **Crop** command or the Cropping tool. We'll also offer suggestions for better scanning and discuss the types of images you can acquire and files you can import into Photoshop, including PhotoCD and images you've gotten on the Internet. Finally, information on saving and exporting files will close out the chapter.

RESIZING AND RESAMPLING USING IMAGE SIZE...

The image of a child shown in Figure 14.1 is saved on the CD-ROM. It is 6.56 inches x 4.48 inches and was scanned at resolution of 100 ppi for good-quality Web reproduction. The file size is 287 K. To resize the image yet keep the same resolution, we select **Image Size...** from the Image menu, which gives us the Image Size dialog box (Figure 14.2):

Figure 14.1 Image before resizing.

- At the top of the Image Size dialog box are the current file size, width, and height.
- Under this are the print size and resolution. Notice the correlation between size in pixels and in inches.

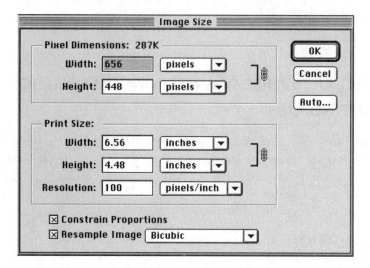

Figure 14.2 *The Image Size dialog box.*

- At the bottom are boxes to indicate if you want to constrain proportions and if you'd like to resample the image.

- Note that with the **Proportions** box checked, the width and height are joined together and a Link icon appears to the side. This allows proportional scaling. With the Proportions box unchecked, the link disappears. Unlink the dimensions if you want to change the height more than the width, for instance.

RESIZING DOWN

Keeping the resolution at 100 ppi, we change the width to 4 inches and the height automatically and proportionately reduces to 2.732 inches, as the file size reduces to 107 K.

RESAMPLING UP

Increasing the resolution while maintaining the size of the image can be done, but it is not recommended. The new pixels have to be created by interpolation based on the present pixel values, resulting in an image that looks out of focus. If you absolutely must resample up to increase resolution, try applying the Unsharp Mask filter (under the Filter menu) to increase apparent sharpness.

RESIZING UP WHILE MAINTAINING RESOLUTION OR RESAMPLING UP

You can use the Image Size box to increase the size of an image while keeping the resolution the same or increasing the resolution. To achieve either increase, Photoshop must add pixels where there were none before, and this can degrade image quality.

INTERPOLATION

Whenever you resize, resample, scale, skew, distort, change perspective, or rotate an image, the values of the new pixels are determined by interpolation. Photoshop offers three interpolation methods, which you can choose by selecting **Preferences:General** from the File menu:

- Bicubic interpolation, the default choice, is recommended by Adobe as being the most precise, although the slowest, method.

- Nearest neighbor interpolation is much faster than the bicubic method because it simply divides each pixel into more of the same color, but the lack of precision inherent in Nearest Neighbor can cause a jagged appearance, especially if an image is transformed more than once.

- Bilinear interpolation is a compromise between the first two methods. It is neither as precise nor as slow as bicubic, but it is more precise than the faster nearest neighbor method.

PASTING AND RESOLUTION

A Photoshop file cannot have images with different resolutions, so if you paste an object scanned at a high resolution into a low-resolution file, the pasted-in object will expand in size. The solution is that you might need to resize the object before pasting it in. For example, if you're pasting a 200-ppi circle into a 100-ppi background, you will need to reduce the size of the circle by one-half if you want it to appear the same size in the destination file as it does in its file of origin. Conversely, if you're pasting a low-resolution image into a high-resolution file, the object will shrink in size and you'll need to resize-up accordingly.

EXERCISE 12.1: ADDING TO AN IMAGE USING CANVAS SIZE

You can add area around an existing image without changing resolution by using the **Canvas Size...** command from the Image menu:

1. Create a new file, 2 inches x 2 inches, with a resolution of 72 ppi.

2. Fill the entire file with a solid foreground color of your choice. Deselect the image and select **Canvas Size...** from the Image menu. The Canvas Size dialog box will open (Figure 14.3).

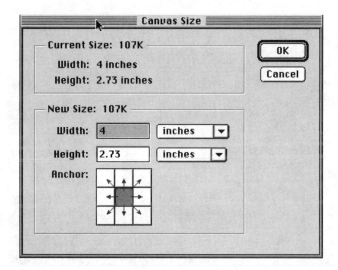

*Figure 14.3 Use **Canvas Size...** to add new area around an image.*

3. Make the new image 4 inches x 4 inches. Enter these numbers in the New Size Width and Height boxes. The placement diagram indicates where the original image will be placed when new space is added. Click on the upper-left-hand box to see how placement can be changed. Then click back in the center. Click **OK** to approve the change.

4. The original image is centered in a larger file, 4 inches x 4 inches. Press the **Option** (Mac) or **Alt** (PC) key while clicking on the file size box to see that the size of the file has been changed but that its resolution remains the same.

CROPPING IMAGES

Photoshop offers two ways to crop an image: you can use the **Crop** command from the Edit menu or the Cropping tool from the Toolbox.

Cropping Using the Crop Command

1. Using the Rectangular Marquee tool, drag to select the area to be cropped (Figure 14.4).

Figure 14.4 *Cropping using the Rectangular Marquee tool.*

2. Select **Crop** from the Edit menu. The part of the image outside of the selection border will be eliminated (Figure 14.5). This method of cropping is suitable when you do not want to rotate, resize, or resample the image simultaneously.

Figure 14.5 The image after cropping.

Cropping Using the Cropping Tool

When you crop using the Cropping tool you can adjust image size and resolution and even rotate the cropped area, all in one operation:

1. Press the **Marquee** tool and keep it pressed until the fly-out menu offers you the tool options. From this menu, select the **Cropping** tool. Double-click the **Cropping** tool (Figure 14.6) to open the Cropping Options palette.

2. Set the dimensions that you want for the final image and the resolution. (We want to crop an area 2 inches x 2 inches square.) If you wanted to resample up or down at this point, you could change the resolution.

3. Click and drag the **Cropping** tool on the image to select the area to be cropped. Release the mouse button when you are pleased with the crop.

4. If you wanted to rotate the marquee, you would bring the mouse outside the selected area. The pointer turns into an arrow with a curve. Now drag as you would using a Transform tool.

Figure 14.6 Cropping tool.

5. To scale the selection, simply grab a handle. If you press **Shift** while dragging, you will constrain the proportions.

6. To make the crop, press **Return** or **Enter**.

OPENING FILES AND IMPORTING IMAGES

Opening Files

Files saved in the following formats can be opened in Photoshop 4.0: Photoshop 4.0, Photoshop 3.0, Photoshop 2.5, Photoshop 2.0, Amiga IFF, BMP, EPS, Filmstrip, GIF, GIF89a, JPEG, MacPaint, PCX, PDF, PhotoCD, PICT File, PICT Resource, PIXAR, PixelPaint, PNG, Raw, Scitex CT, Targa, TIFF, and TWAIN-scanned files.

Using the Open... Command

When you open a file using the **Open** command under the File menu you will be able to see the file format when you click on a file you want to open as well as a preview of the file to be opened (Figure 14.7).

In Windows, you can use the **Open As** command to open a file with a missing or incorrect file extension or one that doesn't appear in the Open dialog box.

N O T E

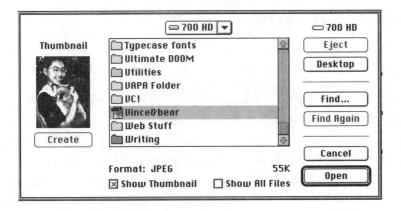

Figure 14.7 *Opening a file using the Open command.*

Importing Files Using the Acquire Command

As previously mentioned, some scanners allow you to scan while you're running Photoshop, in which case the scanning software is reached using **Acquire…** (File menu). The **Acquire…** command is also used to import files in other formats, including EPS files saved using JPEG compression, anti-aliased PICT files (created in programs such as MacDraw and Canvas), PICT Resources, and images to be scanned via the TWAIN interface. Video frame grabs are also brought into Photoshop by using the **Acquire…** command.

To acquire a file using an import module:

1. Select an **Acquire…** module from the File menu.
2. Depending upon your choice, you may be presented with a File Open box, a dialog box requesting additional information, or another screen specific to the manufacturer of the module.

Importing PhotoCD Files

Files saved using Kodak's PhotoCD format can be opened using **Open…**. A PhotoCD dialog box will give you the choice of color mode and resolution. Select **Lab Color** if you plan to use the image for color separations. The RGB mode opens the file in RGB format, and the grayscale mode removes the color information from the file.

SAVING YOUR WORK

Just as Photoshop lets you open and manipulate images with many different file types, it also lets you save files in a wide variety of formats. Among these Save formats are Photoshop (which includes versions 2.5–4.0), Photoshop 2.0, BMP, CompuServe GIF, EPS, Filmstrip, JPEG, PCX, PICT File, PICT Resource, PIXAR, PNG, Raw, Scitex CT, Targa, and TIFF.

These formats will appear in the pop-up menu of the Save dialog box when you choose **Save...** or **Save As...** from the File menu.

If you do not see these names on your menu, it could mean that they are not presently in your Plug-Ins folder and that you will need to install them properly. If the format appears but is grayed-out, it means that the option is unavailable with the type of file you want to save. Photoshop also offers several export modes, which can be found under the Export... submenu under the File menu. Images can be exported to Adobe Illustrator with the **Paths to Illustrator** command under **Edit:Export**.

SAVING A FILE

You can save a file using either the **Save** or **Save As...** command. The **Save** command saves a file in its existing format. In the case of a newly created file, the default is the native Photoshop 4.0 format. The **Save As...** command allows you to save a file in another format.

To save a file:

1. Select **Save** from the File menu.
2. When the dialog box opens, enter your name for the document in the text box.
3. Select a file format from the pop-up menu. Click **OK**.

To save a file in a different format:

1. Select **Save As...** from the File menu.
2. When the dialog box opens, enter the file name.
3. Choose a different file format from the pop-up menu. Click **OK**.

Photoshop 4.0, 3.0, 2.5, and 2.0 Files

Photoshop's native format is not encoded and supports all the possible image modes listed under the Mode menu for the version of Photoshop you are using. You can also save mask channels, which are part of a document when you use this format. The disadvantage of this format is that it is not supported by some page layout and illustration programs, and it takes up a lot of space because the files are not compressed.

TIFF Files

TIFF (Tagged-Image File Format) is a paint-type format that is widely accepted for desktop publishing. TIFF files can be reduced in size using LZW (Lempel-Zif-Welch) lossless compression, and they can be exported to many layout programs, including Aldus PageMaker and QuarkXpress. *Lossless* means that no data is lost when the file is compressed. If you have included mask channels with your image, the TIFF format allows you to save them.

PICT Files

Like TIFFs, PICT files can contain grayscale or full-color bitmapped images. PICTs can be exchanged between different programs and are perfect for many graphics applications, including object-oriented drawing programs, multimedia, and video. However, there is disagreement about the usefulness of PICTs in page layout applications. PICT documents can be quite compact, especially when an image contains large areas filled with the same color. In fact, a simple black-and-white RGB image of a white circle on a black background that appears to be 900 K in size when viewed in Photoshop takes up only 32 K on the disk when saved in PICT format. PICT files can be saved with mask channels when 32-bit/pixel resolution is selected, but not when JPEG compression is selected.

EPS Files

Encapsulated PostScript (EPS or EPSF) is a desktop-publishing standard, accepted by most illustration and layout programs. The images in files saved in the EPS format are described by many lines of written, coded commands. This format is different from PICT and TIFF files, for example, where the image is described in a bitmapped form. Because the EPS format cannot be viewed directly in a layout program, you have the option of saving a PICT preview along with your file, which allows you to place the image on the page more accurately.

BMP Files

The standard bitmap image format for computers running on the MS-DOS or Windows platforms. If you specify Run Length-Encoding compression (RLE) you will add lossless compression similar to the LZW in the TIFF file format. You will need to specify the operating system format (Microsoft Windows or OS/2) as well as the bit depth in the BMP Options dialog box.

JPEG Files

In the last couple of years, JPEG (Joint Photographic Experts Group) has come to be one of two popular formats of images displayed in hypertext on the World Wide Web. In the JPEG format, undetectable amounts of data are dropped, resulting in a smaller file size. Although this is a lossy method, the quantity of missing data is usually not noticeable, and it is actually less than the other popular hypertext format, GIF. When JPEG is chosen, the dialog box asks you to decide upon the amount of image compression and the image quality you request. Notice that there is an inverse relationship between the two—the better the quality, the less the compression; the better the compression, the lower the quality.

Filmstrip Files

When you open a Filmstrip file created in Adobe Premiere, you can save it again in the same format. This option is not available with other files.

CompuServe GIF and GIF89a Files

GIF files (Graphics Interchange Format) are most commonly seen on the World Wide Web and other hypertext services. Grayscale, bitmapped, and indexed color images can be saved in this format, with resolution from 1 to 8 bits per pixel.

GIF89a (found under **File:Export**) lets you specify transparent areas in the file and enables you to save in RGB format.

PCX Files

IBM PC-compatible computers use PCX format. Many different Photoshop modes (including RGB, Grayscale, Bitmapped, Lab, and Indexed Color) can be saved in the PCX format.

MacPaint Files

The format for MacPaint files is used to transfer black-and-white (Bitmapped mode) images to other applications. The MacPaint dialog box gives you two-page placement choices.

PICT Resource Files

Popular in the Macintosh world for moving graphics files between programs, PICT Resource Files can be especially useful for transferring files that have large areas of solid color. This can be helpful for archiving alpha channels that are stored in black and white.

PIXAR Files

Images can be saved in the PIXAR format for export to high-end PIXAR work-stations.

PNG Files

The PNG format is a lossless compression method intended for use on the World Wide Web. Select **Adam 7 for Interlace** if you want the image to display gradually with increasing detail while being downloaded.

Raw Files

The raw files format is sometimes used when you want to save an image for use on a different computer platform. In this binary format, the file information consists of a stream of bytes. In each channel, pixel brightness is described on a scale of 0 to 255, with 0 as black and 255 as pure white.

Scitex CT Files

Only CMYK and grayscale images can be saved in the Scitex CT format, which is used for very sophisticated image processing. Although you can convert a Photoshop file directly into the Scitex format, you need additional utilities (available from Scitex) to transfer files to a Scitex system.

Targa Files

Use the Targa (TGA) format to save a file to be used on a system with a Truevision video input/output board. You do not have to save files in TGA format to use them with Truevision's NuVista video boards for the Macintosh.

EXPORTING A FILE

In addition to saving files in the previously mentioned formats, you can also export files using the special plug-in modules available under **File:Export**. These options include GIF89a for viewing on the Web, compressing EPS files with JPEG, and exporting paths to Adobe Illustrator. To use an Export module, simply select **Export** from the File menu and choose one of the formats. When the corresponding dialog box appears, enter the appropriate data and click **OK**.

Exporting Photoshop Paths to Adobe Illustrator

At times, you may want to export a path created with the Pen Paths tool so that it can be modified in Adobe Illustrator. For example, you might want to add some Illustrator-modified text to a Photoshop image. This is how to do it:

1. Create a path using the Pen Paths tool.

2. Save and name the path as you learned earlier.

3. Select **Paths to Illustrator** from the Export submenu (File menu). Save and name the file. It will have the suffix *ai*.

4. Open this new file in Adobe Illustrator. It will look the same as it did in Photoshop, and crop marks will designate the size of the image it came from.

5. Add any extra objects or text. Text can be placed on the path, inside a closed path, or separate from the path.

6. Save the path with the appropriate Adobe Illustrator preview.

7. Use the **Place** command (File menu) to place the path in Photoshop. It will fit perfectly with your original Photoshop image.

WHAT YOU'VE LEARNED

Resizing and Resampling

- Resizing adds or subtracts pixels from the image through the process of interpolation.

- Resize or resample an image using the **Image Size...** command.

- Add additional space around an image using the **Canvas Size...** command.

- Crop images using **Edit:Crop** command or the Cropping tool. You can rotate and resample an image when you crop with the Cropping tool.

Opening and Importing Images

- Open files using the **Open...** command.

- Import files using the Acquire modules.

Saving and Exporting

- Save files in a variety of formats using Photoshop's **Save** and **Save As...** commands.

- If save formats do not appear under the Save dialog box pop-up menu, their respective plug-in modules might not be properly installed.

- Save formats, which are grayed-out, are not available for that specific image mode.

- Export files to other applications using format choices from the Export submenu.

Working with Color

In this chapter...

307

A Colorful World

It's simply not possible to play with Photoshop for very long without wanting to dip your fingers into the color. Case in point: in every chapter thus far we've experimented with color in various ways without actually getting serious and saying, "Okay now: let's learn about color in Photoshop."

The fact is, Photoshop and the other computing tools that support it have made designing with color easy. It is tempting to blithely work away without a full understanding of how color works and how it can best be put to work for you, but go the distance and take it a step further. Although the effortless color that Photoshop can provide is often good enough, the full beauty corrected and properly thought-out color can bring to your images can make all the difference between just okay and truly tuff.

The Picker Palette

To progress to image color correction, it's helpful to know more about how Photoshop works with color and some of your color management options.

The Eyedropper

The Eyedropper and the Picker palette (Figure 15.1) work together to provide complete color information about an image, right down to the color values of individual pixels.

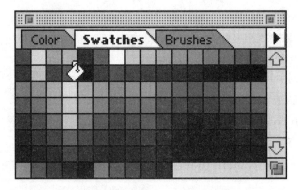

Figure 15.1 *The Picker palette.*

This precision sampling method is called the *point sample* mode, and it can be set by double-clicking the **Eyedropper** tool to bring up the Eyedropper Options palette, where it may be selected from a dropdown list. (Two other modes are 3 x 3 average, which samples a 3 pixel x 3 pixel area, and 5 x 5 mode, which samples a 5 pixel x 5 pixel area.)

EXERCISE 15.1: EXPLORING COLOR PALETTE COLOR MODELS

The Color palette has sliders that can be used to adjust colors in any of five color models: Grayscale, RGB Color, HSB Color, CMYK Color, and Lab Color. The color bar at the bottom of the palette can display hues in any of four different spectrums: RGB, CMYK, grayscale, or a foreground-color/background-color continuum. The sliders and color bar can be set independently; that is, you can view a CMYK color spectrum while the sliders are set for RGB. You could, for example, set RGB colors using only CMYK hues, if you wished (thereby avoiding out-of-gamut, or unprintable, colors). You can examine the color of any pixel with one of these models. Each gives unique information about the image.

Select a color with an RGB value of 241, 164, 21. Making sure that you have the **RGB Mode** chosen, set your color sliders so that your numbers are the same. Change the color model by opening the submenu on the right side of the Color palette. Click on the arrow to open the submenu. (Changing the model will not convert the color mode of the image.)

The RGB model tells us that the pixels in the red channel are almost fully illuminated at 241, the green pixels are less brightly lit at 164, and the blue pixels are dim at 21. The HSB model describes a color's hue, saturation, and brightness. In this model, hues are expressed by their position on the color wheel, measured in degrees, with red occupying the 0° position. Continuing around the wheel, yellow is at 60° with respect to red, green is at 120°, cyan at 180°, deep blue is at 240°, and magenta at 300°. The saturation and brightness are both expressed in percentages. Our foreground color, gold, appears at 39° on the color wheel, with the saturation at 91% and the brightness at 95%.

The CMYK model expresses the color in terms of percentages of cyan, magenta, yellow, and black—the component colors of four-color process printing.

The Lab model describes the color in terms of luminosity, an *a* component and a *b* component. *Luminosity* is defined as a percentage from 0, black, to 100, white. The *a* component measures the color along a continuum from green to magenta, and the *b* component measures the color along a scale from blue to yellow. The Lab model is recognized as an international standard for mathematically defined color and is the preferred mode when you import PhotoCD images. You might find this mode useful if you want to change the brightness of a color separately from its color. To demonstrate, move the L slider from 77 down to 50 and back to 77 again. When the *a* and *b* components are centered, the color presented is a shade of gray.

The Grayscale model measures "color" value on a scale from white to black, with 0 as black and 255 as white. The letter *K* (as in CMYK) represents the word black. Use this model when you work with grayscale photographs.

NOTE The expression black-and-white photograph is a misnomer. On the computer, scanned continuous tone photographs are represented with 256 shades of gray. The only Photoshop images that are truly black and white are 1-bit images.

COLORS THAT CAN'T BE PRINTED

Return to the HSB mode and drag the hue slider all the way to the left to select a vivid red. A warning icon appears (Figure 15.2), indicating that the color you have selected is out of gamut—it cannot be reproduced accurately on paper using CMYK inks. (Some colors in the RGB color model will give you the same warning.) A somewhat darker shade of red is offered as a substitute color in a small color box to the right of the warning icon. This color is suggested as a printable alternative, based on the Printing Inks Setup you indicated in the Color Setting preferences under the File menu. If the image you are working on will be printed, click on the substitute offered to change to an in gamut color.

Figure 15.2 Warning icon indicates out-of-gamut color.

CREATING NEW COLORS

Photoshop gives you several ways to create new colors other than sampling them from an image:

- Select colors or create colors "by the numbers" using the Photoshop Color Picker.
- Adjust the sliders in the Colors palette.

EXERCISE 15.2: CREATING COLORS WITH THE PHOTOSHOP COLOR PICKER

The Photoshop Color Picker gives you exquisite control over color selection. The picker opens by default when you click the foreground or background color icon on the toolbox or in the Colors palette (Figure 15.3). The choice of Color Picker (Photoshop, Apple, or Windows) is set in the **Preferences:General** submenu under the File menu.

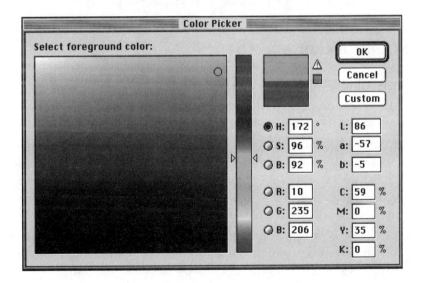

Figure 15.3 The Photoshop Color Picker.

Using the Photoshop Color Picker

Use the Photoshop Color Picker for the following purposes:

- To create a color in any of the color models by entering numbers in the boxes.
- To view all four color modes at the same time and see how changing one affects the other. (This is especially helpful to see how RGB or HSB changes affect the CMYK model.)
- To select a color directly from the color field, the large colored area on the left side of the box:
  1. Double-click the foreground color to open the Photoshop Color Picker if it is not already open.
  2. The large colored rectangle is the color field. To the immediate right is the Color slider. Farther to the right is a smaller rectangle that is divided to show the present color and any new color you'd like. As you drag the mouse around the color field, the color at the top of the small rectangle will change, as will the numbers that represent each of the color modes available in Photoshop.

The Color Picker and the HSB Model

1. Drag upward using one of the small triangles on the Color slider. With the **H** button clicked, the slider changes the hue. Click in the bottom of the small rectangle to reset the color to red.
2. Click the **S** button. Now the large color field shows the entire spectrum, decreasing in brightness toward the bottom. As you drag a triangular slider, the saturation of the color changes. When you drag the circular mouse pointer around the color field, you select colors of varying hue and brightness, but with constant saturation.
3. Click the **B** button. The large color field now displays the spectrum, decreasing in saturation. Dragging the triangular slider changes the brightness of the color as it graduates to black. Dragging the mouse in the color field changes a color's hue and saturation but not its brightness.

The Color Picker and the RGB Model

You can also view each color component separately using the RGB model. Click the **G** button to display the green component. In this view, the red and blue values are displayed in the large color field along its vertical and horizontal axes. The Color slider represents the brightness of the green pixels in the image. As you increase the value of the green pixels by raising the triangles on the slider, the brightest red changes to yellow. (In the RGB additive color model, green and red combined at full brightness make bright yellow.) Continue your experimentation with the other two component colors.

When you are finished, click in the bottom of the small rectangle to reset the color to red.

CMYK AND LAB COLOR BY THE NUMBERS

Using the boxes assigned to any of the color models, you can enter numbers to create any color. The CMYK model represents colors as percentages of cyan, magenta, yellow, and black. The Lab Color model expresses colors as numbers from –128 to +127 for each of its luminance a and b components.

SELECTING CUSTOM COLORS

Photoshop supports custom color inks from several systems, including the ANPA (American Newspaper Publishers' Association) Color System, the DIC Color Guide, Focoltone Colour System, the Trumatch Swatching System, the Toyo 99 ColorFinder 1050 System, and several varieties of the Pantone Matching System. You need to have a swatch book from the manufacturer of the ink you plan to use to see exactly how your selected colors will print:

1. Click the **Custom** button in the Photoshop Color Picker. When the Custom Colors dialog box opens (Figure 15.4), a custom color will be automatically selected that is nearest to the current foreground color.

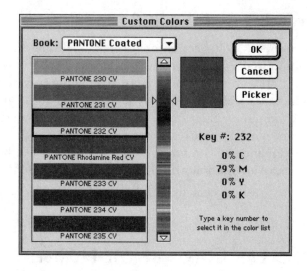

Figure 15.4 Custom Colors selector.

2. Change the color swatch book being used with the pop-up menu.

3. To select a color, enter the manufacturer's swatch number or drag the triangles on the scroll bar to view all the choices.

4. The Custom Colors box also shows you the color's CMYK percentages. Click **OK** to select a color or click **Picker** to return to the Photoshop Color Picker.

Depending on your platform, you can specify use of either the Apple or Windows Color Picker instead of the Photoshop Color Picker under **File:Preferences:General**. Neither offers the range of modes that the Photoshop picker does. If you want to use one of these pickers, consult the documentation that shipped with your computer's operating system.

EXERCISE 15.3: CHANGING THE COLORS ON THE PICKER PALETTE

To add a new color to the Swatches palette:

1. Choose one of the color selection tools to prepare your custom color (i.e., the Eyedropper tool or the Color Picker).

2. Move the Eyedropper tool to the first open space in the bottom row of the Swatches palette. As the tool turns into a Paint Bucket, click to add the color to the palette (Figure 15.5).

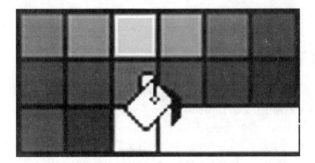

Figure 15.5 *Adding a new color to the Swatches palette.*

To remove a color from the Swatches palette:

1. Press the **Command** key (Mac) or **Ctrl** key (PC) as you position the pointer over the swatch you added to the palette.

2. When the pointer turns into a pair of scissors, click to cut the color from the palette.

CHANGING OR INSERTING A COLOR ON THE SWATCHES PALETTE

Press the **Shift** key and position the Paint Bucket over the swatch you want to change. Click to replace a swatch with a new color. To insert a color between two existing colors, press **Shift-Option** (Mac) or **Shift-Alt** (PC) keys simultaneously as you click with the Pointer/Paint Bucket tool.

USING CUSTOMIZED SWATCHES PALETTES

If you create a new Swatches palette, you can save it using the **Save Swatches** command, which appears on the Swatches palette fly-out menu. A saved palette can be loaded at another time using the **Load Swatches** command. Opening a saved Swatches file automatically appends it to the open Swatches palette. If you want to return to the Default color palette (the one that you open when Photoshop is launched for the first time), reload the Photoshop colors file. As with the Brushes palette, the Picker, and Swatches palettes that are loaded when you quit Photoshop will be the ones that load when you start the program again.

COLOR CORRECTION

Unlike many of the other Photoshop skills you have learned, precise color correction is a complex art and science, one that volumes have been written about. This section will provide a color correction overview along with an introduction to the basic Photoshop tools and techniques. In other words, it's a foundation from which you can build your own expertise.

Analyzing the Image

It's a good idea to take a long, hard look at the image you'll be correcting in order to determine just what corrections need to be done to go about fixing it:

- Is the image too dark or too light?
- Is there a predominant color cast to the image? This is common with commercially printed photographs. You will often see a definite green or magenta cast that you could do without.
- How is the contrast of your image? Is it muddy? Is the contrast too high?
- Are there no true whites and blacks?
- If the surface of the print was texturized, you can end up with a speckled look when the image is scanned. It's not always possible to remove all of this artifact, but you can try to minimize it.

After you have scanned the image and before doing any corrections, make a copy of the original using the **Calculate:Duplicate** command from the Image menu (Figure 15.6). In this way, you can experiment with changes and if necessary make a fresh copy from the original to try other changes.

*Figure 15.6 A copy of my lovable equine Annie was made using the **Calculate:Duplicate** command. In this way, if I make her color crazy, it isn't catastrophic.*

Click the **Preview** box in any of the following dialog box windows to see the changes in the image as you make adjustments.

N O T E

If you make a change in one of the Adjust submenu dialog boxes and don't like the preview, press the **Option** key (Mac) or **Shift** key (PC), and the Cancel button will turn into a Reset button while it's depressed. Click the **Reset** button to restore the image to the way it was before. Continue making adjustments. You can use the **Reset** button as many times as you wish.

SHORTCUT

CORRECTING THE IMAGE

Step 1: Adjusting the Brightness and Contrast

Open the Levels dialog box by selecting **Image:Adjust:Levels** (Figure 15.7). The graph you see is called a *histogram,* and it is used to measure the numbers of pixels at each of 256 brightness levels. The horizontal axis displays the range of these pixel values—0 (black) is on the left and 255 (white) is on the right. The vertical axis measures the number of pixels at each level. This particular histogram for my photo of Annie tells us that there is a preponderance of dark pixels in this image. When a histogram displays this kind of pattern, it means that the lights and darks are not distributed evenly throughout the image, which we know is true, because we see that the image is too dark overall. In addition, there are few pure black pixels (far left) and pure white pixels (far right), which means that the shadows and the highlights are compressed, resulting in decreased contrast.

SHORTCUT

One way to adjust an image as painlessly as possible is to use Adjustment Layers. Choose **New Adjustment Layer** from the Layers palette. Then work with the levels as though you were working directly with the image. The big advantage at this stage is that, should you be unhappy with your adjustments, it's easy to turf the adjustment layer and start over.

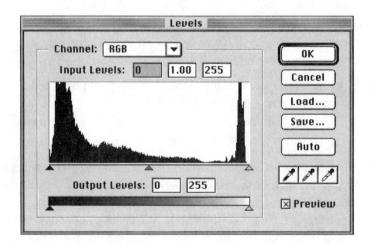

Figure 15.7 Use levels to adjust brightness and contrast.

Using the Auto Command in Levels

The easiest way to adjust the levels is to click the **Auto** button and let Photoshop apply its own suggested changes. This resets the white point and the black point and redistributes the gray values of the pixels in between (Figure 15.8). Afterward, the histogram shows that the pixels fill the complete range from white to black.

You'll find that setting Auto Levels are more effective with some images than others. Your best bet is to do the eyeball test. Does it really look better after the Auto Levels have been set? In the case of the Annie photo, it really doesn't. Best to work on these manually.

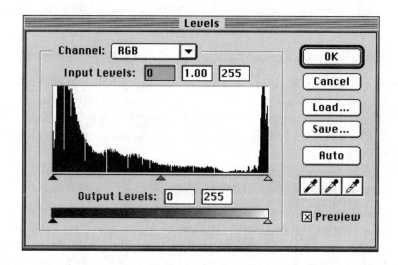

*Figure 15.8 Levels after using the **Auto** command.*

Setting Black and White Points Manually in Levels

If you want more control, you can use the Eyedroppers in the Levels window to set the black and white points. Make sure the Info palette is open and that the HSB and RGB color models are displayed. If they are not, select them from the Info Palette Options submenu, on the fly-out menu on the Info palette.

Select the **White Eyedropper** tool and drag it around the image while watching the Info palette. We are looking for the lightest white in the image, which we find at 90% brightness in one of the hot spots. Select that point by clicking.

Next, we use the Black Eyedropper tool to select the darkest black in the image (the deep shadows in the lower right). The combination of these two choices redistributes the pixels from pure white to pure black.

If you prefer, you can reset the white and black points by moving the position of the white and black triangles on the input sliders (upper scale). Or, you can enter numbers in the Option boxes. The three boxes represent the black, gray, and white triangles, respectively. Use the numbers 0–255 in the white and black boxes. We'll come back to the gray triangle later.

Although we are making changes to the entire document in this demonstration, you can apply changes to any one of an image's component channels by selecting the specific channel with the pop-up menu. This applies to CMYK files as well.

Adjusting Contrast Using the Levels Input Sliders

Below the histogram in the Levels dialog box are the output sliders—a black triangle on the left and a white triangle on the right. Moving the black triangle to the right reduces the contrast in the shadows and lightens the image. Moving the right triangle to the left reduces the contrast in the highlights and darkens the image.

Using the Brightness/Contrast Dialog Box

The Brightness/Contrast dialog box (**Image:Adjust:Brightness/Contrast**) provides a simpler, but less-controlled way to adjust your image (Figure 15.9). While Levels gives you five ways to change brightness and contrast for each channel (three input controls, two output controls), the **Brightness/Contrast** command gives you only two. Another significant difference is that Levels presents a histogram so that you can see where you are potentially losing information. The Brightness/Contrast dialog box lacks this. Photoshop makes it easy for you to work at your comfort level.

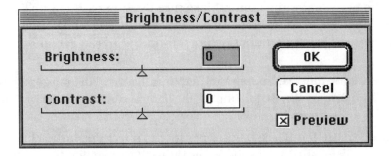

Figure 15.9 *The Brightness/Contrast dialog box.*

Step 2: Adjusting the Midtones

The center (gray) triangle slider in the Levels histogram is used to adjust the midtones, which are called the *gamma values*. Dragging this triangle to the left lightens the midtones. Dragging it to the right darkens the midtones while leaving the highlights and shadows alone. You can also move the gray triangle by entering numbers from 9.99 to 0.1 in the Center option box. The default value 1.0 lies exactly in the middle of the range.

Step 3: Selecting a Neutral Tone to Remove a Color Cast

Most of the greenish cast in my Annie image is removed by resetting the black and white points in Levels. Some of the remaining cast can be taken out by selecting a neutral tone with the Levels Gray Eyedropper tool. You will want to magnify the image with the Zoom tool to look for a neutral-colored pixel before doing this. A neutral-colored pixel is one in which the R, G, and B are present in equal amounts.

Saving and Loading Levels Settings

You may find it convenient to save the adjustments you make to an image, especially if you are processing a batch of photographs that were taken under the same conditions or if you are retouching a series of video frames. Save your settings by clicking **Save** and saving them as a file. This file can be loaded later by clicking **Load**.

Step 4: Fixing the Color Balance

Adjusting Color Balance with the Sliding Scales

Select **Image:Adjust:Color Balance** to open the Color Balance dialog box (Figure 15.10). There is still some green in my image, which we can remove by clicking each of the **Midtones**, **Highlights**, and **Shadows** buttons and dragging the Magenta/Green slider very slightly away from the green. The colors on these three sliders are complimentary. For example, to reduce red, drag toward cyan; to reduce magenta, drag toward green; to reduce blue, drag toward yellow. Click the **Preview** box to see the changes as you make them.

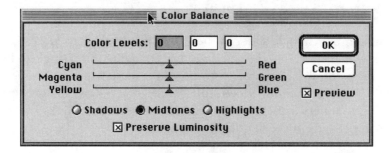

Figure 15.10 *Use Color Balance controls to adjust the color in the shadows, midtones, and highlights.*

Adjusting Color Balance by the Numbers

You can also make color changes by entering numerical values in the Color Balance option boxes. Each of the boxes represents one of the scales, with +100 as the right-side color and –100 as the color on the left. For example, to adjust the Cyan/Red scale toward red, you would enter a positive number in the first box. To adjust the Magenta/Green slider toward magenta, you would enter a negative number in the second box.

Step 5: Correcting the Hue and Saturation

We'll demonstrate hue and saturation correction with another image: a bright red amaryllis belladonna (Figure 15.11), which we'll change to a burnt sienna color. If you want to follow along, open the Amaryllis Sienna image from the Chapter 15 folder on the CD-ROM.

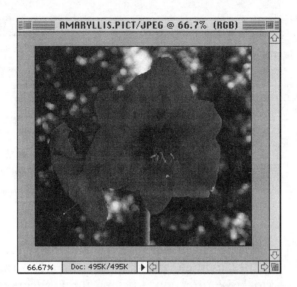

Figure 15.11 *The Amaryllis Sienna image from the Chapter 15 folder on the CD-ROM.*

1. We use the Magic Wand tool, anti-aliased, with the Tolerance set to 100 to select much of the red color. We added left-out parts of the image by encircling them with the Lasso tool, holding down the **Shift** key. Then, the **Quick Mask** option was checked and the stamens were painted so that they would not be selected when the mask was loaded on the flowers.

2. The completed selection was saved in a new channel.

3. The Blur More filter (**Filter:Blur:Blur More**) was applied two times to the channel with the saved selection. This makes a smoother transition at the edge of the selection border.

4. The selection was loaded onto the image by selecting **Load Selection** from the Select menu.

5. We opened the Hue/Saturation dialog box by going to **Image:Adjust:Hue/Saturation** (Figure 15.12).

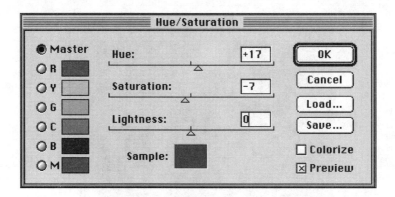

Figure 15.12 *Hue/Saturation dialog box.*

6. The Hue slider was moved to +17 to change the selected color area from red to gold. This is the same thing as moving 17° around the color wheel in a clockwise direction. Clicking the **Eyedropper** tool in the image selects the color and puts it in the sample box. As you adjust the hue, the sample color box shows you the change.

7. By dragging the Eyedropper tool around the image, we noticed in the Info palette that areas of this changed color were out of gamut for four-color printing, so the saturation was reduced (−7) until the color value was acceptable. (The Info palette shows you Eyedropper-sampled color values before and after correction in your choice of color models.)

Hue and saturation settings can be saved and loaded to work on a series of similar images so that you don't have to reset the sliders to correct each one.

N O T E

At the left of the Hue/Saturation dialog box is a series of buttons indicating the three primary additive colors (RGB) and the three primary subtractive colors (CMY). You can adjust the hue, saturation, and brightness of each color component separately as well as adjust the Master color. (Master is the default when you open this dialog box.)

N O T E

Step 6: Adjusting Final Details

We return now to the image of Annie the Equine. We found the image background too sharp and distracting. We used the Magic Wand tool to select Annie and her foreground, and then inversed the selection. The inversed selection was then given a slight Gaussian blur to soften the background and thereby provide less distraction. Finally, we thought about using a small Paintbrush tool in the Hue Painting mode to change the eye color to blue. This would have preserved all the eye detail and affected only the color. However, after we'd played with that, the sight of an Arabian mare with bright blue eyes was just too silly, so we deleted that layer.

Step 7: Sharpening the Image

Scanning often reduces the sharpness of an image because the data in the artwork has to go through a layer of glass to be picked up by the sensors. To regain some of the sharpness of the original, apply the Unsharp Mask filter to the image when color correction is completed (**Filter:Sharpen:Unsharp Mask**). This filter brings back definition by sharpening the parts of an image where there are significant color changes between adjacent pixels (Figure 15.13).

Figure 15.13 The color-corrected and finished image.

COLOR CORRECTING USING THE VARIATIONS COMMAND

If you're from the "I'll know it when I see it" school of color correction, you're going to love the **Variations** command (under the Adjust submenu on the Image menu; Figure 15.14).

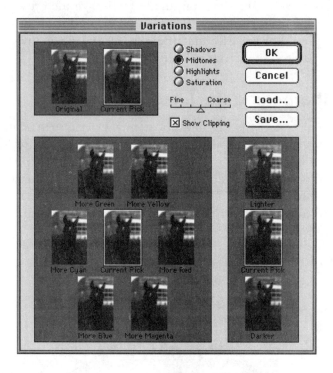

Figure 15.14 *The Variations dialog box lets you select adjustments visually.*

 The **Variations** command can be a useful learning tool. Because you can see what each adjustment actually does to your image, you gain a more complete understanding of what adjustments do to your image in a very practical sense.

NOTE

The **Variations** command displays your original image, surrounded by an array of color correction variations represented as thumbnail images.

- The picture in the middle (the current pick) displays the status of the image. Every time you click on a thumbnail, the change is applied to the current pick.

- Change the color cast of the image by clicking on the thumbnail image that adds more magenta, red, cyan, blue, yellow, or green.

- Change the brightness by clicking on a brighter or darker thumbnail.

- Click the buttons to adjust the color separately for the highlights, shadows, and midtones. You can also change the color saturation.

- As you approach the color you want, move the slider from coarser to finer. This applies change in smaller and smaller increments.

- When you make changes to the shadow and highlight areas, there's a danger that some of the values may be clipped or converted to pure black or white, which you probably don't want. Areas that would be clipped when the change is applied are highlighted in a bright neon color when the **Show Clipping** option box is checked (the default position). Uncheck the box to turn this option off.

- To start over, click the **Original** image thumbnail.

- Clicking **OK** applies the changes to the image.

ADDITIONAL IMAGE ENHANCEMENT TOOLS

Using Curves

The **Curves** command (**Image:Adjust:Curves**) offers subtle control over the brightness, contrast, and gamma levels in an image. This is control that is far beyond that offered by the Levels and Brightness/Contrast dialog boxes.

Although this is an introductory-level book, we are discussing the **Curves** command so that you'll be somewhat familiar with its functions. For a complete explanation, refer to the Photoshop *User's Guide.*

The Brightness/Contrast dialog box lets you change an image globally, with no difference between the way the changes are applied to the highlights, midtones, and shadows. The **Levels** command adds more control, allowing you to change the shadows, highlights, and midtones separately. The **Curves** command goes all out and lets you change pixel values at any point along the brightness level continuum, giving you 256 locations at which you can make corrections. For simplicity, we are demonstrating with a grayscale photo, but the same principles apply to color images.

Our mission photograph has been deliberately darkened and the contrast reduced (Figure 15.15), so that we can correct it using **Curves**. We open the Curves dialog box by selecting **Adjust:Curves** from the Image menu (Figure 15.16):

Figure 15.15 Mission before.

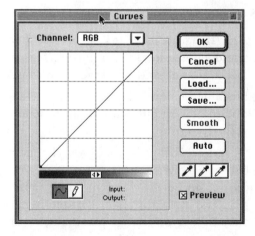

Figure 15.16 Curves dialog box.

- The horizontal axis maps the brightness values as they are before image correction. The vertical axis maps the brightness values after correction.

- Each axis represents a continuum of 256 levels, divided into four parts by finely dotted lines. In the Default mode, the lower-left-hand corner represents 0, 0 (pure black) and the upper-right-hand corner is 255, 255 (pure white).

- If you wanted to reverse the way that the scale is represented, you can click on the central arrows. This places white on the left and black on the right and measures levels in percentages instead of brightness values.

- Whenever you open the window, the graph begins as a straight line because unless changes are made, the input will be exactly the same as the output—a direct 1:1 correlation.

- When you use the Eyedropper tool from the toolbox to click on the image, a circle appears on the graph to show you the value of the pixel being sampled. At the bottom of the Curves dialog box, you can read the pixel's input and output values. When we read the pixels in this image, we see that what should be the brightest pixels are only at level 79—far too dark—and what should be the darkest pixels have a brightness of 29—too light.

- Click the **Preview** button to see the changes as you make them.

Use the Auto Button to Set the White and Black Points

As we click on the **Auto** button, the darkest pixels in the image (the deep shadows) are reset to black, and the lightest areas (the clouds) are remapped to white. As in the Levels dialog box, this is the easiest way to make corrections, but it doesn't use the subtle power of the **Curves** command any more than the **Auto** button did in Levels.

Reset the Black and White Points with the Levels Eyedropper Tools

1. Starting over with the bad image, we selected the black paint-filled Eyedropper tool and clicked it on the darkest part of the image. This

identifies a new black point, and the contrast immediately starts to improve.

2. Then we selected the white paint-filled Eyedropper tool and clicked it in the brightest part of the image (pixels in the clouds). The contrast is now adjusted.

3. Let's see what's happened to the Curves graph (Figure 15.17). The two dark endpoints at the end of the graph moved. When the mouse pointer is positioned over either of these endpoints (without clicking) we can read the input and output values. The endpoint at the far right indicating the white pixels has been moved from x, y = 255, 255 to 79, 255. This means that the murky gray cloud pixels that were at level 79 before the change (input) have been remapped to an output level of 255 (pure white). The endpoint at the far left has also moved. From an original position of 0, 0 it has moved to 29, 0. This means that pixels that were previously at a brightness level of 29 (washed-out murky shadows) have been remapped to 0 to produce black in the very darkest part of the shadows. Figure 15.18 shows the finished image.

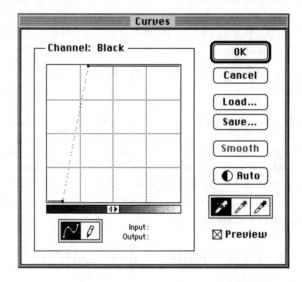

Figure 15.17 Curve after adjustments.

Figure 15.18 Image after curve adjustment.

If you click at any point on the curve other than the endpoints, a control point will be added that shows your position. You can remove a control point by dragging it downward until it is completely off the graph. The shape of the curve will seem to bend momentarily, but it will spring back unaffected.

Use Curves to Adjust Midtones

Midtones are parts of an image with color values that range from 25% to 75% of the total value range. After you've set a new white point and black point, you may want to manipulate the midtones by adding and moving additional control points, which are between the two extremes.

Common Curve Corrections

- Flattening a curve lowers contrast. When we take our corrected bell tower image and flatten the curve by raising the black endpoint and lowering the white endpoint (Figure 15.19), we lower the contrast in the image.

- An S-shaped curve increases contrast, especially in the highlight and shadow area. Using a curve like this also helps to define the midtones (Figure 15.20).

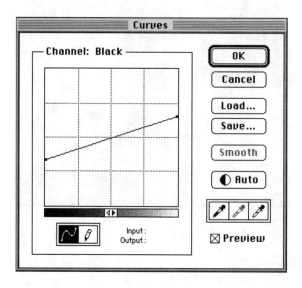

Figure 15.19 *Flattening a curve lowers contrast.*

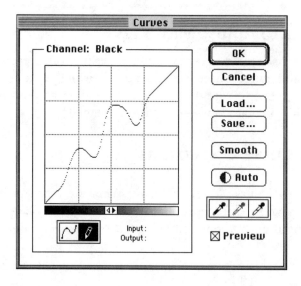

Figure 15.20 *Arbitrary map drawn with pencil and smoothed.*

Creating an Arbitrary Map

For ultimate control, Photoshop lets you draw a curve with the precise shape you'd like. This kind of curve is called an *Arbitrary map*.

1. Using the corrected bell tower image, we open the Curves dialog box and select the **Pencil** icon.

2. We draw a shape that has several peaks and valleys in the midtone range, and press the **Smooth** button to smooth out the shape (Figure 15.20).

3. The result is an interesting posterized effect. Arbitrary maps provide many creative possibilities for grayscale and color images.

Colorizing Images with the Colorize Option

Use the **Colorize** option in the Hue/Saturation dialog box to change the color of any selected area to a new, solid color. (This is not like the Hue slider, which changes individual pixels based on their present color values.) Here's how:

1. If you don't have a scanned black and white image of your own to colorize, Open the Orpheus image from the Chapter 15 folder on the CD.

2. Open the Hue/Saturation dialog box by selecting **Image:Adjust:Hue/ Saturation**.

3. Click the **Colorize** button. The image will turn red immediately because red is always the starting point for this option. (Red, you'll remember, is at 0° on the color wheel.)

4. Drag the Hue slider to –30, or enter **–30** in the Option box. The hue should change to magenta. Pure white pixels and pure black pixels are not colorized because colorization affects only gray pixels (from value 1 to 254). Click **OK**.

5. With the selection border still active, change the foreground color to vivid gold (255, 148, 8 in RGB model) and the background color to robin's egg blue (0, 182, 230). Double-click the **Gradient** tool and set the blending mode to overlay. Drag over the magenta area with the Gradient tool to create a linear fill with these colors.

Figure 15.21 The Orpheus image from the Chapter 15 folder on the CD-ROM.

6. Open the Hue/Saturation dialog box again, click **Colorize**, and drag the Hue slider to –30. Once again, the area is completely magenta. Only the brightnesses of the underlying pixels create variation in the color.

7. Hold down the **Option** key (Mac) or **Shift** key (PC) to change the Cancel button into a Reset button, and click the **Reset** button. Click the checked **Colorize** box to turn off this option.

8. Now drag the Hue slider to –30. The gold will turn to red, and the blue will change to a sea-green hue, with the intermediate colors as a brownish blend between the two. This demonstrates the difference between using the **Hue** command with and without Colorize.

To colorize a grayscale document, you must convert it to RGB mode.

N O T E

USING THE MAP COMMANDS

Invert

The **Invert** command turns an image into its negative—black becomes white, white becomes black, and colors turn into their opposites across the color wheel.

Equalize

Using **Equalize** balances the brightness and contrast of an image so that the pixels represent the entire range of values, from black to white. When you equalize an image, Photoshop looks at all the pixels, and finding the brightest and darkest ones, averages all the brightness values in between. This redistributes pixels and generally improves the contrast in an image. However, in some cases, it may lighten the picture too much.

Threshold

Threshold allows you to change images (grayscale or color) into high-contrast black and white images without converting the file mode into a bitmap:

1. Choose **Map:Threshold** from the Image menu or press **Command-T** (Mac) or **Ctrl-T** (PC). The Threshold dialog box contains a histogram that shows you the distribution of pixel values.

2. Move the slider to set the threshold level. All pixels to the right of this point will be turned white, and all pixels to the left will be changed to black. If the **Preview** button is checked, you can see the change as it happens.

Threshold is ideal for making high-contrast images that can be traced in an illustration program (such as Adobe Illustrator) and turned into PostScript outlines (Figure 15.22).

Figure 15.22 *After processing with the* **Threshold** *command.*

Posterize

A grayscale or color photograph can be changed so that pixels are reassigned to a limited number of gray or brightness levels. This results in a posterized effect:

1. Choose **Map:Posterize...** from the Image menu.
2. When the Posterize dialog box appears (Figure 13.23), enter the number of levels you wish. You can preview the change by clicking the **Preview** button (Figure 15.24).

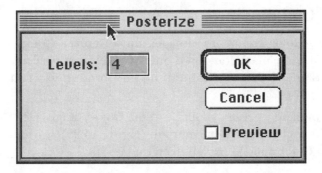

Figure 15.23 Posterize dialog box.

Figure 15.24 The Posterized image.

OTHER COLOR CORRECTION OPTIONS

Photoshop offers many options for colorization. Here are a few more of them.

Replace Color

The **Replace Color** command (**Image:Adjust:Replace Color**) allows you to create a temporary mask composed only of pixels in a particular color range and then to adjust the hue, saturation, and brightness of those values to change the color.

This command operates similarly to the Color Range selection tool; even the dialog boxes have much in common (Figure 15.25). To adjust color using the Replace Color dialog box you need to:

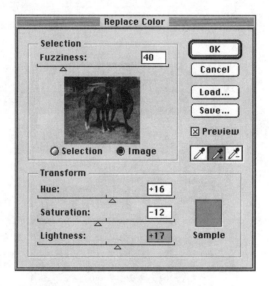

Figure 15.25 *Replace Color dialog box.*

- Select an area of the image you want to modify (if you don't want to change the whole image).
- Use the Eyedropper tool to sample colors to be replaced. Use the + and – Eyedroppers to add or subtract hues from your selection.
- Adjust the Fuzziness slider to provide the tolerance you want (to select more or fewer pixels close to the color you've chosen).
- Drag the Hue, Saturation, and Brightness sliders to change the color.
- If you check the **Preview** box you can see the effects of your changes on the screen.

• Click **OK** to apply the effect to your image.

Selective Color

The **Selective Color** command (**Image:Adjust:Selective Color...**) lets you change colors by modifying the amount of ink used to produce a given color. That is, you can add 10% or another amount to any particular ink that will be used to print an image. To use this command follow these steps:

1. First, make sure you're viewing the RGB channel of your image. The command won't work if you're viewing any other channel.
2. Choose **Adjust:Selective Color...** from the Image menu.
3. Select the color to be adjusted from the dropdown Colors list (Figure 15.26).

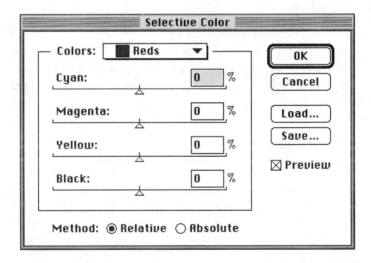

Figure 15.26 *Selective Color dialog box.*

4. Choose the method for adjusting the colors. Selecting **Relative** adds or subtracts colors from existing CMYK values; **Absolute** controls the amount of color in absolute percentages, regardless of the amount currently in the original image.
5. Drag the sliders to make your adjustments.

6. If **Preview** is checked, you can see the results on your image.

7. You can save or load adjustments for reuse.

8. Click **OK** when finished.

Desaturate Command

The **Desaturate** command is nothing more than a quick way to switch to tones to grayscale, without changing mode. Suppose you wanted to change the tones of an RGB image or a portion of such an image to gray, but then continue to work on the image in RGB mode. You might wish to change a color photo to gray and then add color callouts. The long way to do this would be to change to grayscale mode and then back to RGB. The **Adjust Desaturate** command (**Image:Adjust Desaturate**) does the same thing in one step.

Sponge Tool

Don't forget about the color corrections you can make with the Sponge tool, the third Toning tool on the fly-out menu on the Toolbox, after Dodge and Burn. Sponge can selectively desaturate colors in small areas of your image, producing color corrections in sections that you don't want to apply to the entire document.

Quick Edit Feature

The Quick Edit feature of Photoshop can be used when working with colors to allow you to experiment with a section of an image. That's especially useful when you want to try out some corrections on a very large file and don't want to wait while Photoshop applies your changes to the entire image. Quick Edit can also be helpful for applying filters to small sections of an image as a test. To use Quick Edit, follow these steps:

1. Choose **File:Import:Quick Edit...**.

2. Select the file you want to edit.

3. When the image of the file appears on the screen, use the selection tool to mark off the portion of the image you want to edit. Click **OK**.

4. Only the section of the image you specified will be loaded.

5. When you save the file portion, it will be restored to the original file in the correct position.

WHAT YOU'VE LEARNED

Picker Palette

- Evaluate a color's components using any of five color models: RGB, HSB, CMYK, Lab, and Grayscale.
- Use the Eyedropper tool to sample a single pixel or the average of pixel values in a wider area.
- A warning icon (triangle with exclamation point) alerts you if a color cannot be printed.
- Create new colors in the scratch pad.
- Add new colors to the existing color palette with the Eyedropper tool.
- To remove colors from the color palette, press **Command** (Mac) or **Ctrl** (PC) as you position the mouse pointer over the unwanted color swatch.
- Insert a color using the Paint Bucket tool between two color swatches on the palette.
- Save, load, and append color palettes using the pop-up menu.

Color Pickers

- Create new colors by the numbers using the four color models in the Photoshop, Windows, or Apple Color Picker.
- Change the style of Color Picker in the **Preferences:General** submenu under the File menu.
- Select custom colors from a variety of color matching systems.

Color Correction and Image Enhancement

- Use a histogram to determine the distribution of pixels in an image.
- Adjust image brightness and contrast using the input and output scales in the Levels dialog box, by adjusting sliders in the Brightness/Contrast dialog box or by creating a new curve in the Curves dialog box.
- Use the **Auto** command in the Levels or Curves dialog box to set the white and black points automatically.
- Use the **Black** and **White Eyedropper** tools in the Levels or Curves dialog box to set white and black points automatically.
- Adjust midtones of an image with the **gamma level indicator** in Levels.
- Adjust midtones even more precisely using the **Curves** command.
- Draw a custom curve as an arbitrary map using the **Curves** command.
- Use the **Color Balance** command to change the color balance of an image.
- Use the **Hue/Saturation** command to change the hue, saturation, and lightness of an image or to colorize an image.
- Use the **Variations** command to change an image by selecting from multiple image correction possibilities.
- Use the **Invert** command to turn color or grayscale values into their exact opposites (e.g., making a negative of a positive image).
- Use the **Equalize** command to improve the contrast in an image.
- Use the **Threshold** command to turn a color or grayscale image into a high-contrast picture.
- Use the **Posterize** command to turn a color or grayscale image into a graphic with flat areas of gray or color.

Other Tools

- The **Replace Color** command can be used to replace only particular colors in an image.
- The **Selective Color** command can be used to adjust the amount of ink used to print a color.

- The **Desaturate** command changes all tones to gray without changing modes.

- The **Sponge** tool can remove color from portions of an image.

- **Quick Edit** can let you work with only a portion of a large image.

CHAPTER 16

Applying Filters to Images

In this chapter...

- How to apply and use a filter
- Artistic filters
- Blur filters
- Brush stroke filters
- Distort filters
- Noise filters
- Pixelate filters
- Render filters

- Sharpen filters
- Sketch filters
- Stylize filters
- Texture filters
- Video filters
- Other special filters
- Creating your own filters

APPLYING FILTERS TO IMAGES

Filters are the magic of Photoshop—and they're great fritterware if you want them to be. It's possible to know nothing about the program, yet apply filter after filter to an image for hours of fun and, sometimes, beauty.

So filters are fun.

But let's add a little knowledge and a direction. Filters are still fun, but now the magic really begins. Not only can you make things *look* cool, you can also add practically unimaginable special effects and enhancements to all or part of an image.

As you've seen in various chapters of this book, filters can be applied to an entire image or to only a selected part or layer of a document to blur or sharpen the image, distort it, or add other transforming special effects. Some filters are built into Photoshop, and others are plug-in modules, which must be dragged into the Plug-Ins folder in order to appear under the Filter menu. You can also purchase additional Plug-In filters from third-party vendors or obtain shareware filters from numerous sources. Some of these "after market" filters are really great.

HOW TO USE A FILTER

1. Use one of the selection tools to select part of the image to be filtered. If no area is selected, the entire file will be filtered (Figure 16.1).
2. Select a filter from the Filter menu. Some filters have dialog boxes, while others do not. If there is a dialog box, enter numerical values and/or other choices and click **OK** to apply the filter (Figure 16.2).

Figure 16.1 *The unfiltered image.*

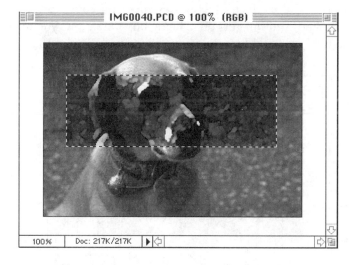

Figure 16.2 *The* **Artistic:Watercolor Filter** *has been applied to the Marqueed portion of the image.*

You can undo the effects of a filter after it has been applied simply by using the **Undo** command or pressing **Command-Z** (Mac) or **Ctrl-Z** (PC).

SHORTCUT

You can stop a filter from being applied while it is in progress. This can be helpful if you change your mind while a very slow filter is being used.

N O T E

If the Filter menu is grayed-out when you try to apply a filter, it's because you're trying to use it on an inappropriate file type. Filters can't be applied to files in 16-bit grayscale, 48-bit RGB, Bitmap mode, or indexed color mode. To apply a filter to one of these files, change the file's mode from the Image menu.

FADING A FILTER

You can "edge down" the effects of a filter by choosing **Filter:Fade** after any filter has been applied. You will get you a dialog box that allows you to adjust the opacity of the filter and add blending mode controls (Figure 16.3).

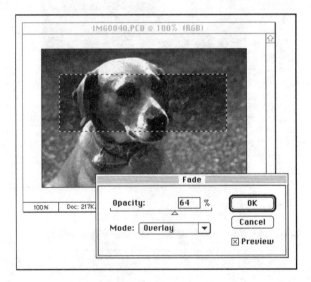

Figure 16.3 By selecting **Filter:Fade** *you can renegotiate the way the filter was applied.*

ARTISTIC FILTERS

Photoshop 4 ships with 15 Artistic filters. These filters all add a painterly quality to the images they're applied to. Almost all of them allow you to input your own parameters, and the results you get from each application will be quite different. The examples shown in Figures 16.4–16.18 should give you an idea of the range of results you can expect. Use them as a rough guide for your own work. Of course, on color images, you can expect the results to be quite a bit more striking.

Figure 16.4 Colored pencil.

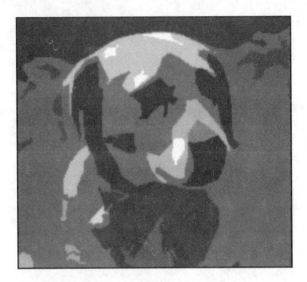

Figure 16.5 Cutout.

Figure 16.6 Dry brush.

Figure 16.7 Film grain.

Figure 16.8 Fresco.

Figure 16.9 *Neon glow.*

Figure 16.10 *Paint daubs.*

Figure 16.11 Palette knife.

Figure 16.12 Plastic wrap.

Figure 16.13 Poster edges.

Figure 16.14 Rough pastels.

Figure 16.15 *Smudge stick.*

Figure 16.16 *Sponge.*

Figure 16.17 *Underpainting.*

Figure 16.18 *Watercolor.*

BLUR FILTERS

Photoshop gives you six ways to blur an image. All can be found under the Blur submenu under the Filter menu:

- The Blur filter smoothes out an image by blurring it (Figure 16.19).

Figure 16.19 Blur.

- The Blur More filter is comparable to applying the Blur filter three or four times.
- The Gaussian Blur filter lets you select the amount of blur to apply (Figure 16.20). When you choose **Gaussian Blur**, a dialog box appears. Enter a number from 1 to 100 to determine the radius of the blur. Higher numbers provide more blurring.

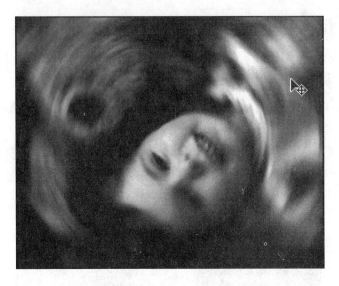

Figure 16.20 Gaussian Blur 3.0.

- The Motion Blur filter simulates the blur seen when a moving object is photographed with a slow shutter speed. To set the direction for the blur:

1. Set the angle degree (–90° to +90°) as a numerical value or change the angle by rotating the diameter line in the circle.

2. Set the distance of the blur (values can range from 1 to 999).

3. Paste a copy of the image back on top of the blur and tinker with the composite controls. The Motion Blur can completely obliterate the image.

- The Radial Blur filter creates two kinds of soft blur around a central point (Figure 16.21). The **Spin** option blurs the image as though it is being spun around a central axis. The **Zoom** option blurs the image as though taking a photograph while moving a zoom lens. The higher the number entered in Amount, the greater the blurred effect. Click and drag the dot in the Blur center box to reposition the center of the blur.

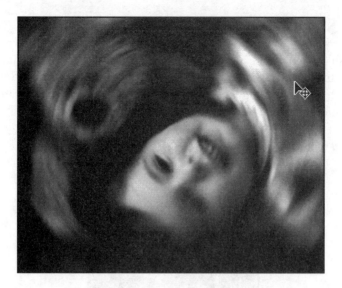

Figure 16.21 Radial Blur.

• The Smart Blur is entirely configurable (Figure 16.22).

Figure 16.22 Smart Blur.

BRUSH STROKE FILTERS

Eight Brush Stroke filters again give you the option to add a painterly, artistic dimension to your images. Most can be configured in several different ways. The examples shown in Figures 16.23–16.30 are just a rough indicator of what you can achieve.

Figure 16.23 The original image.

Figure 16.24 Accented edges.

Figure 16.25 *Crosshatch.*

Figure 16.26 *Dark strokes.*

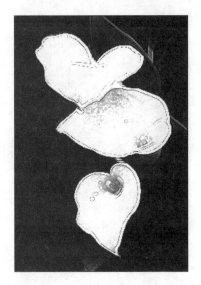

Figure 16.27 Ink outlines.

Figure 16.28 Spatter.

Figure 16.29 Sprayed strokes.

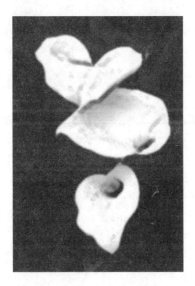

Figure 16.30 Sumi-e.

DISTORT FILTERS

The Distort filters change the geometry of the image, bending and shaping it into a new form.

The Pinch filter squeezes the image inward or outward, depending upon whether the percentage of pinch is a positive or negative value. A positive value (up to 100%) pinches the image inward; a negative value (down to −100%) expands it outward.

The Polar Coordinates filter distorts an image or a selection from rectangular to polar coordinates or from polar coordinates to rectangular.

The Ripple filter creates ripples on the surface of an image or a selected part of an image. Enter values from 1 to 999 in the Amount box (in the Ripple Filter dialog box) to set the size of the ripples. Set the ripple frequency as small, medium, or large.

The Shear filter lets you distort the image according to a curve that you drag in the Shear Filter dialog box. When you select **Shear** from the Distort submenu, the dialog box shows a graph with a single line in the center. Drag on this line to create a distortion curve. Choose **Wrap Edge Pixels** to wrap the image to fill the area left vacant when the image is distorted. Choose **Repeat Edge Pixels** to fill the empty area with more pixels of the same color or grayscale value.

The Spherize filter distorts an image as though it was wrapped around a sphere. The numerical value you enter in the Amount box (in the Spherize dialog box) determines the amount of spherization. Values can range from −100 to +100. The filter will be applied in the direction specified: normal, horizontal only, or vertical only.

The Twirl filter twirls the image around a central point. Parts closer to the center are twirled more.

The Wave filter performs a similar function to the Ripple filter. However, the Wave filter gives you more creative possibilities:

- You can have from 1 to 999 wave generators.
- The *wavelength* is the distance from one wave crest to the next wave crest. The maximum and minimum can be any number from 1 to 9999.
- A sine wave is a periodic, smooth, rolling wave. A square wave changes instantly in amplitude, resulting in a square form. A triangular wave has a triangular form. To see the difference between these waves, create a

new RGB or grayscale file and draw a single horizontal black line on a white background. Apply each of the wave shapes.

- The horizontal and vertical scale amount can vary from –9999% to 9999% percent.

- Refer back to the Shear filter for a description of how undefined areas can be filled (wraparound versus repeat edge pixels).

The Zigzag filter creates the effect of ripples in a pond (although only one of the dialog box options actually bears that name). To use the Zigzag filter:

1. Set the Amount of distortion—it can range from +999 to –999.

2. Ridges indicates the number of times the zigzag reverses direction from the start at the center of the image to the outer edge.

3. Choose **Pond Ripples** to displace the image to the upper-left-hand or lower-right-hand corner, depending upon whether a positive or negative value is entered for the amount of distortion. Choose **Out from Center** to displace the image outward (with a positive amount value) or inward (with a negative amount value). The **Around Center** option displaces the image around the center, moving it clockwise or counterclockwise, depending upon whether the amount is positive or negative.

The Displace filter is the most complex of the distort filters. It uses the brightness values in one file (a displacement map) to indicate how the pixels in the target image will be moved to create a distorted effect. The files do not have to be the same size or resolution or even the same mode for this to work. In fact, a color displacement map can be used on a grayscale file, although a bitmap file cannot be a displacement map because it does not have 256 brightness levels. The displacement map can be anything: a gradient, a pattern, even a photograph. When the pixels in the displacement map have a value of 0, there is maximum negative displacement. A value of 255 produces maximum positive displacement, and a value of 128 (a midtone gray) produces no displacement at all. When a map has more than one channel, the first channel affects the horizontal displacement, and the second affects the vertical displacement. When there is only one channel, the displacement takes place along a line that expresses the ratio between the vertical and horizontal displacement.

Use the Displace filter in this way:

1. Open a file that you want to distort with the Displace filter (Figure 16.31).

Figure 16.31 The original image.

2. Select **Displace** from the Distort submenu of the Filter menu. A dialog box will appear.

3. Change the horizontal and vertical scale to determine the magnitude of the displacement. When both scale factors are 100%, the displacement cannot be more than 128 pixels. We've set both factors in this case to 50%.

4. When the displacement map and image to be filtered are not identical in size (which is usually the case), you can decide how the map will be modified to fit the image. It can be stretched to fit or tiled, which means repeated over and over again like a pattern. Undefined areas will be filled by wrapping the image around the opposite side(s) of the window or by repeating edge pixels, as explained earlier. When you've made your settings, click **OK**. An Open File dialog box will appear.

5. Select an Adobe-provided displacement map from the Displacement Maps folder in your Plug-Ins folder. Click **Open**. (You can also create your own displacement maps.) After filtering with the map, the image changes. Figures 16.32–16.38 show some possibilities.

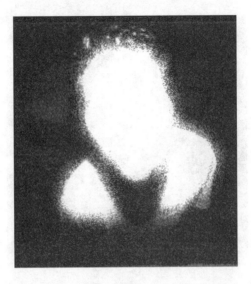

Figure 16.32 Diffuse glow.

Figure 16.33 Displacement (with Mezzotint displacement map).

Figure 16.34 *Glass.*

Figure 16.35 *Pinch.*

Figure 16.36 *Ripple.*

Figure 16.37 *Shear.*

Figure 16.38 Twirl.

NOISE FILTERS

Noise filters modify an image by adding pixels with randomly distributed color values. Noise filters can be used as a basis for interesting textured backgrounds, or they can blur an image.

The Add Noise filter gives a grainy appearance, depending upon how much noise is added (Figures 16.39 and 16.40). When you select the **Add Noise** filter, the Add Noise dialog box lets you determine the amount of noise (32 is the default). This noise can be added uniformly throughout the image (**Uniform** option) or distributed along a bell-shaped curve (**Gaussian** option).

Figure 16.39 *The original image.*

Figure 16.40 *Add noise.*

The Despeckle filter finds areas in an image in which color changes occur and blur all parts of the image except those areas. Despeckle is often used on video frame grabs to reduce noise and smooth out the appearance of the image.

The Dust and Scratches filter can be used to obscure physical defects in the image, such as dust artifacts or scratches on the original scanned print or the negative it was made from. A Threshold slider and preview lets you examine the defective area of your image and see how it will be affected before applying the filter.

The Median filter is also useful for noise removal. The brightness values of adjacent pixels are averaged, which causes the image to blur.

PIXELATE FILTERS

Use the Pixelate filters to give an image an impressionistic or painterly effect.

The Color Halftone filter makes the image look as though it was printed with an oversized halftone screen (shades of Andy Warhol). Each channel of the image is divided into rectangles, and these rectangles are subsequently replaced with circles of varying size, depending upon the brightness of the original rectangle (Figures 16.41 and 16.42).

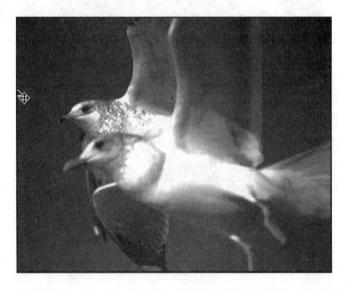

Figure 16.41 *The original image.*

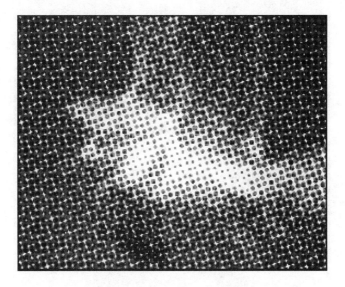

Figure 16.42 *Color halftone.*

In the Color Halftone dialog box, enter values of 4 to 127 for the maximum radius of the dot. Select a screen angle (the angle of the dot from true horizontal) for each channel. (An RGB image will have three channels, a CMYK image will have four, and a Grayscale image will have only one.)

The Crystallize, Mosaic, and Facet filters break the image up into small cells after gathering pixels with similar color values together.

Using the Crystallize filter, the cell size can be from 3 to 999 pixels and will have a polygon shape (Figure 16.43).

The Mosaic filter breaks the image into square blocks. The cell size can be set from 2 to 64 pixels (Figure 16.44).

The Facet filter breaks the image into groups of similarly colored pixels.

The Fragment, Mezzotint, and Pointillize filters further modify your image by breaking it up into additional patterns (Figures 16.45–16.47). Your best bet with any of these is to try them out for yourself to see the effects they produce.

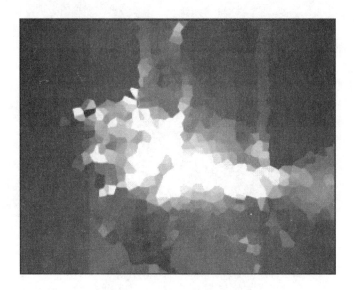

Figure 16.43 Crystallize.

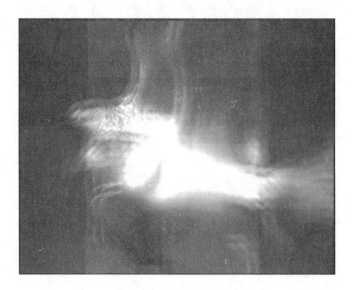

Figure 16.44 Fragment.

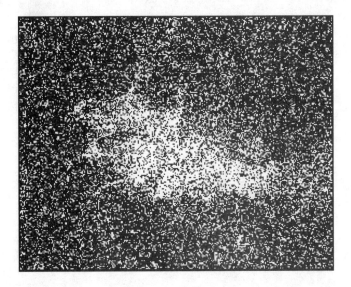

Figure 16.45 *Mezzotint.*

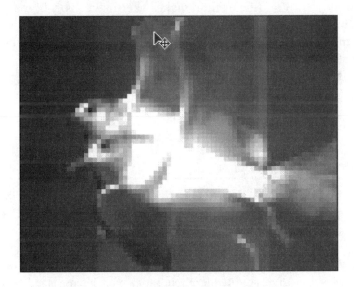

Figure 16.46 *Mosaic.*

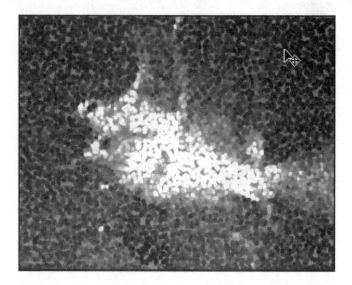

Figure 16.47 Pointillize.

For example, the Pointillize filter makes the image look like a pointillist (French impressionist) painting, created with a pattern of small dots. The background color of the canvas will appear between the dots. Cell width can vary from 3 to 999 pixels.

The Fragment filter copies an image four times and lays the copies back down, each one offset from the other. It reminds me of the effect you get when you shake the camera while taking a picture.

RENDER FILTERS

Render filters make some startling changes to your image. The Clouds filter produces quick and dirty (and quite realistic) cloud effects in a selected area (Figures 16.48 and 16.49).

NOTE

Want still more boffo clouds? Try holding down **Option** (Mac) or **Alt** (PC) while choosing **Filter:Render:Clouds** for a more intense cloud pattern.

The Difference Clouds filter calculates its cloud effects based on the underlying image, producing a partial reversal of some parts of the image (Figure 16.50).

Figure 16.48 *The original image.*

Figure 16.49 *Clouds.*

Figure 16.50 Difference Clouds.

The Lens Flare filter simulates the effect of a bright light (like the sun) shining into the lens (Figure 16.51). In the Lens Flare dialog box, the brightness can vary from 10% to 300%.

Figure 16.51 Lens Flare.

The Lighting Effects filter allows you to place and manipulate lights as if you were in a photographic studio. It's easy to create some amazing lighting effects with this filter

The Texture Fill filter lets you fill a selection with a texture based on a Photoshop 2.5 or 3.0 grayscale file, which is applied to the image as a background texture.

SHARPEN FILTERS

The Sharpen filters work the same way the Sharpen tool does—they increase contrast between adjacent pixels, which makes a blurry image look sharper (Figures 16.52 and 16.53).

Figure 16.52 The original image.

Figure 16.53 Sharpen.

The Sharpen and Sharpen More filters make an image seem more in focus. Be careful that you do not oversharpen an image, as this can create an unnatural appearance. Sharpen More can bring out more detail in the image.

The Sharpen Edges filter examines a file looking for areas of abrupt color transitions. These "edges," not the entire image, are then sharpened.

The Unsharp Mask filter also serves to sharpen an image (Figure 16.54). The unfortunate choice of name makes it sound as though it is going to unsharpen (blur) the image, but in fact it makes a soft-focus image look crisper. When we grab video frames, we sometimes apply the Median filter to remove noise and then apply the Unsharp Mask filter to increase edge contrast. The Unsharp Mask filter is also useful for processing scanned artwork.

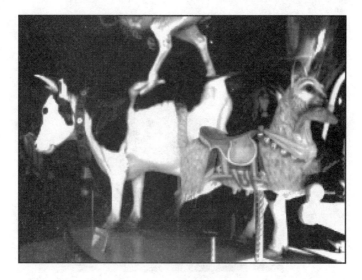

Figure 16.54 Unsharp Mask.

In the Unsharp Mask dialog box, you will adjust the amount, radius, and threshold of the filter:

- The Amount can vary from 1% to 500%—the larger the number, the stronger the effect.

- The Radius value refers to the area around edge pixels. Radius values can range from 0.1 to 100 pixels. The larger the radius, the more pixels away from the edges will be affected. A lower radius number means that only the edges will be sharpened.

- The Threshold value specifies the amount of contrast (differentiation in brightness) that must exist between adjacent pixels before the edge is sharpened. The threshold value is expressed as a level, from 0 to 255. When the threshold is set to a low level, it means that little contrast is needed for the effect to be applied, so therefore, the effect of the filter will be more noticeable.

SKETCH FILTERS

These are more happy painterly filters. These filters mainly add the types of effects one would get with a pencil-based medium. Figures 16.55–16.68 show a few examples.

Figure 16.55 *The original image.*

Figure 16.56 *Bas Relief.*

Figure 16.57 Chalk and Charcoal.

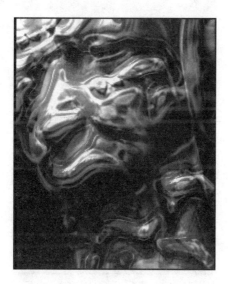

Figure 16.58 Chrome.

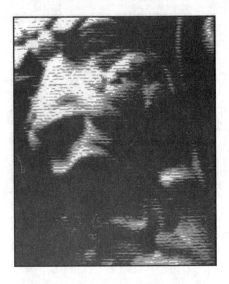

Figure 16.59 Conte Crayon.

Figure 16.60 Graphic Pen.

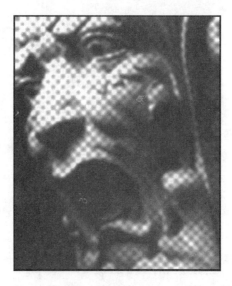

Figure 16.61 *Halftone Pattern.*

Figure 16.62 *Notepaper.*

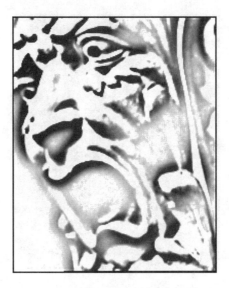

Figure 16.63 Photocopy.

Figure 16.64 Plaster.

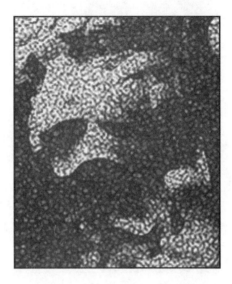

Figure 16.65 Reticulation.

Figure 16.66 Stamp.

Figure 16.67 *Torn Edges.*

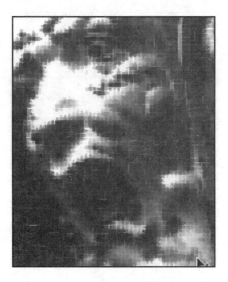

Figure 16.68 *Water Paper.*

STYLIZE FILTERS

Stylize filters produce additional effects.

The Diffuse filter randomly moves the pixels within a selected area so that the image appears broken up and in softer focus (Figures 16.69 and 16.70). The Normal option in the Diffuse Filter dialog box moves the pixels without regard to their color value. The **Darken Only** option replaces light pixels with darker pixels when the filter is applied. The **Lighten Only** option replaces dark pixels with lighter pixels when the filter is applied.

Figure 16.69 *The original image.*

Figure 16.70 Diffuse.

The Emboss filter makes an image appear to be either raised or stamped (Figure 16.71). To demonstrate the effect, add your initials in black type to a white background. Deselect the floating type. Select **Emboss** from the Stylize submenu of the Filter menu. Set the angle to 150°. (A positive number will create an embossed effect. A negative number will create a stamped effect.) Set the height of the emboss to 5 pixels—the higher the pixel amount, the more raised (or lowered) the effect. Finally, set the Amount—values can range from 1% to 500%.

The Extrude filter turns a selected area into a cluster of objects, each with a three-dimensional appearance (Figure 16.72). These block-like objects can have a pyramidal or four-sided appearance. In the Extrude dialog box, the Size box determines the length of an object's base and the Depth box determines how far an object seems to stick up. You can choose to have the objects protrude at random heights, regardless of the brightness of the original image (**Random** option), or you can choose to have the brighter parts of the image protrude more than darker parts (**Level-Based** option).

Figure 16.71 Emboss.

Figure 16.72 Extrude.

The Find Edges filter locates edges in an image (areas with noticeable changes in brightness as in Figure 16.73 where the white hibiscus meets the dark foliage) and outlines them with black.

Figure 16.73 Find Edges.

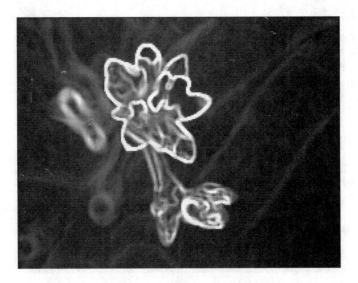

Figure 16.74 Glowing Edges.

The Trace Contour filter also seeks the areas of brightness change and outlines them thinly (Figure 16.75). When the Trace Contour dialog box opens,

enter a number from 0 to 255 to set the threshold level for tracing. In addition, you can determine whether the upper or lower edge is traced.

Figure 16.75 Solarize.

The Solarize filter blends a negative and positive version of the image, which is nice for exotic effects (Figure 16.76).

Figure 16.76 Tiles.

The Tiles filter sounds as though it's the same as the Mosaic filter, but it's quite different. The Mosaic filter groups similarly colored pixels into square blocks and colors each cluster according to the dominant color of the group (Figure 16.77). The Tiles filter simply breaks up the image into pieces like a jigsaw puzzle. You can determine the number of tiles (in any direction) the image will be broken into as well as the maximum offset for each of the pieces. The empty spaces can be filled with either background or foreground color or the original image or an inverse of the original image.

The Wind filter places small horizontal lines in the image to make it appear as though it's being blown (Figure 16.78). The Wind effect is the mildest. Blast and Stagger represent increasing intensities.

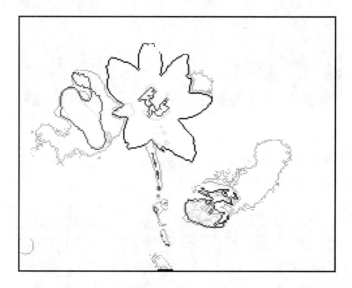

Figure 16.77 *Trace Contour.*

Figure 16.78 Wind.

TEXTURE FILTERS

Six texturizing filters let you add textures to your image. Figures 16.79–16.83 show a few examples of what these filters can do.

Figure 16.79 The original image.

Figure 16.80 Craquelure.

Figure 16.81 Grain.

Figure 16.82 Mosaic Tiles.

Figure 16.83 Patchwork.

VIDEO FILTERS

These filters were created specifically for use in video applications, although you could certainly use them on any image for artistic effect.

The NTSC Colors filter, when applied to a color image, restricts the range of colors to those that are preferred for television use. When colors are too saturated, they tend to bleed. You might see this from time to time when someone who wears bright red clothing on TV looks like a fuzzy tomato. Rather than desaturating an entire image using the **Hue/Saturation** command, you can apply the NTSC Colors filter on a file before exporting it to videotape.

The De-Interlace filter removes either odd or even scan lines from a video frame grab.

OTHER (SPECIAL) FILTERS

The Custom filter, which you can design to suit your needs, allows you to change a central pixel and surrounding pixels according to parameters, which you set. When you open the Custom dialog box, you see a grid of boxes (Figure 16.84). You will enter different values in these boxes to create the filter.

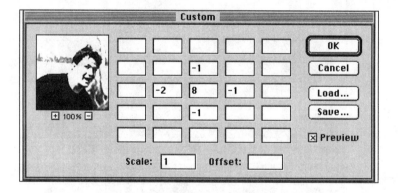

Figure 16.84 *Custom dialog box.*

- In the center box, enter a number from –999 to +999. This represents the number by which a pixel's brightness will be multiplied.

- There are eight boxes immediately adjacent to the central box. These boxes represent pixels above, below, to the right and left, and diagonally adjacent to the central pixel. The default filter places a value of 5 in the center, surrounded by –1s above, below, and on the right and left sides. When you apply this filter, the image is sharpened. Try changing the negative ones to positive ones—the image will look overexposed like a bad photocopy. Press **Command-Z** (Mac) or **Ctrl-Z** (PC) to undo.

Reset the values to the default and try changing only the far left –1 to a –2 (Figure 16.85). The result will look similar to an inverted version of an image processed with the Find Edges filter.

Figure 16.85 *Custom filter applied to image.*

For additional information on the mathematics of setting the scale and offset values, see the Adobe Photoshop *User's Guide.*

The High Pass filter looks for the highlights and brightest areas in an image and emphasizes them. Values for the pixel radius can be between 0.1 and 100; the lower the number, the stronger the filter effect.

Keep a notebook or word processing document in which you record your Photoshop experiments. You never know when you'll need to dig up a particularly dazzling or time-saving effect.

NOTE

The Maximum and Minimum filters are helpful when you want to modify a mask (alpha) channel. The Minimum filter enlarges black areas and reduces white areas. The Maximum filter does just the opposite: it enlarges white areas and reduces black areas. In trapping terms, the Minimum filter is like a spread, and the Maximum filter is like a choke.

The Offset filter moves an image a specified amount horizontally and vertically, depending upon the values you indicate in the Offset Filter dialog box. The image can be moved plus or minus 30,000 pixels in either the horizontal or vertical direction.

The part of the image that is vacated can be filled in three different ways:

- It can be filled with the background color (Set to Background).
- It can be filled with pixels from the opposite side of the image (Wrap Around).
- It can be filled with repeating pixels (Repeat Edge Pixels). If the image is being moved only to the right, the vacated area would be filled with a repetition of the pixels on the left-hand edge of the moved area.

USING THIRD-PARTY FILTERS

Photoshop comes with an wonderful range of plug-in filters that can certainly keep you going creatively for a long time. Adobe has also cleverly planned it so that third-party vendors can develop additional filters. These filters can be added to Photoshop easily; simply drag them into your Plug-Ins folder.

The larger the file size, the longer it takes Photoshop filters to be applied. Some third-party vendors have developed faster versions of Photoshop's most frequently used filters. Daystar Corporation offers accelerated filters such as Unsharp Mask, Gaussian Blur, Blur, Blur More, Sharpen, Sharpen More, and High Pass. These filters are used in conjunction with Charger, Daystar's Photoshop acceleration board.

WHAT YOU'VE LEARNED

- Use filters to apply special effects to a selected part of an image or to the entire image.

- Use the Artistic filters to make the image appear as though it were created in another medium.
- Use the Blur filters to make the image appear in softer focus.
- Use the Brush Strokes filters to give your image a painterly look.
- Use the Distort filters to change the shape of the image.
- Use the Noise filters to blur or change the texture of an image.
- Use the Pixelate filters to beautifully alter the pixels.
- Use the Render filters for different painterly effects.
- Use the Sharpen filters to bring the image into sharper focus.
- Use the Sketch filters to give your images a "hand-done" look.
- Use the Stylize filters to make an image look painted, to modify contrast, or to define and process "found" edges in an image.
- Use the Texture filters to alter the images textural appearance.
- Use the Video filters to import images from video into Photoshop and export Photoshop images to videotape.
- Create, save, and load custom filters to change an image to fit to your specific needs.

CHAPTER 17

Channel Calculations

In this chapter...

- Using channel calculations
- Duplicate calculation
- Constant calculation
- Lighter and darker calculations
- Add and subtract calculations
- Difference and multiply calculation
- Screen and blend calculation
- Composite calculation

WHAT ARE CHANNEL CALCULATIONS?

To delve into everything that you can do with channel calculations in combination with each other could be the subject of a book in itself. This chapter is offered as a brief introduction with a few simple exercises. After that, you're on your own to practice and experiment, both with combining channels or layers within a single document and merging them between documents.

You've learned in earlier chapters that a *channel* is where information is stored. In Photoshop, separate layers can contain their own channels. There are three channels in an RGB image or layer (Figure 17.1), four in a CMYK image, three in a lab image, and so forth. In addition, of course, there are mask (alpha) channels, where you can store selection borders and masks.

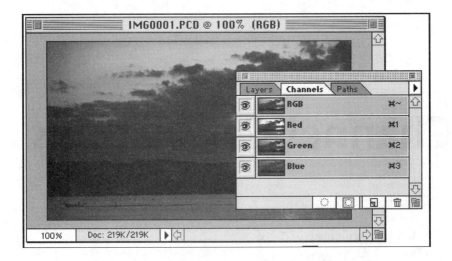

Figure 17.1 An RGB image and its channels.

Channels can also be added, duplicated, composited, blended, and combined in a variety of ways to create special effects. All the possibilities are listed under the **Image:Calculations** and **Image:Apply Image...** submenus.

The Calculate dialog box lets you combine channels or layers from one existing image. The Apply Image dialog box lets you merge channels or layers from two images. Both work in a similar way: you select the source document/channel/layer and the target document/channel/layer and then specify how corresponding pixels in each will interact to produce the result pixel in the finished image. You can use all the merging modes discussed in earlier chapters, such as Lighter, Darker, and Screen. We'll use some of the simpler modes in this chapter to introduce channel calculations.

ABOUT CHANNEL CALCULATIONS

It will come as no surprise that Photoshop accomplishes painterly effects by performing math functions based on pixel brightness in one or more of the channels being manipulated. Some calculations involve only one channel, others involve two channels or two channels plus a mask from one of the channels. Whenever you use a channel calculation that involves two or more channels, the channels must be of exactly the same size and dimension in pixels. Unless the source channels are the same size, Photoshop cannot compare pixels because they are in the same location in both files.

Although each type of calculation has its own requirements, you will generally do the following:

1. Select one or more source images, masks, or both using the pop-up menus provided in the Calculations or Apply Image dialog boxes.
2. Enter any additional values required, such as offset values, or indicate other "specials" such as Invert.
3. Select a destination file. (Most of the time, this will probably be **New** because you don't want to replace and therefore wipe out information in an existing channel.)
4. Click **OK** to carry out the calculation.

In the next section, we will introduce several of the key channel calculations with easy exercises that show how they operate. Although channel operations can be used to create extremely sophisticated graphics, these demonstrations are deliberately "no-frills" so that you can see how the calculations operate in their purest form.

EXERCISE 17.1: CHANNEL CALCULATIONS

Duplicate Calculation

The Duplicate calculation duplicates the information in one channel and places it in another channel. This can be a new or existing channel. Use Duplicate to copy a mask from one document into a new channel in another document. You can also use Duplicate to create an extra copy of an image when you want to experiment with different effects but don't want to harm the original. When you duplicate an RGB image, all three component channels are copied, but associated alpha channels are not copied. These channels must be duplicated separately into the new document. Using the Duplicate calculation is the fastest way to make a copy of a document:

1. Create an all-white RGB image, 200 pixels x 200 pixels square. A resolution of 72 ppi is fine.

2. Type a large solid black *O*. Pick a bold font; we used 220 point Adobe Garamond. Save the file in Photoshop format as **Original O** (Figure 17.2).

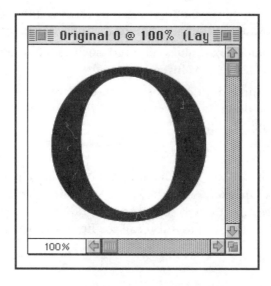

Figure 17.2 Original O.

3. Select **Duplicate** from the Image menu.

4. When the Duplicate dialog box appears, enter a new name for the copy. Click **OK**.

5. A second document that is identical to the first will be created. Save this file, naming it **Dupe O** (Figure 17.3).

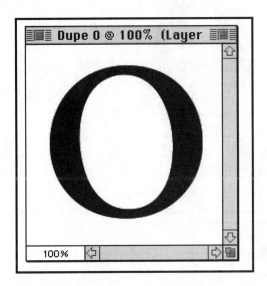

Figure 17.3 Dupe O.

Lighter and Darker Calculations

The Lighter calculation compares the pixel brightness values of two channels, makes a copy of whichever pixels are lighter, and places the copy into a destination channel. To demonstrate:

1. Create a new RGB document, 200 pixels square.

2. Use the Photoshop Color palette to create a gray color in which the pixels in each of the R, G, and B channels have a brightness of 150 (150, 150, 150). Fill the image with this color and save the document as **150 Gray**.

3. Choose the **Lighter...** command from the Apply Image submenu. Set Source as **Dupe 0**, and set the target as **150 Gray**. If you click the **Preview** box, you'll be able to see the effects immediately (Figure 17.4).

Figure 17.4 *Lighter dialog box and preview of 150 Gray.*

4. The file will contain a gray *O* with a brightness value of 150 against a pure white background. When Photoshop compared the two files, the white background in **Dupe O** was brightest (255 versus 150), so it was placed in the destination file. However, for pixels the area of the black *O*, the gray (150) was brighter than the black (0), so in this area the gray pixels were placed in the destination. Save this new file as **Gray O** (Figure 17.5).

For practice, follow the same procedure and use the same files to create a new channel based on the Darker calculation. Your image will be a black *O* on a gray (150) background.

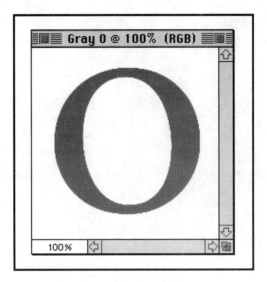

Figure 17.5 Gray O.

Add and Subtract Calculations

The Add and Subtract calculations allow you to add the pixel values of two files, placing the sum (or difference) in a destination file:

1. Create a new RGB file, 200 pixels x 200 pixels. Use the Rectangular Marquee tool to select the vertical left half of the image. Fill the selected area with solid black. Fill the right side of the image with a lighter gray in which all R, G, and B pixels have a brightness of 128. Name this file **Black/128 Gray** (Figure 17.6).

2. Select **Add...** from the Apply Image submenu. When the Add dialog box appears, select **150 gray**, **RGB channel** as the source. The target will be **Black/128 Gray**, **RGB channel**. The destination should be a new document with a new channel. Leave the scale at the default of **1**, with an offset of 0. Click **OK**.

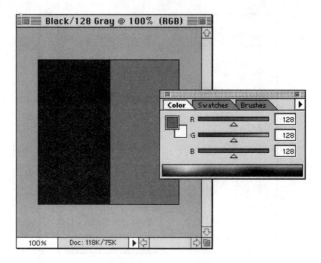

Figure 17.6 *Black/128 Gray.*

3. The combined file will also appear to be divided in half. The left side will have a gray level of 150 because it is the sum of gray (150) from Source 11 and black (0) from Source 2. The right side will be white because it is the sum of gray (150) from Source 1 and gray (128) from Source 2. The sum of these brightness values is actually more than 255, but it is represented as 255, white. Save this new file as **150 Gray/White** (Figure 17.7).

For practice, follow the same procedure with the **Subtract...** command. When a Subtraction calculation results in a negative value, a black pixel (0 brightness) is placed in the destination.

For technical remarks regarding the Add and Subtract equations and the use of the Scale and Offset factors, see the documentation that came with your Photoshop application.

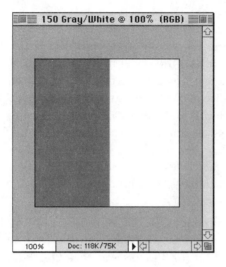

Figure 17.7 *150 Gray/White.*

Difference Calculation

Use the Difference calculation to create a new file based on the difference in pixel brightness between two channels:

1. Create a new RGB file 200 pixels x 200 pixels and fill it completely with white. Save and name this file **All White**.

2. Select **Difference…** from the Apply Image submenu. When the dialog box opens, select **All White** as the source and **150 gray** as the target. Click **OK**.

3. All the R, G, and B pixels in the new file will have a value of 105—the difference between Source 1 (255) and Source 2 (150).

Whenever the difference in a Difference calculation turns out to be a negative number (e.g., –60), Photoshop ignores the negative sign and creates pixels in the destination file using the absolute value of the difference (60).

Multiply Calculation

The Multiply calculation multiplies the brightness values of the pixels in each of two channels and divides the result by a constant (255), which is the greatest possible pixel brightness. The effect of multiplying one channel by another is like looking at two slide transparencies together in a slide viewer. What you can do with this and other calculations is really limitless. Here we'll demonstrate one possible application:

1. Duplicate your starting image, **Original O**, by clicking the **Invert** button in the Duplicate dialog box before clicking **OK**. Name this new document as **Inverted O**.

2. Select all (**Command-A** on the Mac, **Ctrl-A** on the PC) of the **Inverted O** file and select **Gaussian Blur** from the Blur submenu of the Filter menu. Set the blur for **3** pixels and click **OK**.

3. Using the Rectangular Marquee tool, drag a square around the blurred white inverted *O*. Move the *O* 3 pixels to the right and 3 pixels down by using the keyboard directional arrows. Deselect the selection. Save the change you've made to **Inverted O** by pressing **Command-S** (Mac) or **Ctrl-S** (PC).

4. Select **Multiply...**. Set **Original O** as the source and **Inverted O** as the target. Click **OK**. Your completed image will be a black *O* with a glowing white drop shadow.

5. Save the file as **White Shadow O**.

Screen Calculation

Just as the Multiply calculation is similar to sandwiching and projecting light through two positive transparencies, the screen calculation is like sandwiching and printing two photographic negatives.

1. Select **Screen...**.

2. When the dialog box opens, select **Original O** as the source and **Inverted O** as the target. Click **OK**.

3. Your new document will look like a white 3-D donut. Name the file **White 3D Donut**.

More Uses for the Apply Image Command

I use this command all the time when I want to make a simple change to a finished image. It allows me to keep individual portions of an image in separate documents and then combine them to create the final image. To make a change, just go back to the original documents, modify them, and then combine them using **Apply Image...**.

WHAT YOU'VE LEARNED

- Use the Calculate commands to combine images from more than one channel.

- Use **Duplicate...** to make either an exact copy of an image or an inverted copy.

- Use **Constant...** to fill a document with a shade of gray.

- Use **Add...** and **Subtract...** to add or subtract pixel values in two different channels, putting the result into a destination channel. A scale amount can be used to average pixels, and an offset value can be added to lighten or darken the new image.

- Use the **Lighter...** and **Darker...** commands to compare pixel values in two channels, putting a copy of the lighter or darker pixels into a destination channel.

- Use the **Difference...** calculation to compare the pixel values in two channels, putting the difference into a destination channel.

- Use **Multiply...** and **Screen...** to create special effects by manipulating the pixels in the two source channels.

CHAPTER 18

Image Conversion and Duotones

In this chapter...

- Image conversion
- Color tables
- Creating duotones, tritones, and quadtones

415

This chapter will discuss the different Photoshop image types and ways that you can convert images from one type to another. To review the differences between RGB, CMYK, and other image types, see Chapter 15.

IMAGE CONVERSION

Unless you plan to work exclusively in RGB mode (e.g., if you're creating only color images for multimedia or video output), you need to learn to convert images from one image type to another so that they can be printed or published on the Web. If a lot of your work is output-based, the most common conversion you will encounter will be to change images from RGB mode to CMYK mode. When you perform this conversion, the colors that are expressed in terms of their red, green, and blue channel components are first converted to three channels of luminance, an *a* component, and a *b* component in the lab mode. They are then converted into the four channels of the CMYK mode—cyan, magenta, yellow, and black.

Remember that because you're converting from an additive color mode to a subtractive mode, the colors will not be exactly the same, and there's no going back once values have been changed. Always keep a copy of your original file before you do an intermode conversion. That way, if you don't like the results, you can begin again.

Converting an image from one mode to another is easy: you simply select the new mode from fly-out menu found under **Image:Mode** (Figure 18.1). The only exception to this is when you convert an image to the indexed color mode, in which case you have a number of different options.

Figure 18.1 *Selecting a new mode.*

IMAGE MODES

Table 18.1 lists the modes available when you select **Image:Modes**.

Table 18.1 Image Modes at a Glance

Bitmap	Smallest amount of information per pixel. Since most of Photoshop's tools are not available to bitmapped images, you're more likely to be converting from bitmap than to it.
Grayscale	Useful for converting a color photo into a high-quality black and white image.
Indexed Color	Most useful when you are working with a limited number of colors (e.g., in preparing images for the World Wide Web).
RGB	The Photoshop default for new images. This is the way your monitor "sees."
CMYK Mode	Cyan-magenta-yellow-black: the colors required for process printing. Converting to CMYK creates a color separation and is the last step before output for traditional printing.
Lab Mode	Even though you'll probably never use Lab color, it's a good thing to know about because it's the color method Photoshop uses to convert documents.

Table 18.1 Image Modes at a Glance (continued)

Multichannel   Another one you probably won't need, but it's good to have. If you
were to convert a duotone for printing in Scitex CT, you would use
Multichannel mode.

If you are preparing a file for eventual output, you are best served doing any
required editing in RGB and then converting to CMYK as the last prepress step
before it leaves your computer.

N O T E

CONVERTING AN IMAGE TO THE BITMAPPED MODE

Bitmapped images contain the smallest amount of information per pixel—only one black or white bit. Bitmapped images cannot be edited with most of Photoshop's tools. The image can be inverted, flipped horizontally and vertically, and rotated in 90° and 180° preset directions, but free transform, effects, and other commands, including filters, are not available (they appear grayed-out on the menu). To get a bitmapped look and have access to all of Photoshop's tricks, convert an image to bitmapped mode and then convert it back to grayscale again (or onward to RGB), where you can filter and rotate to your heart's content.

Recall that a grayscale image contains 8 bits per pixel and can represent 256 levels of gray. However, a bitmapped image has only 1 bit per pixel, which represents only black or white. During the conversion process, Photoshop lets you decide how each of the 8-bit pixels should be handled. The look of the image depends upon the conversion option you choose. In general, conversion progresses like this:

1. With the grayscale image open, choose **Bitmap** from the Mode menu.
2. When the Bitmap dialog box appears (Figure 18.2), set the output resolution.

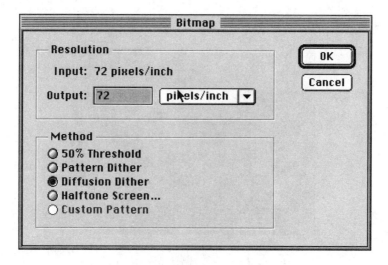

Figure 18.2 Bitmap dialog box.

3. Select the conversion method, and click **OK**.

BITMAP CONVERSION METHODS

Photoshop gives you five bitmapped conversion methods to choose from, each with a distinctive look.

50% Threshold

You'll recognize this feature from the **Threshold** command introduced earlier. When a grayscale image is converted using this method, all pixels with a value over 128 are turned into white pixels; those below 128 are converted to black pixels (Figure 18.3).

Figure 18.3 50% threshold conversion.

Pattern Dither

The gray levels in the image are converted using a pattern that looks vaguely similar to a cross-stitched sampler (Figure 18.4).

Figure 18.4 Pattern dither conversion.

Diffusion Dither

The diffusion dither evaluates and converts grayscale pictures in such a way as to reduce the amount of error inherent in image conversion. The soft, diffused effect makes this conversion method a favorite—it is reminiscent of a mezzotint (Figure 18.5).

Figure 18.5 Diffusion dither conversion.

Halftone Screen...

Using this option, you can convert a grayscale image to bitmapped mode and make it look as though it were prepared with a halftone screen:

1. With a grayscale image open, select **Bitmap...** from the **Image:Mode** menu to begin the conversion.

2. When the Bitmap dialog box appears, select **Halftone Screen...**.

3. The Halftone Screen dialog box will open (Figure 18.6). Choose **lines per inch** or **lines per centimeter** and enter a number for the screen frequency. Your printer can advise you of the correct frequency for the publication.

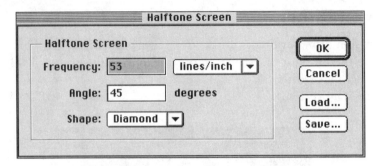

Figure 18.6 Halftone Screen dialog box.

4. Enter a number for the angle of the screen. Although screen angles can vary from −180° to +180°, 45° is customary for most halftone screens.

5. Select the shape of the halftone dot. Choices include **Round, Diamond, Ellipse, Line, Square,** and **Cross.** Click **OK.** The sample image was processed at 133 lines per inch (lpi), with a 45° screen in a line pattern (Figure 18.7).

Figure 18.7 Halftone Screen conversion.

6. You can save these halftone screen settings for future use. They can be convenient if you plan to process a batch of images.

Custom Pattern

You can also define a custom pattern and use it as a simulated halftone screen:

1. From the File menu, open the **Brushes and Patterns** folder that came with Photoshop. Inside this folder, find **PostScript Patterns** and open it. Select one of the patterns and click **Open**. I chose **Intricate Surface**. A small patterned square will appear.

2. Choose **Select All** and choose **Define Pattern** from the Edit menu.

3. With your grayscale image open, choose **Bitmap....** Then choose **Custom Pattern** in the dialog box, and click **OK**. The grayscale will be converted and the pattern applied (Figure 18.8). You can also use this technique with custom patterns that you create.

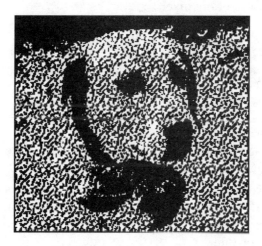

Figure 18.8 *Custom pattern conversion.*

CONVERTING IMAGES TO GRAYSCALE MODE

Both bitmapped and color images can be converted to grayscale.

Converting Bitmapped Images to Grayscale

1. With your bitmapped image file open, select **Grayscale** from the Mode menu. You'll see a Grayscale dialog box asking for a size ratio, which is a ratio for scaling down the image.

2. Enter a ratio of **1** to keep the image at the same size. A ratio of 2 makes the converted image half the size.

Converting Color to Grayscale

All the color information in an image is discarded when you convert an image from color to grayscale. The only information that remains is the grayscale level (i.e., luminosity) of the pixels.

CONVERTING IMAGES TO COLOR

CMYK Conversion

Before you can print a color separation, you must convert your RGB, lab, or indexed color image to CMYK. (If a lab image is being printed on a PostScript Level 2 color printer, you do not have to convert it.)

A CMYK conversion splits the image into four channels (cyan, magenta, yellow, and black). As an intermediate step, the image is converted to the lab model, and a color table is built, which will serve as a reference for the creation of CMYK color values.

It's not a good idea to convert back and forth between RGB and CMYK multiple times because the colors have to be recalculated with each conversion, which leaves room for error. Use the **Mode:CMYK Preview** command to view a "soft" copy of the image in CMYK without actually converting.

For additional information about saving and loading color separation tables, see the Adobe Photoshop *User's Guide.*

Lab Color Conversion

You can convert any image to lab color without affecting the original color values. As mentioned in Chapter 15, the lab color mode is useful for changing the brightness of an image separately from changing the hue or saturation. To convert to lab color mode, choose **Lab Color** from the Mode menu. Lab color is the best choice when you want to export an image to another system.

Indexed Color Conversion

Like a grayscale image, an indexed color image can have only one channel. Every pixel in that image contains 8 bits, which allows 256 colors to be used— just like a grayscale image's 256 gray levels.

   Conversion from RGB to indexed color can be useful when you have to export an image to another program that can handle images of only a limited size or number of colors, such as publishing via the Internet or for a multimedia program. Grayscale images can also be converted to indexed color mode, where color can be added by editing the image's color table:

1. With your color image open, select **Indexed Color** from the Mode menu.

2. When the Indexed Color dialog box appears (Figure 18.9), enter the Palette type, Color Depth, and Dither options.

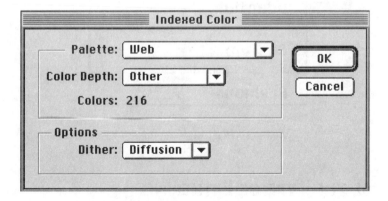

Figure 18.9 *Indexed Color dialog box.*

CHOOSE THE TYPE OF COLOR PALETTE

Several different color palettes can be used with indexed color images (Figure 18.10). The Exact palette replicates the exact colors used in an image when it has 256 or fewer colors. The System palette uses your system's standard default 8-bit color table. The Web palette uses the palette most often used by current World Wide Web browsers. The Uniform palette creates a palette from a sampling of colors in the spectrum. The Adaptive palette looks at the image and chooses a range of colors based on the most prominent colors in the image. The Custom palette allows you to create a color table to your own specifications. You can edit the color table to create a different range of colors to be applied to the image. For batch processing, selecting **Previous** allows you to apply the most recently defined color table to the current image. You can choose **Previous** only if you have converted the image using either the Adaptive or Color palettes.

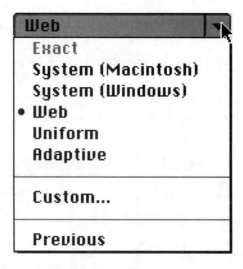

Figure 18.10 *Available color palettes.*

CHOOSE THE TYPE OF DITHERING

Dithering creates colors that are not in the designated color table. If you're using the System palette, the following three dithering options are available:

- **None**. Colors are not dithered. Missing colors are replaced with the closest nearby colors. This can create a somewhat posterized effect with abrupt transitions between image colors.
- **Diffusion**. Pixels are added without obvious patterning.
- **Pattern**. Pixels are added at random to simulate missing colors. The pattern is pronounced and looks like a needlepoint cross-stitch.

If you are using an Adaptive, Custom, or Previous palette, only **Diffusion** and **None** are available. If you are using an Exact palette, there are no missing colors in the table (because 256 or fewer are being used); consequently, there is no need for dithering.

EDITING A COLOR TABLE OF AN INDEXED COLOR IMAGE

You can change the color table associated with an indexed color image, thereby changing the colors represented in the image. RGB, CMYK, and grayscale image color tables can be edited when the image is converted to indexed color:

1. With the indexed color image open, select **Color Table...** from the Mode menu.

2. When the Color Table dialog box opens, click or drag to select the range of squares whose color you want to change. The range can be all the squares in the table (256) or just one.

3. The Color Picker will appear. If you are changing only one color, select the new color and click **OK**.

4. If you are changing a range of colors, Photoshop will create a blend of the beginning and ending colors. The first time the Color Picker opens, you will be asked to select the first color. Click **OK** after you've made your choice. Then the Color Picker will reopen, asking for the last color. Click **OK** again. The color table now shows blends of the colors you select (Figure 18.11).

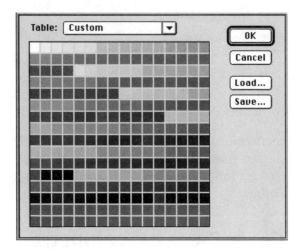

Figure 18.11 Edited color table.

TYPES OF COLOR TABLES

Four different types of color tables can be accessed from the Table pop-up menu. The Grayscale color table shows the full range of 256 grayscale tones from 0 (black) to 255 (white). The Spectrum color table shows the rainbow of colors in the visible spectrum. The System color table shows the Macintosh or Windows System color palette, with 256 choices. These colors are not arranged as a gradient. The Black Body color table shows a range of colors based on the colors emitted as a black body radiator heats up. The gradient proceeds from black to red, orange, yellow, and white.

Color tables can be saved and loaded. Use the **Save...** and **Load...** buttons in the Color Table dialog box.

CREATING DUOTONES

Grayscale images do not have to be printed with only black ink. When they're printed using colored ink, they are called *monotones*, *duotones*, *tritones*, or *quadtones*, depending upon the number of inks used. Monotones are printed with one color of ink that is not black. Duotones, tritones, and quadtones are printed with black ink plus one, two, or three additional colors. For simplicity, we'll refer to them all as *duotones*.

Why Print Duotones?

Although a grayscale image might contain much subtle detail, when it is printed using black ink in a single pass on a press, only about 50 gray levels are reproduced. Sometimes two passes of black ink are used, or occasionally, one pass each of black and gray ink, to increase the tonal range. Another alternative is to print that second pass using a colored ink. This gives the image a slight tint and creates an image of much greater depth.

Although duotones can look something like tinted color images, they are not created in the RGB or CMYK mode. Instead, they are converted from grayscale to duotone mode by selecting **Duotone...** from the Mode menu. Duotones begin with one channel, like grayscale images, although additional mask channels can be added in which to save selections.

Converting an Image into a Duotone

Only grayscale images can be converted into duotones. If you want to create a duotone from a color image, you must first convert it to a grayscale image. The grayscale-to-duotone conversion process is easy. For the finished Orpheus duotone (Figure 18.12), see the Chapter 18 folder (within the Exercises folder) on the CD-ROM.

Figure 18.12 Orpheus duotone.

1. With the grayscale image open, choose **Duotone...** from the Mode menu.

2. When the Duotone Options dialog box appears, select your choice of **Monotone, Duotone, Tritone,** or **Quadtone** from the pop-up Type submenu (Figure 18.13).

3. Next, select the ink color by clicking on an empty box.

4. As soon as you click, the Custom Colors dialog box will appear. You can select a custom color or click the **Color Picker** button to select a color with the Color Picker.

5. Finally, adjust the duotone curves for each ink. A duotone curve determines how the ink color is applied to the shadows, midtones, and highlights of an image. To adjust a curve, click the curve box adjacent to the ink color swatch.

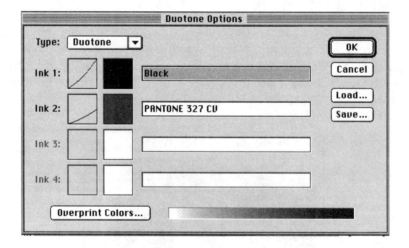

Figure 18.13 *Duotone Options dialog box.*

6. The Duotone Curve dialog box will open (Figure 18.14). Before you adjust the curve, the graph represents a straight linear relationship between the brightness of a pixel and the size of dot used to print it. The horizontal axis indicates the input values, and the vertical axis indicates the output values. The density of the ink increases as you go up the vertical axis. The lightest values (highlights) are at the lower-left side of the graph, midtones are in the center, and the darkest values (shadows) are at the upper right.

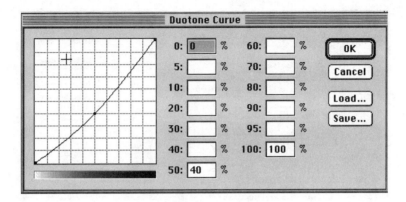

Figure 18.14 Duotone Curve dialog box.

7. You can adjust up to 13 points along the curve by clicking and dragging on the curve.

8. You can also adjust the curve by entering numbers in the boxes. By default, a 10% highlight pixel will be printed with a 10% dot of ink, a 60% midtone pixel with a 60% dot of ink, a 90% shadow pixel with a 90% dot of ink, and so forth. You can change these relationships by specifying that a larger or smaller ink dot be used to print a given percentage of the image. For example, when you enter **80** in the 100% box, an 80% ink dot will be used to print the 100% shadow area. A duotone curve must be specified for each ink you plan to use.

9. Two unscreened inks printed on top of each other are called *overprints*. Overprints can also be specified in the Duotone Options dialog box. For advanced technical information about creating and viewing overprints and viewing individual duotone colors in a multichannel format, see the Adobe Photoshop *User's Guide*.

10. For duotones to reproduce correctly, the inks must be printed in a particular order, and halftone screens must be indicated for the optimum angle. As a rule, the darkest duotone inks should print first, followed by successively lighter ones. Ask your printer for his or her recommendation.

11. To set the halftone screen frequency, dot shape, and screen angle, open **Page Setup....** Click the **Screens...** button to access the Halftone Screen dialog box (Figure 18.15). Click the **Auto** button to let Photoshop calculate the best screen angle and frequency.

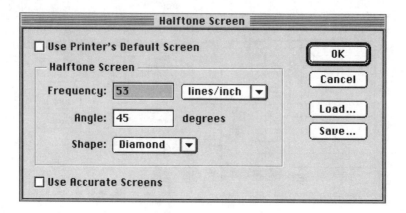

Figure 18.15 Halftone Screens dialog box.

12. Duotones can only be saved in Photoshop, EPS, or Raw formats. To save a duotone as a TIFF image, you must first convert it to an RGB file. Be sure to save a separate copy of the duotone in the Photoshop format first (under a different name) in case you want to go back and make changes to the original.

WHAT YOU'VE LEARNED

Image Conversion

- Convert images from one mode to another by selecting a new mode under the Mode menu.

- Images must be converted to grayscale before conversion to bitmapped mode.

- When converting to bitmapped mode, five conversion methods are available: 50% Threshold, Pattern Dither, Diffusion Dither, Halftone Screen..., and Custom Pattern.

- Bitmapped images can be converted back to grayscale (and then to RGB) for editing with all the Photoshop tools.

- Convert images to CMYK mode in preparation for printing and creating color separations.

- Convert images to lab color mode for export to other systems.
- Convert images to indexed color mode for export to applications that can only use images with smaller file sizes.

Color Tables

- Edit the color table of an indexed color image to change the colors in the image.

Creating Duotones

- Create monotones, duotones, tritones, and quadtones from grayscale images.
- Adjust duotone curves to describe how the ink or inks are applied to the highlights, midtones, and shadows of the image.

CHAPTER 19

Photoshop and Internet Publishing

In this chapter...

- Introduction to Web publishing
- File formats for Internet publishing
- Digimarc watermarking
- Cross-platform gamma correction

Manipulating Images for an Additive Light Medium

In the not-so-distant past when we talked about Photoshop—or any image manipulation software for that matter—we were talking exclusively about manipulating images for reproduction in some hard format (i.e., offset printing, laser printing, etc.). There's a huge step in there, one we've devoted whole chapters of this book to and that entire volumes have been written on: taking that which is created and viewed on a computer and reinterpreting it for an entirely different medium.

Things have changed. These days, you are just as likely to have some use for your image that doesn't involve output and that will entail others seeing it in the very medium in which it was either created or manipulated: the computer screen.

In keeping an edge on other image manipulation programs—something Adobe has been very good at doing—the latest versions of Photoshop include features for publishing and otherwise presenting your images in their best light on the World Wide Web and other electronic media.

Photoshop and the Internet

If you are interested in manipulating images for inclusion on a page on the Internet's World Wide Web, Photoshop is a good starting point. Many features of the most recent versions of Photoshop lend themselves to efficient electronic publication.

These include:

- Easy GIF89a, PNG, and JPEG image conversion for Web use.
- The **Actions** command, which allows a series of commands—including image mode and file type conversion—to be executed easily and for large batches of files.
- Digital watermarking to provide authorship information for registered users of Digimarc's watermarking filter.
- Specifiable Web color palette for converting an image to indexed color.

PREPARING AN IMAGE FOR INTERNET USE

Whenever we create an image in Photoshop, we are generally thinking in terms of final output and the way that others will view our creation. If the image is to be used in a magazine layout, we have think about how to prepare the image so that, when we output the film the printer will be able to reproduce the image as closely as possible to our original vision.

In Web use, final output is several steps closer and almost entirely in our own control. Output in this instance will be computer screens, not unlike our own and—potentially—all over the world. Because Internet data is still mainly carried by telephone lines, we have to try to keep file sizes small so that they transmit quickly. Also, because our image will be viewed on different computer platforms using different browsers, we have to try to correct in advance for potential discrepancies in lighting and gamma delivery.

CHOOSING A GRAPHICS FILE TYPE

If you had total control of how your image would be viewed on the Web, deciding on a file format would be easy: you'd choose to deliver it how it looked best. But because of the variables of size and various platforms, we have to choose the format that will make it:

- Smallest and easily read
- Most accessible to the widest number of browsers
- Shown to best advantage

At present, there are three basic file types for delivery of still images via the Internet. All three are easily supported by Photoshop 4:

- *GIF.* As of this writing, most images you view on the Web are saved as GIFs (Graphics Interchange Format). GIF allows 1-bit transparency and a palette of a maximum of 256 colors. When you save an image as a GIF file, you can specify how the image will load. If you select **Interlace** from the file options, the image will download gradually in ever-increasing detail. Every Web browser on the planet supports the GIF compression scheme, so you can safely include GIFs on your Web page and know that people will be able to view them.

- *JPEG.* When you save a file as JPEG (Joint Photographic Experts Group) you retain all of the color information of an RGB image; GIF does not. The downside is that JPEG compression works by tossing out information not deemed necessary to rendering the image. This makes for lossy and imperfect compression because data lost can't be recovered, so the file you save will be inferior to the one you started with. On the whole, though, JPEG files tend to be slightly smaller than GIF files and the format is just as widely accepted.

- *PNG.* PNG (Portable Network Graphics) file format is being developed as an alternative to the GIF format for displaying images on the Web. PNG is exactly like GIF, only more so. That is, PNG not only retains all color information of the original file, it also retains the alpha channels. In addition, PNG is a lossless compression method so none of your valuable bits of data get dropped in the translation. Of course, we can't have all this good stuff without some bad stuff. PNG files are larger than JPEG or GIF files. Also, as of this writing, browsers are only beginning to support the PNG file format. Once it becomes widely accepted, however, I predict we'll be seeing a lot more of this nondestructive format on the Web.

EXERCISE 19.1 EXPERIMENTING WITH FILE FORMATS FOR THE WEB

Let's work with the different file formats and see how they look and how they work:

1. Open an image you'd like to include on a Web page. If you don't have one handy open **IMG0039.PCD** from the CD-ROM. This image is from the Hyogensha Royalty Free Stock Photo Collection Vol. 0 and is a huge, high-res file. Getting it down to a size that will be acceptable for Web use while retaining the beauty of the image will be quite a feat. Choose **256 x 384** from the Kodak PhotoCD dialog box (Figure 19.1). This will give you an image of 288 K, which is 5.333 inches wide and 3.556 inches high, a good starting point for this exercise.

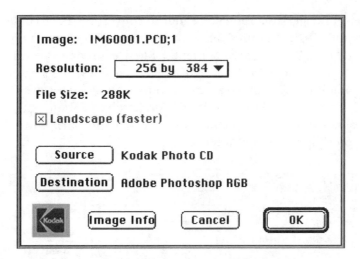

Figure 19.1 *The Kodak PhotoCD dialog box.*

2. The image has been given to us full-frame as you can see by the edge of the filmstrip visible around the edges. Using the Rectangular Marquee tool, crop the image to a size and shape that pleases you (Figure 19.2). This will prepare the image for saving and reduce the file size slightly to boot.

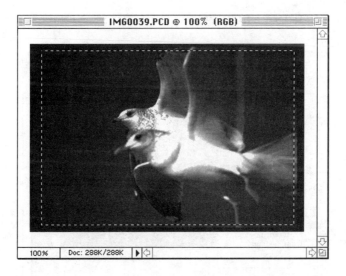

Figure 19.2 *Using the Marquee tool to crop the area you'd like to work with.*

3. Select **Image:Mode:Indexed Color** to convert the file to indexed color (Figure 19.3). Choose **Web** as the palette option, as this image is destined for a Web page. Note that the file size is reduced considerably: to 84 K from 250 K in the case of my own crop. At the same time—and depending on your computer setup—you'll note a drop in overall image quality and tonality. Don't worry, we're just getting ready for the realities of the Web. Just in case we crash and burn, save it now as a Photoshop file simply as **birds**.

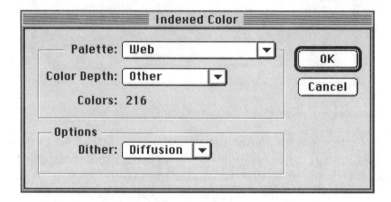

Figure 19.3 *The Indexed Color dialog box.*

4. Choose **File:Export:GIF89a** (Figure 19.4) to save the file as a GIF.

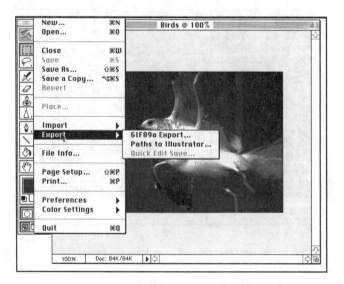

Figure 19.4 *Exporting a file as a GIF89a.*

5. After choosing the **Export** plug-in, you'll get a dialog box that gives you transparency options. You would request transparency if, for example, this image was going to lay on the default gray background of a Web page. Since this is not the case, we can leave the transparency options alone for now. Click **OK**. Call the file **birds.gif** and note that Photoshop may already have appended the **.gif** suffix so that you don't have to.

6. If you look at your file at the operating-system level, you'll see it's reduced in size a great deal: 33 K on my Mac, but your mileage will vary.

7. Because you exported the file rather than saving it, your indexed color file is still as it was in Photoshop. Go back to it now, and save it as a Photoshop file called **Bird**.

8. Choose **File:Save As CompuServe GIF**. Name the file **BirdsCS.gif** so you'll be able to tell it from its sister file when you're done. If you check at this point, you'll note that the GIF file saved in this way is about 20 K larger than the exported file. While 20 K isn't significant in the normal course of things, when it comes to Web graphics files, that 20 K can be very important.

9. Close the CompuServe GIF file and open your Photoshop file **Birds** once again.

10. Once again, choose **File:Save As**, but this time choose **PNG**. This time, give **Birds** the suffix **.PNG** (Figure 19.6).

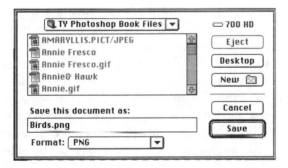

Figure 19.6 Choose PNG from the save options.

11. Another dialog box opens, this one offering PNG options (Figure 19.7). To have the image interlace when it is downloaded, make sure **Adam7** is checked under Interlace. For filter, choose **None**. Press **OK**.

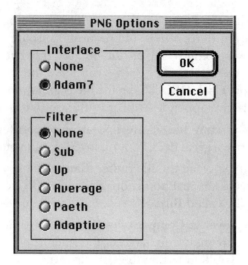

Figure 19.7 The PNG Options dialog box.

12. At your operating-system level, you'll see that you have created a file that is about 25% smaller than the original Photoshop file, although it is not as small as either of the GIF formatted files.

13. To save our birds as a JPEG we must first convert them to RGB by choosing **Image:Mode:RGB Color**. Next, choose **File:Save As:JPEG**. Remember to call this file **Bird.JPG** so you can tell it from the others.

14. You'll be presented with the JPEG Options dialog box (Figure 19.8). The slider attached to the numeric value box and the fly-out menu to indicate low- to high-quality work together to determine the size of your JPEG file as well as the desired quality. Although this will largely be determined by your own bandwidth, how you're using this image, and how important speed is in relation to absolute beauty, by taking the middle path in this instance I ended up with a 33 K file—small enough, but still detailed. For format options, check **Standard Baseline** to ensure that the largest number of browsers will be able to successfully view your file.

15. You have now created three Net-ready files (four if you count the extra GIF file). Any of these could be tagged in HTML (the subject of yet another book) and uploaded to a server for inclusion with a Web page to be viewed by most browsers.

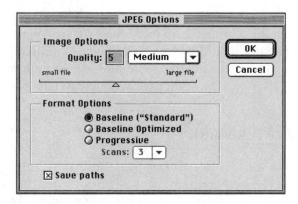

Figure 19.8 JPEG Options dialog box.

Conclusion?

Here's how my bird files stacked up size-wise: yours will be similar, depending on your original image and the crop you chose (Figure 19.9). The original file cropped and converted to indexed color came in at 110 K. Both the JPEG and exported GIF were 33 K. The CompuServe GIF was 55 K and the PNG file was a whopping 66 K, although all of its data was left intact.

As you will have realized by going through the exercise, there are many possible permutations on the saves you made. For instance, saving the JPEG as lower quality might not make an appreciable difference to the image's Web viewability, but it might save you some valuable file space, making it faster to download. On the other hand, a file with a lot of detail might benefit from a higher-quality treatment. The best thing to do is experiment with the various formats as well as the various possibilities within those formats to find what works best for you, your images, and the Web site you're working on.

PROTECTING YOUR ARTWORK

For as long as people have been "publishing" their images on the Web, artists have been concerned about people stealing their work—and not without some justification. An image that can be viewed on a browser can be lifted almost as easily as it's looked at, and this opens a whole can of creative worms.

While there continues to be no easy answer, the latest version of Photoshop has tried to address this concern. Working together with the

Digimarc Corporation, Photoshop 4 includes a filter that enables you to embed an electronic watermark into your image that will make it possible not only for you to prove your authorship of the image, but will allow prospective clients who have gotten their hands on it to find you through your watermark. That's the theory, anyway. The reality will take time to tell.

WHAZZA WATERMARK?

If you hold a nice piece of letterhead paper up to the light, you'll see the paper's watermark. The paper company's logo or even the paper variety's name are embedded into the paper during its manufacture. The watermark is an intrinsic part of the paper and will follow it through its lifetime.

WHAZZA ELECTRONIC WATERMARK?

In theory, an electronic watermark works in just the same way. Digimarc's entry adds your personal code as noise to your image's lightness channel. This watermark is invisible and doesn't mess with the image's integrity. When a watermarked image is loaded into Photoshop 4 (Figures 19.9 and 19.10), the copyright symbol is displayed, letting the would-be Web thief know that this is a protected image.

Figures 19.9 and 19.10 Before (19.9) and after (19.10) watermarking with the Digimarc filter.

Several organizations and companies have been cooking up watermarking schemes to help protect creators whose images appear on the Web. We're mentioning Digimarc's entry in these pages because they've managed to get theirs included with Photoshop 4. That tacit endorsement of their system might be all Digimarc needs to launch properly, and a proper launch is what is needed. None of the watermarking schemes will be very effective without a lot of support from the market. That's not said to put the onus on you to make Digimarc successful. Rather, it's up to you to watch them and the watermarking industry in general to see how it progresses and then back a horse that looks like it's going to be a flyer.

WATERMARKING NUTS 'N' BOLTS

The mechanics of how to watermark an image is well covered both in the documentation that accompanies Photoshop 4.0 as well as by the Digimarc Corporation themselves at their Web site at http://www.digimarc.com, but just so you know exactly what's involved, we'll give you a simple overview here.

Watermarking Step by Step

1. All the physical stuff you need to read and embed digital watermarks a la Digimarc is included with Adobe Photoshop 4.0, but to watermark an image yourself, you need to be listed in Digimarc's database of artists and photographers. You register with them for a fee and are assigned a Creator ID and then listed in their database.

2. You can register with Digimarc via the Web or via fax, and both registrations can be initiated directly from Photoshop 4.0.

3. Once you have a Creator ID, you apply the watermark as you would any filter (by choosing **Filter:Digimarc:Embed Watermark**). You can apply the filter to as many images as you want.

4. If you have the Digimarc Watermarking filter installed in Photoshop, the program will automatically look for watermarks when you load an image. You can tell at a glance if the image is watermarked because the copyright symbol will appear in the image's title and status bars (Figure 19.10).

Figure 19.11 A GIF file ready for the Web.

5. If you come across a watermarked image (and you know because the ©
is showing), and you want to find out more about the image's author,
choose **Filter:Digimarc:Read Watermark**. When the reader has finished
looking at the image you'll get a dialog box (Figure 19.12) giving you
the Creator ID number so that you can look up authorship information
with them via the Web or fax-back.

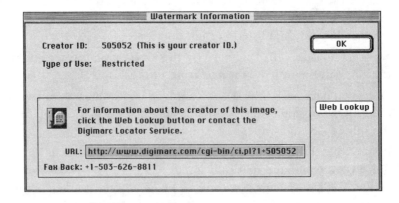

Figure 19.12 Creator ID dialog box.

6. Once you have information on the file's creator, you can then contact them for permission to use the image, or commission them to do an image like it for you.

CROSS-PLATFORM GAMMA CONSIDERATIONS

In their ultimate wisdom, the powers-that-were-hardware-designers have determined that the correct gamma setting for a Macintosh monitor is strikingly different from that for a PC. In the natural course of design, this affects us not at all: once we have everything nicely calibrated, off we go. Until, again, our output is targeted for Web distribution.

Put more simply, what looks like a perfectly color-corrected image on a Web browser on my Mac will look quite dark and hideous on my PC's browser. Fortunately for PC users, the reverse is not true. That's because—due to their monitor's gamma settings—they have already made the image lighter than the Mac user would have. What you—as the designer whose creations will be viewed on many computer platforms—must do is find a good average or light and brightness that will ensure that all viewers get full impact from your images.

The easiest way to make this happen is to make your Mac images slighter lighter than what looks perfect to the eye on your monitor.

Preparing the Mac Image

1. Your perfect **.gif**, **.jpeg**, or **.png** file is ready to go (Figure 19.11).

2. Choose **Image:Adjust:Brightness/Contrast** to slightly bump up both adjustments.

3. With the **Preview** box checked (Figure 19.14), slide both sliders until you've reached a brightness and contrast that looks just a little too light to be perfect. Remember, you're going for an average that will look good on all platforms.

Figure 19.13 Selecting Brightness/Contrast from the Adjust dropdown menu.

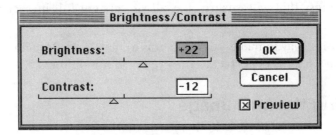

Figure 19.14 The Brightness/Contrast dialog box.

WHAT YOU'VE LEARNED

Preparing an Image for Internet Use

- Acceptable file formats are GIF, JPEG, and PNG.
- GIF and JPEG are the most popular formats and create the smallest files.

- PNG retains the most information, but not all viewers presently can read them.

Protecting Your Authorship

- Watermarking in theory and practice.
- What is a watermark?
- How does it work?

Cross-Platform Gamma Considerations

- The Web is viewed across many platforms.
- Mac-prepared images will appear dark when viewed on a PC.
- To compensate, Mac images must be brightened for cross-platform viewing.

CHAPTER 20

Producing Color Separations

In this chapter...

- Calibrating the monitor
- Producing a color separation

SYSTEM CALIBRATION

To have satisfactory printed results, your monitor must be properly calibrated so that the image on the screen matches the printed output as closely as possible. A number of factors and variables affect the screen-to-print conversion. These include the lighting conditions in the room, the color temperature of the phosphors in the monitor, the paper the image will be printed on, and the inks used to print it. Each of these elements can be adjusted during the calibration process.

Photoshop provides two types of calibration software:

- The monitor display is adjusted with the Gamma control panel device. This control affects only the look of the monitor.

- The rest of the software is accessed from within Photoshop through the Monitor Setup, Printing Inks Setup, and Separation Setup dialog boxes by selecting the **Color Settings** Preferences fly-out menu from the File menu. These controls affect how an image in the RGB mode is converted into a CMYK mode in preparation for printing.

WHY CALIBRATE YOUR SYSTEM?

As discussed in earlier chapters, there are inherent differences between the color you see on your computer monitor and the color that appears on the printed page. A color monitor is an RGB device, which works in the additive color system. Printed materials, on the other hand, are created using the subtractive color system. The gamut of colors that can be represented on an RGB monitor is much larger than the gamut of colors that can be printed using CMYK inks.

Hardware differences also contribute to variations. Two monitors, even identical models from the same manufacturer, may portray the same document differently. Room lighting also affects the image. Natural skylight coming in through a window is generally bluish, while incandescent light is reddish, and fluorescent has a greenish tint. If you change lighting conditions, you change the way the image appears, and you will make color correction changes accordingly, for better or worse. When we work, we generally keep the room darkened with no light "spill" from windows. We don't sit very close to our monitors, but if we did, we would be careful not to wear bright colors that might reflect on the image.

Like monitors, printers can also produce results that vary widely from model to model and unit to unit. So how do you get consistent output with so many variables? The best solution lies in carefully calibrating your system and working with service bureaus known for doing high-quality work.

EXERCISE 20.1: CALIBRATING YOUR SYSTEM

Calibrating Your Monitor

You'll use the Gamma control panel device supplied with the original Adobe Photoshop program disks to calibrate your monitor so that colors are displayed properly. If you have a monitor that comes with proprietary calibration software, use that instead.

Do not use Adobe calibration software together with third-party calibration software. If you do, the monitor will be miscalibrated:

1. Turn on your monitor and leave it on for at least a half hour. The device needs to be warmed up to provide a stable display.

2. Adjust the room lighting conditions. You will need to keep the room this way after calibration, so make sure it's something you can live with. Adjust the brightness and contrast controls on your monitor and tape them down so they cannot be accidentally bumped and changed.

3. Set the monitor background color to a neutral light gray. On the Macintosh, open the **Gamma** control panel. On a PC, choose **File:Color Settings:Monitor Setup** and click **Calibrate** in the Monitor Setup dialog box. Figure 20.1 shows Photoshop's gamma tools for monitor calibration.

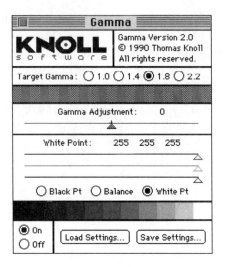

Figure 20.1 *Gamma control panel.*

4. Choose a target gamma from the top of the window; 1.8 is right for most images destined for print or display on the Macintosh. Select **2.2** if you will be outputting images onto videotape. (Jot down these and the following settings. You will need to use them again soon when you work with Monitor Setup.)

5. To set the white point, get a white piece of paper that closely matches the stock on which you'll be printing. Hold it up to the monitor, making sure that the light falling on the monitor is the same as the light falling on the paper. Click the **White Pt** button and adjust the sliders so that the white of the monitor matches the white of the paper.

6. Drag the Gamma Adjustment slider so that there is no difference between the solid gray rectangles and the patterned gray rectangles.

7. Click the **Balance** button. Drag the three sliders to remove any color cast from the gray squares in the gray bar below.

8. Click the **Black Pt** button and again drag the sliders to remove any color cast from the darkest (shadow) squares in the gray bar below. If you need to, adjust the color balance and gamma again.

You can save different settings to load and use with different paper stocks.

MONITOR SETUP

Your next step will be to enter Monitor Setup information.

1. Open Monitor Setup (**File:Color Preferences**). A dialog box will open (Figure 20.2). The information you enter takes into consideration the way your monitor displays an image. These options also affect how an RGB image is converted to a CMYK image.

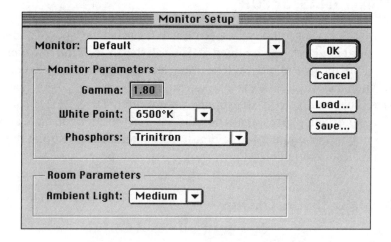

Figure 20.2 Monitor Setup dialog box.

2. Select the type of monitor you are using from the pop-up menu.

3. On the Mac, find the gamma value that you entered in the Gamma control panel and enter it in the Gamma dialog box. On the PC, you will have already entered a value here when you calibrated your monitor in the last step. The default is 1.8 unless you have a specific reason to change it.

4. Set the white point from the pop-up menu. Use 6500°K unless you are using third-party calibration software that says you should do otherwise. The **Custom** selection lets you enter any value you'd like.

5. Set the monitor type with the Phosphors pop-up menu. You will probably find your monitor on this list. If you do not, choose **Custom** and enter the RGB chromaticity values provided by the monitor manufacturer.

6. Set the ambient light conditions in the Room Parameters dialog box. Medium lighting means the image on the screen is about as bright as the room lighting. Low and high are room-light levels that are dimmer or brighter than the screen image.

7. Click **OK**. Remember, these are considered Preferences so the changes won't take place until after you've shut down and restarted Photoshop.

PRINTING INKS SETUP

Printing Inks Setup lets you be very specific with regard to the types of papers and inks your print-targeted work is aimed at. You will specify the kind of paper you'll be printing on, the type of ink you'll be using, and the dot gain you expect on the printer. When halftone dots are printed on paper, they can spread out, darkening the image. The absorbency of the paper is an important factor in calculating dot gain. More absorbent paper spreads dots farther. You will adjust dot gain after you print a proof and examine it with a densitometer, an instrument that measures dot gain or the amount of ink in the proof.

CHOOSING INK COLORS

1. Select **Printing Inks Setup** from the **Preferences:File** menu to open the dialog box (Figure 20.3).

2. The default choice for Ink Colors, **SWOP** (coated), means it's expected that you will print your image on coated paper using standard Web off-set proofing. Use the pop-up menu to select a different ink type. If you choose **Custom**, you will be presented with another dialog box. Ink colors are represented by their CIE values (an international standard), and these values can be adjusted after you print a color proof. You'll learn more about this later in this chapter.

3. Adjust the dot gain after you've run a color proof and examined the proof with a densitometer. The default dot gain is 20%. Click the **Use Dot Gain for Grayscale Images** box if you will be creating grayscale images and want to see how dot gain will affect the look.

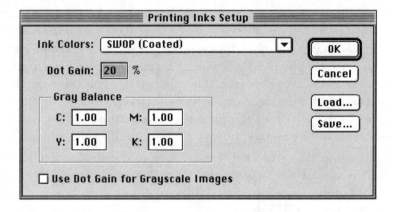

Figure 20.3 *Printing Inks Setup dialog box.*

WARNING

If you convert an image from RGB to CMYK and later change the Monitor Setup or Printing Inks Setup, you must revert to the original RGB image and convert the file again. If you do not reconvert it, the color separations will not reflect these new settings.

THE COLOR PROOF

After calibrating your monitor and making printing ink adjustments, it's time to print a color proof of a CMYK image. You will later compare this image to what you see on your monitor and make further adjustments to make the two match as closely as possible. For your test proof, you can use one of the color files that ships with Photoshop, or you can create an image directly in CMYK mode and use that. (Don't use an RGB-to-CMYK conversion for this test.)

Adobe recommends that you include the following elements in your test image:

- A CMYK image of your choice. Make it colorful. It's a good idea to have an image with skin tones.
- Four color swatches. Each swatch should be 100% of one of the CMYK colors—100% cyan, 100% magenta, 100% yellow, and 100% black.

- Four additional color swatches. Each swatch should combine two or three colors at 100% value—100% magenta and 100% yellow combine make red; 100% cyan and 100% yellow make green; 100% magenta and 100% cyan make purple; and 100% of each cyan, yellow, and magenta together make a murky brownish gray. (This nondescript gray color, by the way, is why four-color printing always includes black as a "color" of ink: even if you print 100% of each of the process colors, a true rich black cannot be achieved. Black generation corrects this, as you'll soon discover.)

- Calibration bars. Add calibration bars to the image by clicking the **Calibration Bars** box in the Page Setup dialog box from the **Preferences:File** menu. You will need these when you examine the printed proof with a densitometer.

After you have assembled a test image, the last step is to print the file.

COMPARING AND CALIBRATING THE MONITOR DISPLAY TO THE PRINTED PROOF

Now comes the moment of truth: comparing your output to the screen image. Chances are you'll need to do some adjustment in the Printing Inks Setup dialog box so that the screen and proof are a good match.

MAKING DOT GAIN ADJUSTMENTS

When the **Use Dot Gain for Grayscale Images** box is checked in the Printing Inks Setup dialog box, the screen shows you what the image will look like, taking into consideration the amount of dot gain. If the screen image looks too dark, use one of the adjustment tools (such as Curves, Levels, or Brightness/Contrast, found under the Image menu) to change it.

If you're proofing a color image, you will need to adjust the amount of dot gain until the screen looks like the printed proof. You can do this visually by inspection or by using an instrument called a *reflective densitometer* to measure the amount of ink on the proof. See your Adobe Photoshop User's Guide for technical dot gain compensation instructions.

NOTE

You can set dot gain compensation within some layout programs. If you are going to use this capability, do not change the dot gain settings in Photoshop. Doubling the compensation will cause the image to print too lightly.

TRANSFER FUNCTIONS

You can print on film as well as on paper. To adjust the dot gain on film, you need to examine the film on a light table using a *transmission densitometer*, which measures the amount of light that is transmitted through the film. Again, if there is a difference between the expected density in any square on the grayscale calibration bar and the actual density of the film in that area as output by the image setter, the image setter may be miscalibrated, and you'll need to make a transfer function adjustment.

1. Open the Page Setup dialog box and click the **Transfer** button to bring up the Transfer Functions dialog box.

2. Decide what the appropriate adjustment should be. For example, if you expect the midtones to have a density of 50%, and they are, in fact, printing at 55%, enter **45%** in the 50% option box (Figure 20.4). The number you enter represents the difference between the correct density (50%) and the amount of excessive density (5%), for example, 50% – 5% = 45%. All four colors should have the same adjustment when you print color separations. These functions can be saved and loaded for processing a batch of similar images.

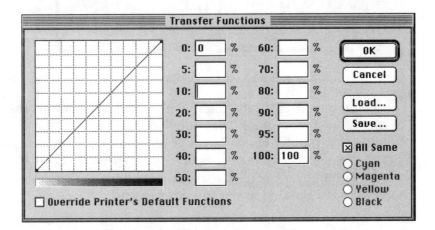

Figure 20.4 Adjusting transfer function values.

ADJUSTING FOR CUSTOM INK COLORS

Although the Ink Colors options in Printing Inks Setup dialog box are usually sufficient for working with most common types of inks, there may be an occasion in which you need to make adjustments for custom ink colors:

1. Open the Printing Inks Setup dialog box (**Preferences:File**). Select the **Custom** option from the Ink Colors pop-up menu to open the Ink Colors dialog box (Figure 20.5).

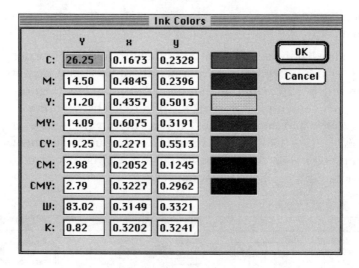

Figure 20.5 Ink Colors dialog box.

2. Using a colorimeter, read the color values of the swatches you created on your printed color proof. Those are the values you need to enter in the various *x, y,* and *Y* option boxes. If you don't have a colorimeter, click the color swatch in the dialog box that matches the color swatch on your printout, and adjust the screen color using the Photoshop or Apple Color Picker until screen and proof match.

ADJUSTING GRAY BALANCE TO REMOVE COLOR CASTS

Sometimes the proof will have a color cast, an overall unwanted color tint. You can compensate for this cast by changing the gamma levels for each channel in the Gray Balance area in the Printing Inks Setup dialog box (refer to Figure 20.3). How do you know what the correct gamma values should be? To determine them, you need to use the **Levels** command, which is accessed from **Image:Adjust:Levels**:

1. With your CMYK calibration image open, select **Adjust:Levels** from the Image menu.

2. Select each of the channels you want to adjust from the pop-up menu at the top of the window (Figure 20.6).

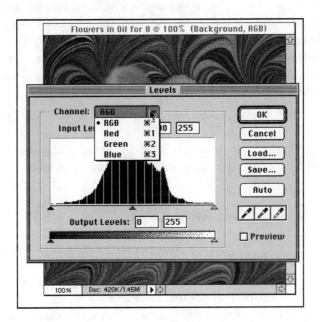

Figure 20.6 *Levels dialog box used with CMYK image.*

3. Move the Input Level Gamma slider (the gray triangle on the top scale) until screen images of each of the basic color swatches (cyan, magenta, yellow, and black) match the proof. Write down the change of gamma for each of the four channels. (Remember that the Gamma option box is the one in the middle.) Be sure to click **Cancel** before leaving the Levels dialog box so that you don't apply the changes to the image itself.

4. Reopen the Printing Inks Setup dialog box and enter the gamma values for each of the channels and click **OK**. The default values before

you apply a change will usually be 1.00. If they are not, multiply the old gamma value by the new gamma value and enter this number.

5. These settings can be saved and loaded so that they can be used with other Photoshop images you may want to process.

EXERCISE 20.2: COLOR SEPARATIONS

Creating a color separation involves converting an RGB image to a CMYK image so that each of the four component channels can be printed with its own plate. Before you convert an RGB image, make a copy of the file (using **Image:Duplicate**) and convert the copy. That way, if you don't like the results of the conversion you can go back to the original, make another duplicate image, and convert again. Converting a document back and forth between RGB and CMYK modes affects image quality adversely.

When Photoshop converts an image from RGB to CMYK, it creates a color separation table. This table is stored in Photoshop's Preferences file in the System folder. Changes made to the Monitor Setup, Printing Inks Setup, or Separation Setup dialog boxes require a new separation table.

MAKING COLOR SEPARATIONS

Adobe suggests the following procedure to create quality color separations:

1. Good separations begin with a correctly calibrated monitor. Instructions on how to do this appear earlier in this chapter. Do not recalibrate your monitor for individual images. It is a "set it and forget it operation." Again, remember that whenever you convert an image from RGB mode to CMYK mode and then change monitor calibration you must go back and reconvert the image again from RGB to CMYK. (You did remember to keep an untouched original copy of the RGB file, didn't you?)

2. Color-correct your RGB file. See earlier chapters for color correction how-to's.

3. Open the Separation Setup dialog box (**File:Color Settings:Separation Setup**) and adjust the settings.

4. Convert the image from RGB mode to CMYK mode (Mode menu). Use Levels or Curves (**Image:Adjust**) to adjust the black and white points.

5. Use the Unsharp Mask filter to sharpen edges and bring the image into focus.

6. Create a color trap to ensure that the image will look good even if there is a slight misregistration of plates on the press.

7. Print the color plates following printing instructions in the chapter on printing and the guidelines in the *Adobe Photoshop User's Guide*.

Black Plate Generation and Undercolor Removal

As discussed earlier, the ink colors cyan, magenta, and yellow combine on the printing press to approximate black, but in actuality they produce a dark, muddy, grayish brown. That's why a black plate (the K of CMYK) is printed along with cyan, magenta, and yellow—to ensure that reproduced blacks are dark and rich. At the same time, some of the cyan, magenta, and yellow are removed from the area where the three process colors overlap and black is added. This is process is called *black generation*, and it is adjusted in the Separation Setup dialog box (Figure 20.7).

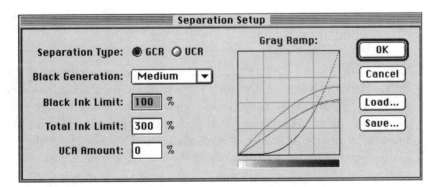

Figure 20.7 *Separation Setup dialog box.*

There are two methods for printing with black ink: undercolor removal (UCR) and gray component replacement (GCR):

- In UCR, black is used to improve clarity and detail in shadow areas, to prevent ink build-up, and to give neutrally colored areas more depth. Neutral colors, composed of equal parts of cyan, magenta, and yellow are all the shades of gray from black to white (e.g., a charcoal briquette, a pewter mug, a doctor's white lab coat). UCR has no affect in areas where cyan, magenta, and yellow are present in unequal amounts because these colors are not neutral.

- In GCR, black is used in combination with colored images, across a wider area of the image and is not just applied to areas with neutral tones. Your printer will advise you about which technique to use, based on your choice of paper and other print shop specifications.

ENTERING SEPARATION SETUP SETTINGS

Open the Separation Setup dialog box (**File:Color Settings:Separation Setup**). On the right-hand side of the window you'll see a graph called a Gray Ramp, which indicates how the neutral colors will be separated if the existing Separation Setup values are used. The horizontal (x) axis of the graph displays all the neutral color values from white to black, and the vertical (y) axis shows how much ink will be used for each value. Each of the four colored curved lines represents one of the process inks:

1. Select the separation type. GCR is the default, and it is commonly used for printing on coated stock. Choose **UCR** for printing on uncoated stock (such as newsprint).

2. Choose the amount of black generation from the pop-up menu (Figure 20.8). Medium is the default with Light and Heavy offering less black and more black, respectively. If you choose **None**, no black plate will be generated. Select **Maximum** when you have large areas of solid black on a white or light-colored background. The **Custom** option lets you reshape the black generation curve. As a starting point, pick a black generation choice that approximates the kind of curve you want, then select **Custom** to refine it. A dialog box will open. Modify the black generation curve by clicking and dragging points along the line. The cyan, magenta, and yellow values will be automatically changed.

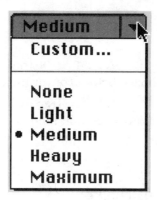

Figure 20.8 *Black generation choices.*

3. Set ink limits. There is a maximum to the amount of ink density a press can print. Your printer will tell you the values to enter for the black ink limit and the total ink limit. By default, the black ink is limited to 100% and the total ink is limited to 300%. These limits are applicable for both UCR and GCR separations.

4. Adjust the undercolor addition amount. To produce more saturated shadows in GCR separations, you may want to reduce the amount of cyan, magenta, and yellow that is removed in areas where black is added. (In other words, to not take away as much undercolor.) The default value is 0%.

Separation Setup settings can be saved and loaded for use with other images.

COLOR TRAPS

When an image is printed on a press, the plates can sometimes move slightly, causing misregistration. Misregistration appears as a small gap between differently colored parts of the image where the paper color shows through (e.g., between a solid yellow sun in a cyan-colored sky). To avoid gaps, you can indicate that areas with significant color differences overprint each other very slightly. When you call for one color to overprint another, you are creating a *trap*.

Photoshop creates traps by spreading the overprinting ink by a specified (and very small) distance. As a rule, four-color images do not need to be trapped. The exception would be when you are using solid tints in a CMYK-mode image:

1. An image must be in CMYK mode to be trapped. Always make a copy of your original RGB image before converting it to CMYK.

2. Select **Trap** (Image menu). In the Trap dialog box, set the unit of measurement (pixels, points, or millimeters) and enter a value in the Width box to designate the amount of anticipated misregistration.

WHAT YOU'VE LEARNED

Monitor Calibration

- Calibrate your system so that the image you see on the monitor matches the printed result as closely as possible.

- Adjust the monitor display through the Gamma control panel software.

- Adjust the color calibration options that affect the RGB-to-CMYK file conversion (Monitor Setup, Printing Inks Setup, and Separation Setup) through the Color Settings submenu of the File menu.

- If you convert an image from RGB to CMYK and then change any of these color calibration options, you must reconvert the file from RGB to CMYK again.

- Always keep a backup copy of an RGB file before you do a conversion. That way, if you change the color calibration options, you can reconvert from RGB to CMYK again. Don't ever lose your original RGB file. Use **Image:Duplicate** to make a copy for conversion.

Monitor Setup

- The specifications you enter in the Monitor Setup dialog box compensate for elements that affect the monitor display (such as room lighting and monitor type), determine how a file is converted from RGB to CMYK, and designate how the resulting CMYK image is displayed on-screen.

Printing Inks Setup

- Adjust the dot-gain compensation to make sure that the image doesn't print too darkly or too lightly (dot loss). Paper absorbency and miscalibration of an image setter can affect dot gain.

- Use the Transfer functions to adjust dot gain when you're printing on film.

- Adjust the Gray Balance to remove color casts. Use the **Adjust:Levels** command to determine the proper gamma amounts to be entered in the Printing Inks Setup dialog box.

Color Separations

- Begin to create color separations after you have calibrated your monitor, printed a color proof, and changed settings in Monitor Setup and Printing Inks Setup to compensate for differences between the monitor image and the printed page.

- Use the Separation Setup dialog box to choose between UCR (Undercolor Removal) and GCR (Gray Component Replacement), to choose the amount of black generation, to set ink limits, and to select **Undercolor Addition** (if desired).

- Select **Traps** from the Image menu to compensate for slight misregistration when a CMYK image is printed. Traps are usually needed only when an image contains areas of adjacent solid color in which the hues are radically different.

GLOSSARY

Acquire

A way of importing a file into Photoshop using a special plug-in module. Scanners and video frame grabbers are often accessed using the Acquire command. You can also use it to import only a portion of a file using Quick Edit.

Actions

Essentially, a function of Photoshop 4 that lets you create macros to automate many things you can do within the program.

Additive color model

RGB is an additive color model. The three components—red, green, and blue—combine in the computer monitor to produce white light.

Adjustment Layers

A special layer, used within the Layers Palette, that lets you try on tonal and color-adjustment effects without permanently altering the image.

Alignment	The position of type with regard to the place the Type tool was clicked. Alignment choices in the Type Tool dialog box are Left, Center, and Right.
Alpha channel	See channel.
Anti-alias	To smooth an edge by adding pixels of an intermediate value.
ATM (Adobe Type Manager)	A control panel device that allows the Mac to create smooth type on the screen (and in Photoshop documents) based on PostScript Type 1 fonts. ATM was automatically installed in your System folder if you used Photoshop's Easy Install option.
BMP	The standard Windows format for bitmap images.
Brightness	One of the three components of a color—hue and saturation are the other two. In an image, brightness ranges from the lightest highlights to the darkest shadows.
CMYK	Cyan, magenta, yellow, and black, the four component colors of four-color process printing. CMYK is one of Photoshop's primary color models and is the one used to make color separations.
Calibration	The process of matching the on-screen image to the printed output.
Channel	One of the layers that comprises all the information in an image. An RGB image has three channels; a CMYK image has four; a grayscale image has one black channel. Photoshop files can have a total of 16 channels, most of which will be added mask (alpha) channels. Bitmapped images cannot have alpha channels.
Clipping path	A path exported with an image when the image is intended to be silhouetted when placed in a pagelayout program.

Color cast An overall tone that dominates a color image, such as excessive magenta or blue.

Constrain To limit in some way. Selections can be constrained to a fixed size. You can constrain the movement of a selection by holding down the Shift key after you begin to move it with the mouse pointer.

Contrast The difference in brightness between different parts of an image. If there is little difference, the image has low contrast. Much difference means the image has high contrast.

Control point A point that can be added to indicate position on a Curves graph.

Crop To cut out part of an image and remove the surrounding area.

dpi (dots per inch) A definition of output device (printer) resolution.

Default A term that describes a standard setting that Photoshop chooses unless you choose otherwise. New documents will open in the default RGB mode unless you change them. Selections saved as masks will appear as white by default in an alpha channel.

Defloat To cause a floating selection to be nonfloating; see also floating.

Defringe To remove the outer edge of pixels from a selection.

Densitometer A device that measures the density of ink in printed halftones.

Direction lines The lines that emerge from a pen path anchor point, which are used to shape a Bezier curve.

Direction points

The dots at the ends of direction lines. Drag on these to manipulate the direction line.

Dithering

A technique of mixing colors of available pixels to simulate colors that are not in the color table.

Dot gain (dot loss)

Increase (decrease) in the size of halftone dots when printed on paper. Absorbent paper results in greater dot gain.

Duotone

A grayscale image that is printed with black ink plus an ink of another color. When two or three additional inks are used, the image is called a tritone or a quadtone.

Edit, as in editing a channel

To paint on, erase, fill, filter, or otherwise manipulate the contents of a channel. A channel can be edited only if its Pencil icon is visible in the Channels palette. The Smudge, Blur/Sharpen, and Dodge/Burn tools are editing tools. However, all the painting tools can be used to "edit" a mask.

Encapsulated PostScript (EPS)

One of the formats used to transfer Photoshop files to Illustrator and to some page- layout programs.

Fill

To cover a selected area with paint or a pattern.

Gradient fills can be linear (applied in a straight line from point A to point B) or radial (radiating outward from a central point).

Floating

A selection is floating when it has been pasted in from another document or has been moved. When type is added to an image, it comes in as a floating selection; see also defloat. When a floating selection is cut or deleted, underlying pixels are not affected.

Font	The name of a typeface, such as Garamond, Helvetica, Optima. Sometimes the word font is used collectively to mean an entire typeface family, such as all Helvetica Condensed faces (light, light oblique, oblique, bold oblique, and so forth).
Gamma	(1) Gamma correction changes the middle values (midtones) of an image along a curve. (2) Gamma also refers to the lightness or darkness of the monitor.
Gamut	A range of color values. Colors that can be viewed on a color monitor but cannot be accurately printed are said to be out of gamut.
GIF (Graphics Interchange Format)	A file type used widely to display graphics on the World Wide Web.
Gray Component Replacement (GCR)	The removal of a combination of cyan magenta, and yellow ink and their replacement with black ink. Similar to UCR, except that GCR uses more black.
Grayscale	An 8-bit image consisting of 256 gray levels, from 0 (black) to 255 (white).
HSB model	A color model that defines the color in terms of hue, saturation, and brightness.
Halftone	A halftone is an image that has been screened (broken down into a pattern of dots) so that it can be printed using a lithographic printing press.
Highlight	The part of a photograph with the lightest areas. It is printed with very tiny halftone dots or no dots at all.
Hue	The component of a color that defines its place on the spectrum or color wheel.

Image	Literally, what you see in an open Photoshop window—the picture.
Input device	A piece of equipment used to digitize an image and get it into the computer, such as a scanner or digitizing tablet.
Internet	The network of networks that carries a variety of online services—including the World Wide Web—around the world.
Interlaced	A description of a composite video signal, in which two fields (one filled with even lines, one filled with odd lines) describe the image. Video monitors display interlaced images; computer monitors do not.
Interpolation	A technique used to add pixels when a Photoshop image is resized.
Invert	To turn the image into its negative-for example, black becomes white and yellow becomes blue. (See also inverse).
Inverse	To select everything in the window that was not previously selected. There is no keyboard shortcut. You cannot inverse when there is nothing selected. See also invert.
JPEG (Joint Photographic Experts Group)	A file format common for displaying photographic images on the World Wide Web.
Kern	To adjust the spaces between adjacent letters so that they fit well next to each other. Called Spacing in the Type Tool dialog box.
Lab color	A color model that describes a color in terms of luminance, plus an a component and a b component.

Layer
A virtual "acetate overlay" that is initially transparent but that can be used to store portions of an image for separate manipulation until you "flatten" the image back to a single layer for output.

Leading
The distance between the baseline of one line of type and the baseline of the next; the space put between lines of type.

Line art
Artwork that is black and white only.

lpi (lines per inch)
A type of resolution used to describe halftone screens.

Luminance
Lightness.

Marching Ants
The oval wiggling shape you see around a selection or a selected area. The *marching ants* around the edge are the active selection border. The selection defines an area in which you can draw, paint, and edit the image.

Midtones
The tones in a photograph that are about halfway between the shadows and the highlights.

Moiré pattern
An unattractive pattern caused when halftone screens are set to the wrong angles.

Navigator
The Photoshop tool that lets you easily navigate and alter the viewing size of a document.

Neutral color
In RGB mode, a color in which red, green, and blue are present in exactly equal amounts.

Noise (Add Noise)
The random pixels added to an image to increase graininess.

Opacity
A measure of the coverage of paint over an underlying area. Low opacity means high transparency and vice versa.

Output device	A piece of equipment, such as a printer or an imagesetter, used to output the image created in the computer.
PDF	A file format used by Adobe Acrobat in electronic publishing.
Pen path	A Bezier curve path created with the Pen tool, found on the Paths palette.
Pixel	The abbreviation for picture element, the smallest part of an image, one dot on a computer monitor. Image resolution is measured in pixels per inch (or ppi).
PNG	A file format developed as an alternative to GIF for display of graphic images on the World Wide Web.
ppi (pixels per inch)	A description of image resolution.
Process colors	The four ink colors used in printing: cyan, magenta, yellow, and black.
Quadtone	Image that is printed with black plus three other colored inks.
Random Access Memory (RAM)	The memory used by the computer to store information while you're working.
Rasterize	To turn a PostScript file or object into a bitmapped image. Rasterization is the process of turning Illustrator documents into Photoshop documents.
Registration marks	Bull's-eye marks that are placed in the margins of a printed CMYK image to make sure that printing plates align properly.
Resampling	The process of changing the resolution of an image. Resampling up adds pixel information through the process of interpolation. Resampling down loses pixel information.

Resolution

A measure of the amount of detail in an image as expressed in units per inch. See specific resolutions—ppi, dpi, or lpi.

RGB model

An additive color model that describes a color in terms of the amount of red, green, and blue light that comprise it.

Saturation

The purity of a color. The saturation of a color is reduced by adding gray (black and white) to it.

Screen frequency

The density of dots in a halftone screen as measured in lines per inch (lpi). A high screen frequency (also called screen ruling or screen resolution) means more lines per inch.

Selection

An area that is chosen by the use of a selection tool, such as a Marquee, the Lasso, or the Magic Wand. Selections are enclosed by "crawling" borders of marching ants.

Shadow

The areas in a photograph that are darkest and, therefore, are printed with the largest halftone dots.

Spacing

See kerning.

Subtractive color model

CMYK is a subtractive color model. The component colors-cyan, magenta, yellow (and black)—combine on paper to produce black. Reflected light bouncing back to the viewer's eye is subtracted with the addition of each layered color.

TIFF (Tagged-Image File Format)

A file format used to take files to various programs and platforms.

Tolerance

A Magic Wand and Paint Bucket setting that determines which color values will be selected/painted.

Tool Tips

Photoshop 4's on-screen descriptions of tool and palette items while working in the program.

Trap

The amount of overlap needed so that there are no white gaps (due to unprinted paper) when two distinctly different colors are printed side by side.

Tritone

A "duotone" type image printed with black plus two other colored inks.

Under Color Removal (UCR)

The removal of process color inks in shadow areas (where they will print as black) and their replacement with black ink.

Virtual memory

Hard disk space that can be used when there is not enough RAM to carry out Photoshop functions.

World Wide Web

A hypertext system for locating and accessing Internet resources. Most often used with a graphical program that allows you to view images meant for public access on a remote computer.

Write-protect

To prevent a channel or a document from being "written" on or edited. A floppy disk can be write-protected by pushing up the little tab at the top of the disk so that you can see through the hole. A channel can be write-protected by turning off its Pencil icon in the Channels palette.

INDEX

50% threshold bitmap conversion, 419-420

A

Accented edge filter, 360
Acquire... (File menu), 299, 469
Actions, 223-225
  Actions palette , 10, 23, 223-224
  Batch, 223
  defined, 469
Adaptive Indexed Color palette, 426
Add (Image:Apply), 409-410
Add Layer Mask icon, 245
additive colors, 49-50, 469
Adjustment Layers, 254-258
  about, 229, 254, 469
  editing by painting, 257-258
  New Adjustment Layer, 254
Adobe Type Manager (ATM), 200
Airbrush
  Airbrush Options, 82
  described, 12
  opacity, 74-75, 82
  pressure, 82
  recommended use, 82
alert box, 29
Aligned clone, 86-88
alignment, 200, 470
alpha channels, 212, 406, 470
Amiga IFF files, opening, 298
anchor points
  defined, 134
  moving, 140
  using few, 146
anti-aliasing, 62, 470
  type, 200
Apply Image (Image menu), 404
  Add, 409-410
  Difference, 411
  Lighter and Darker, 407-408
Arrow tool, 140-141
arrowheads, drawing lines with, 95-96
ASCII encoding, 269
ATM (Adobe Type Manager), 200, 470
Auto Erase (Pencil option), 84-85
background color
  controlling with Color palette, 19
  controlling with Swatches palette, 20, 63
  controlling with Toolbox, 63
  default, 14, 64
  displayed in toolbox, 14
  reversing with foreground, 14
  Transparent, 228

B

background printing option, 266
Backspace, 180-181

Bas Relief filter, 382
base color, 76
Batch, 223
batch processing, 10, 23
Behind painting mode, 79
Bezier curves
  drawing Bezier curves with the Pen tool, 136-138
  fine-tuning Bezier curves, 139-146
bicubic interpolation, 195, 294
Bilinear interpolation, 294
Binary encoding, 269
Bitmapped mode
  50% threshold conversion, 419-420
  about, 56, 417, 418
  Bitmap dialog box, 419
  converting Bitmapped image to Grayscale, 424
  converting to Bitmapped image, 418-423
  Custom Pattern conversion, 423
  Diffusion Dither conversion, 421
  editing limitations, 418
  Halftone Screen conversion, 421-423
  Pattern Dither conversion, 420
bitmapped (painting) programs, 44-47, 49
bits, 52
Black Body color table, 428
black plate generation, 463-465
Bleed... (Page Setup), 265
blend color, 76
Blur filters
  Blur, 357
  Blur More, 323, 357
  Gaussian Blur, 325, 357
  Motion, Blur 358
  Radial Blur, 358-359
  Smart Blur, 359
Blur tool, 13, 104-107, 108
BMP files, 298, 302, 470
Border... (Page Setup), 265
borders
  applying a stroke to a selection, 282
  Modify:Border, (Select menu), 171-172
  modifying, 171-172
  stroking (the border of) a path, 150-152
brightness, 51, 470
Brightness/Contrast dialog box,
  changing Cancel button to Reset, 317
  color correcting with 320
  preview checkbox, 317
brush stroke filters
  Accented edge, 360
  Crosshatch, 361
  Dark strokes, 361
  Ink outlines, 362
  Splatter, 362

  Sprayed strokes, 363
  Sumi-e, 363
brushes
  Assorted Brushes, 71-72
  Brushes fly-out menu, 17
  Brushes palette, 10, 65
  Brush Size and Shape boxes, 17
  changing color , 64
  creating brushes, 68-70
  creating custom brushes, 73-74
  default brush settings, 73
  Define Brush, 74
  loading brushes, 71
  opacity, 74-75
  painting modes, 75-79
  reviewing brush settings, 70
  saving brushes, 70-71
  selecting a brush shape, 65-66
Burn tool (see Dodge/Burn tool)
bytes, 52

C

Calibration bars (Page Setup), 265
Canvas Size dialog box, 295
Caption (Page Setup), 265
CD-ROM contents, xxii
centimeters as unit of measure, 57, 58
Chalk and Charcoal filter, 383
channel calculations, 404-413
  about, 404-405
  Add, 409-410
  Apply Image (Image menu), 404-405
  Calculations, (Image menu), 404-405
  Darker (Image:Apply), 407-408
  Difference, 411
  Duplicate (Image menu), 406-407
  Lighter (Image:Apply), 407-408
  Multiply, 412
  Screen, 412
  source images sizes, 405
  Subtract, 409-410
channels
  about, 212, 470
  alpha channels, 212, 406, 470
  changing order of channels, 215
  deleting channels, 217
  displaying number of channels in a file, 57
  duplicating, 215-216
  editable, 213
  filling with color, 220
  mask channels (alpha channels), 212, 406
  maximum number of channels, 212
  merging, 219
  naming, 217
  saving a selection to an already existing

479

ABOUT THE CD-ROM

The teach yourself... Photoshop 4 CD-ROM contains sample images and demo software.

Full-color Images From the Book

All the images used in the book's exercises are located in the Exercises folder, within each platform-specific folder on the CD. The images are saved in the PSD (Photoshop), JPEG, and TIFF formats, and can be accessed by Macintosh, Windows 95, and Windows 3.1 users. Copy these files onto your hard disk and use them to practice what you learn.

A Library of Stock Images and Photos

A wide array of royalty-free photos (saved in the PhotoCD format) from Hyogensha, Inc. You can find out more about this company at their Web site, http://www.asia-photo.com.

Demo Software and Filters

A demonstration filter from Alien Skin Software and demo software from MetaTools, Extensis (Macintosh and Windows 95 only), and Kudo (Macintosh and Windows 95 only).

For installation instructions, see the ReadMe files on the CD-ROM.